C000193838

The GLOBAL RISE
of POPULISM

The GLOBAL RISE
of POPULISM

Performance, Political Style, and Representation

BENJAMIN MOFFITT

STANFORD UNIVERSITY PRESS

Stanford, California

Stanford University Press
Stanford, California

© 2016 by the Board of Trustees of the Leland Stanford Junior University.
All rights reserved.

No part of this book may be reproduced or transmitted in any form or
by any means, electronic or mechanical, including photocopying and
recording, or in any information storage or retrieval system without the
prior written permission of Stanford University Press.

Library of Congress Cataloging-in-Publication Data

Names: Moffitt, Benjamin, author.
Title: The global rise of populism : performance, political style, and
    representation / Benjamin Moffitt.
Description: Stanford, California : Stanford University Press, 2016. |
    Includes bibliographical references and index.
Identifiers: LCCN 2015047453 | ISBN 9780804796132 (cloth : alk. paper) |
    ISBN 9781503604216 (pbk. : alk. paper)
Subjects: LCSH: Populism. | Communication in politics. | Mass media—
    Political aspects. | Democracy.
Classification: LCC JC423 .M643 2016 | DDC 320.56/62—dc23
LC record available at http://lccn.loc.gov/2015047453

ISBN 9780804799331 (electronic)

Printed in the United States of America on acid-free, archival-quality
paper.

Text composition: Stanford University Press in 10/14 Minion
Cover design: Bruce Lundquist
Cover illustration: iStock.com/PeopleImages

For ASH *and* WILL

Contents

Figure and Tables

Acknowledgements

Although on the surface it looks like writing a book is a solitary affair, it cannot be done without the support, guidance, encouragement and feedback from a whole team of people. I have been fortunate to have many people on my side through the process of working on this book, and I could not have done it without them.

This book was written from 2012 to 2015 across two wonderful institutions on opposite sides of the planet: the University of Sydney and Stockholm University. At Sydney, thanks must first go to Simon Tormey, whose guidance, support, advice and encouragement to "go the bloody hard way" was absolutely essential to this project. Without his many hours of discussion and careful reading, this book simply would not exist. Thanks must also go to John Keane, who gave me the confidence to be bold in my claims, helped me make sense of the shifting media landscape, and whose joie de vivre made the writing and research process so much more enjoyable. His leadership of the Sydney Democracy Network also provided a forum for wonderful conversations with like-minded folks from all over the world that helped shape my thinking, so thanks also to the SDN crew: Giovanni Navarria, Tim Soutphommasane, and Robert Lamb amongst others who offered generous advice. In Sydney, I was also lucky to be located within the Department of Government and International Relations, where a number of staff offered outstanding support—thanks to Betsi Beem, Anna Boucher, Charlotte Epstein, Anika Gauja, Alex Lefebvre, Rodney Smith and Ariadne Vromen—as well as my fellow Ph.D. cohort—David Allinson, Judy Betts, Naser Ghobadzadeh, Stewart Jackson, Stephen Mills, Chris Neff and Colombina Schaeffer—who provided some of the best feedback I received for the book. Away from Sydney, I also wish to acknowledge Richard Howson and Mary Zournazi, who helped guide me on the research path in my undergraduate years.

Acknowledgements

Since graduating from Sydney, I have been located at the Department of Political Science at Stockholm University, which has been a wonderful and supportive place to work. I have benefitted greatly not only from the institutional support from the department but also from the feedback, guidance and advice of my fellow department members. I would particularly like to thank Maritta Soininen, Michele Micheletti and Jonas Tallberg for their generous mentorship and career guidance; Hans Agné, Andreas Duit, Faradj Koliev, Rebecca Lawrence, Ulf Mörkenstam, Alex Segerberg and Thomas Sommerer for their always insightful feedback and critical discussions; and finally, my compatriot Jon Kuyper, for the many hours of talking about things both important and trivial.

A number of other scholars from the world of populism studies have also contributed greatly to this book. Paul Taggart, Catherine Fieschi and Paolo Mancini all read an earlier version of this book, and their comments were invaluable in changing the book in major ways—I hope they can see that reflected here. Similarly, the reviewers of this book for Stanford University Press provided crucial feedback that has improved the book immensely—I am full of gratitude for their efforts. Carlos de la Torre, Yannis Stavrakakis, Cristóbal Rovira Kaltwasser, Duncan McDonnell and Pierre Ostiguy have also generously read over and provided constructive comments on different sections of the book, and their correspondence and advice have been much appreciated. All errors of course remain my own.

Some of the material in this book has been published elsewhere, and I have benefitted from the feedback from reviewers and editors. Elements of Chapters 2 and 3 appeared in 'Rethinking Populism: Politics, Mediatisation and Political Style', in *Political Studies* (Moffitt and Tormey 2014); while a version of Chapter 7 appeared as 'How to Perform Crisis: A Model for Understanding the Role of Crisis in Contemporary Populism', in *Government and Opposition* (Moffitt 2015b). Thanks to publishers of the journals—John Wiley and Sons and Cambridge University Press, respectively—for allowing the revised versions of the articles to be reprinted with permission in the book.

Further gratitude must be extended those sources that generously provided funding for this research: the Australian government (through the Australian Postgraduate Award); the Faculty of Arts and Social Sciences, the Department of Government and International Relations and the Sydney Democracy Network at the University of Sydney; the Australian Political Studies Association; and the Department of Political Science at Stockholm University.

I also wish to extend my gratitude to those at Stanford University Press who have worked on this book throughout the editorial and production process. Thanks to my editors Geoffrey Burn, for his interest and enthusiasm for the project from the outset, and Jenny Gavacs for ensuring smooth sailing throughout the later stages of the process. Thanks must also go to James Holt, John Feneron and Martin Hanft, who have all been extremely helpful and professional in guiding me through the stages of turning a manuscript into a finished book. It has been a pleasure to work with all at Stanford.

I would also like to thank my family and friends. My parents, Greg and Kathy Moffitt, have always encouraged and supported me in all of my endeavours—particularly in regards to education—and this book has been no different. I thank them for their love, support and understanding in moving across different parts of the world over the past decade. I also thank my brother, Matt, and my dear friends Alex Robertson and Bec Graham for welcome distraction and support throughout this process. Thank you also to James and Cathy McAllister, my parents-in-law, who have hosted me many times and provided love and support for my research over the last nine years.

Finally, I dedicate this book to the two most important people in my life: Ash and Will. Nearly every point in this book has been run by Ash, and she has helped me to clarify my arguments and concepts through many hours of conversation. She has read the chapters more than anyone else, and constantly reminded me that "perfection is the opposite of done". More important, Ash has been by my side over the past nine years, with unwavering support, loyalty, warmth and love. As such, the book is as much hers as mine. In the very last stages of writing this book, we also brought the biggest project of our lives into the world—our son, Will—who has delivered us more joy than we knew possible. Together, Ash and Will provide a much-needed antidote to the cynicism that can tend to creep over you while doing research on populism, and make it all worthwhile. The book is dedicated to them.

The GLOBAL RISE
of POPULISM

1   Introduction:
The Global Rise of Populism

Populism returns ... to haunt the sentient world, undeterred by the
bright dawn of democracy and neo-liberalism.
                                     —Knight (1998, 223)

We are seemingly living in populist times. The effects of the Global Financial
Crisis drag on, the Eurozone sovereign-debt crisis continues to threaten the
very existence of the European Union, and more broadly, it is alleged that we
are suffering from a crisis of faith in democracy, with political party membership falling dramatically and citizens finding themselves more and more
disillusioned with mainstream politics. The anger, fury and disgust targeted at
members of 'the elite'—whether the bankers of Wall Street, the bureaucrats of
Brussels, the politicians of leading parties or the cultural warriors of the op-ed
pages—is palpable, with calls for layoffs, imprisonment or even all-out revolution to change the status quo. The time is ripe for canny political actors who
can speak effectively in the name of 'the people' to make great political gains.

And gain they have. Over the past two decades—but particularly in the last
decade or so—populists across the world have made headlines by setting 'the
people' against 'the elite' in the name of popular sovereignty and 'defending
democracy'. Europe has experienced a groundswell of populism in the form of
leaders like Silvio Berlusconi, Geert Wilders, Jörg Haider and Marine Le Pen,
and populist parties throughout the Continent have enjoyed significant and
prolonged political success. Latin America has seen influential left-wing populist leaders change the region irrevocably, with Hugo Chávez, Nicolás Maduro,
Evo Morales and Rafael Correa all gaining the highest office in their respective
countries. In the United States, the Tea Party ostensibly caused the 2013 government shutdown, and figures like Sarah Palin, Ted Cruz and Donald Trump
have shaped the new face of American conservatism. In the Asia-Pacific, populists like Thaksin Shinawatra, Joseph 'Erap' Estrada, Pauline Hanson and Winston Peters have left indelible marks on their respective countries, while Africa
has experienced its own share of heavy-handed populist leaders, witnessing

the presidencies of Yoweri Museveni, Michael Sata and Jacob Zuma. In other words, populism is back—and it is back with a vengeance. What was once seen as a fringe phenomenon relegated to another era or only certain parts of the world is now a mainstay of contemporary politics across the globe. In order to account for this situation, some scholars have spoken of a "populist Zeitgeist" (Mudde 2004, 542), "populist wave" (Krastev 2007, 57) and "populist revival" (Roberts 2007, 3) in different regions of the world in recent years.

Indeed, the academy has paid close attention to such developments, with the academic literature on populism having its own 'populist revival' of sorts over the same period. Although populism has a relatively long—if disjointed and staggered—record in the annals of political science, the concept was given a new lease of life in the mid-1990s by authors who sought to make sense of the emergence of 'new populism' in Europe and 'neopopulism' in Latin America (Betz 1993, 1994; Roberts 1995; Taggart 1995, 1996). This led to a veritable explosion of empirical work on populism in the first decade of the twenty-first century. Populism has also been at the centre of recent debates within political theory, with key figures like Laclau (2005b, 2005c), Mouffe (2005a), Rancière (2006) and Žižek (2006a, 2006b) having engaged with the concept, tackling populism's sometimes paradoxical relationship with democracy. Taken together, these trends have seen populism move from a relatively fringe topic in political studies towards it becoming one of the discipline's most contentious and widely discussed concepts (Canovan 2004; Comroff 2011).

Yet this newfound interest in populism is not confined to the ivory towers of academia. Politicians and journalists have also pounced on the concept in recent years, with populism being portrayed as an imminent danger for democracy: the *New York Times* frets about "Europe's populist backlash" and the *New Statesman* has called populism "a real threat to mainstream democracy under stress". Former Italian prime minister Enrico Letta has similarly labelled populism as a "threat to stability in Europe", and former Mexican foreign minister Jorge Castañeda has called populism "disastrous for Latin America". Yet elsewhere populism is painted as a panacea for our broken democratic systems: the *Atlantic* argues that populism is the only way that the liberal narrative can be fixed, while the *Huffington Post* called 2014 "the year of economic populism".

Despite this widespread interest in populism, we still do not understand a number of aspects of the phenomenon all that well. Questions still abound: why has populism seemingly spread so rapidly across the globe? What do these different manifestations of populism have in common? Does populism really represent a threat to democracy? And perhaps the most basic question of all—what are we actually talking about when we use the term 'populism' today?

The central argument of this book is that in order to answer these questions, we need to *rethink contemporary populism*. This is because populism today has changed and developed from its earlier iterations, embedded as it is within a rapidly shifting political and media communications landscape. While still based around the classic divide between 'the people' and 'the elite', populism's reliance on new media technologies, its relationship to shifting modes of political representation and identification, and its increasing ubiquity have seen the phenomenon transform in nuanced ways that need explaining. In this light, the book contends that we need to move from seeing populism as a particular 'thing' or entity towards viewing it as a *political style* that is performed, embodied and enacted across a variety of political and cultural contexts. This shift allows us to make sense of populism in a time when media touches upon all aspects of political life, where a sense of crisis is endemic, and when populism appears in many disparate manifestations and contexts.

In making this argument, this book has three central aims that all work towards providing the reader with a more comprehensive, nuanced and time- and context-sensitive understanding of contemporary populism. The first aim is to locate populism within the shifting global media landscape. This is an era in which 'communicative abundance' reigns supreme, and where the increasing ubiquity and affordability of communication technologies, together with the exponential increase in the speed and scope of communication and information networks, have led to a situation in which "all spheres of life, from the most intimate everyday milieux through to large-scale global organisations, operate within heavily mediated settings in which the meaning of messages is constantly changing and often at odds with the intentions of their creators" (Keane 2013, 23). In this global environment, idealised views of populism as an unmediated or direct phenomenon that exists between the leader and 'the people' must be abandoned, and its intensely mediated nature needs to be addressed and explored. We are no longer dealing with the romantic notion of the populist speaking directly to 'the people' from the soapbox, but witness a new breed of savvy populist leaders who know how to utilise new media technologies to their advantage. How has the increased mediatisation of the political helped populism? How do populist actors relate to, or use, different aspects of the media to reach 'the people'? And how has the rise of the Internet and social networking changed contemporary populism?

The second aim of this book is to move beyond purely regional conceptions of populism, and instead build an understanding of populism as a *global phenomenon*. Although this is gradually changing, the literature on populism is still marked by an academic ghettoisation, whereby regionally specific studies of the phenomenon (each with its own traditions, definitions and archetypal case studies) tend to remain quite isolated from one another. Research that pushes beyond these regional boundaries remains rare;[1] as Rovira Kaltwasser (2012, 185) notes: "Virtually all studies that have investigated populism so far have focused their empirical and theoretical analyses on one specific region"—and these regions have usually been Western Europe, Latin America or North America. This book pushes beyond these regions by also taking into account figures who are not the 'usual suspects' of the literature—particularly Asia-Pacific and African examples—and comparing populism across regions and countries. Developing a genuinely comparative approach to populism allows us to consider what might link leaders as diverse as Beppe Grillo, Sarah Palin, Rafael Correa and Thaksin Shinawatra. In other words, what really makes these disparate actors all allegedly 'populist'?

In line with developing a genuinely global and media-centred understanding of contemporary populism, the third aim of the book is to develop and put forward a new framework for conceptualising contemporary populism: populism as a political style. While a number of other authors have used the term 'political style' in the populist literature (Canovan 1999; de la Torre 2010; Knight 1998; Taguieff 1995), it has remained relatively underdeveloped, often being treated synonymously with rhetoric, communicative strategies or discourse. This book builds on these authors' influential work to develop a clearer and more thorough concept of political style by moving beyond its purely communicative and rhetorical elements, and emphasising the performative, aesthetic and relational elements of contemporary populism. As Fieschi (2004a, 115) notes, in the past it has appeared that treating populism as a political style "does not seem to do it justice, as the notion of style implies something frivolous or at the very least inessential or superficial. Nothing could be further from the truth as the power of the appeal to people—however ambiguous—should never be underestimated". The book seeks to make clear that political style is in no way "inessential or superficial", but is in fact vital to understanding populism's position in the contemporary political landscape, as well as its malleable and versatile nature. The book clearly unfolds the different constituent parts of populism as thought of as a performative political style by providing a theoretical framework where the leader is seen as *the performer*, 'the people' as *the audience*, and crisis and media as *the stage* on which populism plays out upon. This new vocabulary speaks to the inherent theatricality of modern populism, as well as helping us focus on the mechanisms of representation and performance that underlie its central appeal to 'the people'.

Given that the book has such an ambitious and wide perspective, how does it actually go about rethinking populism and constructing this framework? Working from an interpretivist and interdisciplinary standpoint,[2] the book adopts a three-step approach that seeks to link a number of regional and disciplinary literatures (including area studies, comparative politics, political theory and political communications) on populism together to develop insights into the nature of contemporary populism across the globe. The first step is conceptual, asking *what is populism?* In order to answer this question, the book undertakes a critical review of the extant literature on contemporary populism, locating the key issues and tensions among the four central approaches to populism identified within the contemporary literature (from 1990 onwards). These approaches see populism as an ideology, strategy, discourse or political logic, respectively.

Second, in order to overcome some of the key problems with these approaches, the book develops the concept of *political style*. It does this by examining the term's usage in the literature on populism, before synthesising insights from the fields of rhetoric, political philosophy and political sociology on political style to build a new understanding of the concept. In doing so, it stresses embodied, symbolically mediated performance as a central element for understanding and analysing contemporary political phenomena.

Third, it uses the concept of political style to discern inductively the features of *populism as a political style*. This is done by examining twenty-eight cases of leaders from across the globe who are generally accepted as populists (that is, labelled as populist by at least six authors within the literature on populism), and identifying what links them in terms of political style. This list of populists can be found in the Appendix, and covers populists from not only the usually examined regions of Europe, Latin America and North America but also Africa and the Asia-Pacific over the past twenty years. While using a higher number of cases than usual obviously means a higher level of abstraction (Landman 2008), this trade-off is necessary if we want to examine contemporary populism across the globe in a broad and meaningful way. Our concern here is not to gain in-depth knowledge of any particular case of populism—for that, we have many books and articles that have already been written—but rather to gain knowledge about contemporary populism as a general phenomenon. The cases are thus *instrumental* rather than *intrinsic* (Stake 1995), helping us to "identify patterns and themes" (Grandy 2001, 474) within contemporary populism across the globe, and aiming for "high levels of conceptual validity" and "conceptual refinement" (George and Bennett 2005, 19) without getting bogged down by the details of the specific cases. In other words, the approach used in this book helps us see the 'bigger picture' of what is going on with contemporary populism across the globe.

To gain this wider perspective, the book predominantly relies on secondary sources—and these sources generally take the form of expert analyses of single and comparative cases of populism. While there are certainly pitfalls involved in relying on secondary literature, in this case it has the benefit of providing reputable (and often peer-reviewed) information on the range of cases at hand that simply would have been impossible to cover otherwise, given the regional and linguistic breadth the cases span (Yin 2009). Relatedly, one limitation of the material drawn upon that must be acknowledged is that it is composed of sources or translations available only in English—a result of the author's monolingualism—which means that a number of important sources in other languages have not been considered. Nonetheless, given that the English-language literature on populism has matured and grown exponentially over the past two decades, it is a literature that is indeed worthy of close scrutiny and analysis. Finally, given that a number of these cases are very recent, with the academic literature yet to 'catch up' with empirical developments, this expert analysis is also supplemented with more up-to-date primary and secondary data including biographies, interviews, audio-visual materials, policy documents, newspaper reports and blogs, amongst other sources throughout the book.

As can be seen, the approach of the book is a little different from the usual book-length treatments of populism, which tend either to focus in-depth on a single case of populism, or to undertake a small number of comparative case studies, with each case usually having its own distinct chapter. The book is instead organised around the key themes and topics that are pertinent to contemporary populism—leadership, media, 'the people', crisis and democracy—and uses the cases to explore and illustrate the arguments made about these broader themes. The kinds of theories about populism developed in this book are thus very much of the *middle-range* sociological variety (Merton 1968), with numerous real-world empirical cases working alongside theory to develop broader insights about the phenomenon of populism.[3]

Book Outline

The argument of this book is set out over nine chapters. The next two chapters give background on the currently existing literature on populism and develop the notion of populism as a political style, while the remaining chapters unpack and examine the constituent parts of the performative relationships at play within populism, examining the key actors, stages and audiences of contemporary populism. These are outlined in detail below.

Chapter 2 provides a critical overview of contemporary debates around populism. These conceptual debates can be difficult for outsiders or newcomers to the literature to navigate and decipher, so the chapter seeks to trace the development of the term and lay out the coordinates of the basic positions in the debate for readers. It firstly contextualises the literature by briefly tracing the development of the concept prior to the 1990s, before turning to contemporary debates around the term. It identifies the four central approaches to populism in the contemporary literature—populism as ideology, strategy, discourse and political logic—and outlines the key authors, central arguments and key features of each approach. In doing so, it balances the strengths and weaknesses of these approaches, overall showing that while the *features* of populism that each approach identifies may be valid—for example, nearly all agree on the centrality of 'the people' versus 'the elite' or some Other—there are problems with the social science *categories* they use to describe the phenomenon.

In an attempt to address these categorical issues, and bring the literature up to date to account for the mediatised character of contemporary populism, Chapter 3 develops the concept of political style as a new way of thinking about populism. Synthesising the work of Ankersmit (1996, 2002), Hariman (1995) and Pels (2003) in the fields of rhetoric, political philosophy and political sociology, respectively, it defines political style as *the repertoires of embodied, symbolically mediated performance made to audiences that are used to create and navigate the fields of power that comprise the political, stretching from the domain of government through to everyday life*. It argues that this concept helps us move beyond outdated modes of categorising political phenomena by stressing the performative dimension of contemporary politics. It then uses this concept to understand populism. This is done inductively, by examining the cases of a number of populist leaders from around the world, and determining what links them in terms of political style. The three key features of populism thought of in this way are: *appeal to 'the people' versus 'the elite'; 'bad manners'; and crisis, breakdown or threat.* The chapter then sets out the positive ramifications of using this new conception of populism.

The book then moves on to addressing the key elements of the performative relationship at the heart of populism, examining the phenomenon's performers, stages and audiences. Chapter 4 addresses the specific role of the populist leader as the key *performer* of contemporary populism. It considers the centrality of leaders within populism, and examines how these leaders must negotiate between appearing as both of 'the people' as well as above 'the people' at the same time, balancing performances of ordinariness with extraordinariness. In terms of ordinariness, it looks at populist leaders' 'bad manners' and efforts to distance themselves from 'mainstream' political leaders, and in terms of extraordinariness, it shows how populist leaders present themselves as the embodiment of 'the people', often through performances of strength, health and virility.

Chapter 5 shifts the focus to one of the central *stages* that populism plays out on: the contemporary media landscape. Arguing that the current literature does not sufficiently deal with the mediatic changes occurring across contemporary politics, the chapter examines the links between contemporary populism and the mediatisation of politics, whereby politics is increasingly reshaped and changed as the influence of the media grows. It presents a case for understanding populist actors' nuanced adaption of new media technologies and strategies as a central factor in the spread of the phenomenon, while also reflecting on the role of media control and celebrity within contemporary populism. It finally addresses what the shift from old media to new media has meant for contemporary populism.

Having explored the *performer* and the *stage* of contemporary populism, Chapter 6 turns to populism's central *audience*—'the people'—and maps out the processes involved when populist actors use media channels to construct, portray and render-present 'the people'. Challenging claims that populism is a 'direct' or 'unmediated' phenomenon, it introduces the concept of mediation in order to better understand these processes. It does this by considering the role of images and media spectacles in presenting 'the people' in contemporary populism, examining how 'the people' have been portrayed in the examples of Silvio Berlusconi's advertising campaigns and the 2002 Venezuelan coup against Hugo Chávez. It also utilises Michael Saward's (2010) concept of the 'representative claim' to make sense of how 'the people' are represented, showing that there is a difference between populist audiences (those who are spoken *to* by populists) and populist constituencies (those who are spoken *for* by populists), and that the success of representations of 'the people' relies on both of these groups. The chapter closes by considering the role of key channels of mediation—newspapers, television, the Internet and so forth—in these representations, demonstrating that media are never just neutral 'loudspeakers' for populist performances but actually active participants, often presenting themselves as proxies for 'the people'.

The next chapter returns to another *stage* of populism: crisis. While much of literature contends that crisis is a trigger for populism, Chapter 7 offers a new perspective, arguing that we should also consider how *populism attempts to act as a trigger for crisis.* This is because crisis is never just a 'neutral' or 'objective' phenomenon, but must be performed and mediated by certain actors—something at which populists are particularly adept. Putting forward an understanding of crisis as the 'spectacularisation of failure', the chapter builds a six-step model of how populists 'perform' crisis, examining how this performance allows populists to divide 'the people' from 'the elite' and associated Others, to radically simplify the political terrain, and to present their own strong leadership and simple solutions as a method for stemming or avoiding the crisis. In making this argument, the chapter suggests that we should move from a conception of crisis as something that is purely external to populism, to one that acknowledges the performance of crisis as an *internal feature* of populism as a political style. It shows that while crisis may present an effective stage for populists, it is often the case that populists must play an important role in 'setting the stage' themselves by promoting and performing crisis.

The framework and arguments developed in the previous chapters are drawn together in Chapter 8 in order to tackle one of the most controversial debates on populism: *what is populism's relationship to democracy?* Arguing that populism itself tells us very little about the substantive democratic 'content' of any political project, the chapter undoes the strict binary between populism and democracy that is often invoked in the literature by instead examining both the democratic and antidemocratic tendencies *within* populism as conceptualised as a political style. In doing so, it demonstrates that questions about populism's relationship to democracy should not always be taken at face value, as they often conceal larger questions about what constitutes 'correct' or 'legitimate' forms of political practice.

Finally, the concluding chapter pulls together the arguments made within this book about populism as a political style and discusses the implications for our understanding of the relationship between contemporary populism, media, crisis and democracy. It also identifies new avenues of research in the field of populism opened up by the new conceptualisation of populism developed in this book. It closes by considering the future of populism across the globe, and why we need to continue to pay attention to populism's changing shape.

This book ultimately shows that the rise of populism across the globe over the past two decades is not a fluke, nor just a reaction to structural economic and political factors such as a prolonged global downturn and rising unemployment, along with disenchantment and cynicism with political parties and the ruling elite. Although those factors are undoubtedly important, contemporary populism has also changed, developed and risen as a result of its attunement with the contours of the contemporary political and media landscapes, co-opting media processes and combining politics, media and entertainment in novel and exciting forms. In this context, a new perspective is needed to take account of the shifting character of contemporary populism, its symbiotic relationship with the new media landscape, and how it relates to crisis and democracy in the present day. By conceptualising populism as a political style, and emphasising populism's performative dimension, this book steps outside the mainstream of populism studies and sets out an important new way forward for making sense of contemporary populism.

2   The Problems with Populism

Scholarly reassessment of Populism will never end.
—Hackney (1971, xxii)

A stagnant lexicon is rarely a useful lexicon.
—Gerring and Barresi (2009, 263)

Like many terms in the lexicon of politics, populism is marked by a high degree of contestability. Indeed, it is an axiomatic feature of literature on the topic to acknowledge the contested nature of populism (Ionescu and Gellner 1969a; Laclau 1977; Taggart 2000)—and more recently, the literature has reached a whole new level of metareflexivity, where it is posited that it has become common to *acknowledge the acknowledgement* of this fact (Panizza 2005a, 1). There are two ways this contestability can be read. The first is to argue that the concept of populism has become so widely used—and usually in a derogatory manner to denigrate any political personality we do not like—that it has lost its analytical value and has become meaningless. Some have even suggested retiring the term (Roxborough 1984). By contrast, we can view the continuing debate over populism as an indication that there is something important, promising and resonant about the concept. The combination of constant contestation with populism's surprisingly resilient staying power in the annals of political science can be read as a sign of its vitality and relevance. Indeed, as tentative attempts to bridge the different literatures on populism have taken place over the past decade or so (see, for example, Mudde and Rovira Kaltwasser 2012b, 2013a; Rovira Kaltwasser 2012; Taggart 2000), it is natural to expect some serious intellectual and terminological arguments to occur in this collision between different approaches.

This book takes the latter view: populism matters, and is an important concept for understanding the contemporary political landscape. However, the task of clarifying what we mean when we talk about populism is an important one; all the more so given that the term is now widely used by comparativists, area studies specialists and political theorists. The issue is not merely of academic interest though—as noted in the introduction, many politicians and journalists claim that populism is a threat to democratic politics. If this is the case, much rides on the sharpness of the conceptual tools we use to understand populism.

As such, this chapter provides a map of contemporary debates around populism to discern the key positions and arguments at play in defining the concept. This is particularly useful given that these debates often take part across different literatures, and can thus be difficult to follow. It is structured in two main parts. The first section provides a brief history of the development of the concept in the academic literature prior to the 1990s, tracing its etymological roots from the US Populist Party of the late nineteenth century through populism's conceptual 'journeys' across the twentieth century. The second section identifies the four central approaches in the contemporary literature—populism as ideology; populism as a strategy; populism as discourse; and populism as political logic—and outlines their key arguments. Importantly, it also critiques these approaches, pointing out both the strengths and challenges presented by their conceptualisations of populism. This critique provides the foreground for the argument that is made in the next chapter—that we need to rethink populism, and that populism is best thought of as a political style.

A Brief History of Debates around Populism (1860–1990)

In trying to understand populism, political thinkers have long been split about the nature of the phenomenon and how to approach it—is it a type of social movement, ideology or something else? A brief exploration of the term's early development can help clarify why these blurry delineations have arisen. The intention here is not to provide a complete history of the term, as this has been done well elsewhere (Canovan 1981; Houwen 2011; Taggart 2000)—but rather to provide a historical context for current debates around the meaning of the concept.[1]

In sketching his "brief biography" of the concept, Allcock (1971, 372) argued that until the mid-1950s, "'populism' was merely a label to identify two separate historical phenomena," and that "there [was] no wider significance attached to the word". The first phenomenon that the term referred to was the agrarian movement that led to the formation of the People's Party in the Southern and Midwestern United States in the 1890s. This party, originally formed to oppose the demonetisation of silver, adopted the nickname of 'Populists' early on, drawing from the Latin *populus* ('the people'). The second phenomenon it referred to was the Russian *narodnichestvo* of the 1860s-70s, a movement of

Russian intellectuals who believed that the peasants were the revolutionary class that would bring about Russia's social and political regeneration, and thus considered it their moral imperative to go to 'the people' and educate them in order to bring about the revolution. Given that the term referred to these past movements, populism was considered a subject for historians, not political scientists or sociologists.

However, from the mid-1950s onwards, the term began to be used to refer to a wide array of phenomena, taking its first steps down a long road of what Sartori (1970) might term "conceptual stretching". The earliest attempts came from Shils (1955, 1956) and Lipset (1960), who both identified the McCarthyism of the time as a form of populism. Shils (1956, 100–101) argued that far from being a specific term for progressive rural movements, populism should be understood as a "widespread phenomenon ... [that] exists wherever there is an ideology of popular resentment against the order imposed on society by a long-established, differentiated ruling class which is believed to have a monopoly of power, property, breeding and culture". He claimed that there were two core principles of populism: a belief that 'the people' are sovereign and above their rulers, and the notion of a direct connection between 'the people' and their government. In a perceptive analysis, he also identified a number of features that have lived on in different conceptions of populism that would follow: distrust of politicians and elites, frustration with bureaucracy, anti-intellectualism and demagoguery. By generalising the concept, Shils made it clear that he considered populism as an ideological phenomenon identifiable across various political and historical settings.

Lipset, meanwhile, saw populism as an extremist phenomenon based around xenophobia and anti-Semitism. While Shils was interested in the 'ideological core' of populism, Lipset believed that the link between different forms of populism was an empirical one that could be identified by the common 'social base' of followers of populism. According to Lipset (1960, 173), these followers were the "declining 'liberal' classes living in declining areas" who become so frustrated with their weakened position in society that "their discontent leads them to accept diverse irrational protest ideologies—regionalism, racism, supernationalism, anticosmopolitanism, McCarthyism, fascism".

Throughout the 1960s, the term was applied to an ever-increasing set of phenomena, with the focus moving away from the United States and towards Latin America (Di Tella 1965; Smith 1969). Here the term was applied to movements that forged multiclass urban alliances under charismatic leaders, thus shifting the definition of populism to one that focused on a particular mode of organisation. Leaders such as Juan Perón in Argentina, Lázaro Cárdenas in Mexico, Getúlio Vargas in Brazil and José María Velasco Ibarra in Ecuador serve as key examples of populist leaders under this definition (Westlind 1996). It was also applied to the developing world, where Shils (1960) modified his earlier definition to have it refer to the role of the disillusioned intellectual in Third World countries, while Worsley (1964) used it in regards to dictatorial Third World regimes, adding a colonialist element to the concept.

It is clear that by this stage the term was becoming quite unwieldy; as Mény and Surel (2002, 2) suggest, these extensions had led to the point where "both the concept and the word lost most of their heuristic utility and were generally used as a convenient label to designate unfamiliar or unusual forms of political mobilisation". It is in this context that Ionescu and Gellner organised a conference at the London School of Economics (LSE) in May 1967, bringing together forty-three experts in the field from disparate specialised backgrounds with the explicit aim of defining populism. The edited collection that resulted from the conference, *Populism: Its Meanings and National Characteristics* (Ionescu and Gellner 1969b), has remained a key reference in the literature, with Taggart (2000, 15, emphasis in original) calling it "*the* definitive collection on populism".

As Ionescu and Gellner (1969a, 1) write in the introduction: "There can, at present, be no doubt about the importance of populism. But no one is clear what it is". Perhaps unavoidably, the contributors to the volume do not come to a unified consensus on the phenomenon. Populism is variously analysed as an ideology, a political movement and as a 'political syndrome', amongst other approaches. This eclecticism, although responsible for *some* conceptual advancement, is rather frustrating, with the results veering from unwieldy lists of the descriptive features of populism (Wiles 1969), lists of political phenomena and movements that have been labelled as populist (MacRae 1969), to attempts to delineate the structural conditions of the emergence of populism (Stewart 1969) and specific case studies that make generalisation difficult. The problem here, as identified by Laclau (2005b, 13), is that much of the work in the collection falls into the category of description rather than striving for conceptual specificity. As a result, the overall result of the aforementioned lists and studies is an in-depth portrayal of lots of different things that *might* be populism, but with no real overarching attempt to synthesise the efforts. In this sense, Wiles' (1969, 166) remark, "To each his own definition of populism, according to the academic axe he grinds", is a rather fitting encapsulation of the collection.

It is Worsley's (1969) contribution to the collection that moves beyond some of these conceptual deadlocks and points to a future direction for the study of populism. After comparing populism in various geographical regions, Worsley (1969, 243) concludes that "since there are obviously innumerable differentials between all of these 'social locations', any features common to them all can only be very general indeed. A systematic concatenation of structural properties (e.g. in terms of social composition, leadership, particular policies, etc.) is impossible to delineate". Calling such an approach "singularly unrewarding" (1969, 244), Worsley suggests that only by returning to the generalised abstraction of Shil's original two core principles of populism can the concept be of any use. In this regard, Worsley (1969, 245) claims that populism is not necessarily a type of ideology or movement, but is rather an "emphasis, a dimension of political culture in general, not simply a particular kind of overall ideological system or type of organization". This is a particularly productive move: in signalling a break from the classical approach of attempting to 'discover' populism, Worsley opens up the research agenda for the concept by making it clear that "populism cannot claim any conceptual purity of its own" (Arditi 2007a, 42). As such, for Worsley (1969, 247), populism is not a phenomenon that is specific to a particular era or region, nor is it the unique bastion of any ideological side of politics. It is, rather, "an aspect of a variety of political cultures and structures" (1969, 247).

It is from this nonessentialist position that the seeds for a number of central approaches to populism were sown. Similarly frustrated with 'empiricist' approaches to populism, Laclau argued in *Politics and Ideology in Marxist Theory* (1977) that attempts to define populism by generalising from examples already labelled as populist were redundant, as they basically acknowledge that one already has a conception of populism (however vague it might be). As a result, instead of engaging in the classificatory schemes that had been attempted earlier, Laclau followed Worsley's lead by claiming that the starting point of his analysis was not the 'social base' of the varied phenomena that have been labelled 'populist' throughout history, but rather the question of how the key referent and central signifier of 'the people' is invoked and constructed in different discourses. For Laclau, populism was to be considered a discourse that pits 'the people' against dominant elites and institutions.

A few years later, Canovan's landmark study *Populism* (1981) was published, which opened with the acknowledgement that the troublesome issues around the definition of populism were not actually unique to populism. Referring to the aforementioned 1967 LSE conference, Canovan (1981, 5) suggested that "a conference to define socialism, liberalism, or conservatism would probably have equal difficulty in reaching a conclusion, and would certainly generate a great deal more acrimony in the process". However, Canovan argued that what makes populism particularly problematic is that beyond the People's Party mentioned earlier, populism has not often been used a self-descriptive label: while the debates about what is meant by socialism, liberalism and communism have generally been decided by self-proclaimed socialists, liberals and communists, the lack of a common populist movement or tradition has seen the term defined by external onlookers—and quite often in a pejorative manner.

Moving away from an attempt to find out what populism 'really is', Canovan (1982, 545) embarked on what she would later label a "phenomenological [approach], concerned with description rather than with explanation, aiming at comprehensiveness in preference to theoretical elegance". In this sense, she compared herself to a naturalist who collects insects and categorises them in groups. The result of her approach is a descriptive typology of populism, in which she distinguishes between 'agrarian' and 'political' forms of populism.

Canovan expressed awareness that this approach had as many weaknesses as strengths. She argued that its strength was that it tidied up the jumbled field of populism into a neat classificatory scheme—a worthy endeavour itself, given the breadth of the field. It also demonstrated that populism is not reducible to a single, essential core as "the various populisms we have distinguished are not just different varieties of the same kind of thing: they are in many cases different *sorts* of things, and not directly comparable at all" (1981, 298). On the other hand, such a typology offered no explanatory strength, and it was difficult to see where one could move from it in analytical terms. Indeed, Canovan (1982, 552) herself seemed somewhat disappointed by the results of her exercise, and admitted that her typology "remain[ed] frustratingly unsystematic".

Canovan gradually moved away from her typology, perhaps herself acknowledging its limited usefulness. Like Laclau, she began to focus on the key referent of populism, 'the people', in her research (Canovan 1984, 1999, 2002, 2004), even publishing a book by that very title in 2005. In essence, she has attempted to shed the concept's historical baggage, and aimed to develop a theory of a specific element of populism: something approaching the 'politician's populism' and 'populist democracy' she identified in her original typology, focusing on its stylistic and ideological features.

The Contemporary Literature on Populism (1990 Onwards)

As can be seen, the major theoretical developments in the field of populism discussed thus far came in a relatively staggered and disjointed manner. The reason for this erratic development is that interest in populism as a political concept has tended to spike when empirical phenomena that are labelled as 'populist' capture the politicosocial imagination. For example, the first developments beyond the initial use of the term arrived in the wake of McCarthyism in the United States in 1950s, with the second stage following the end of the 'golden age' (Green 2006) of Latin American populism that lasted from the 1930s to the 1960s. The next (and most pertinent developments for this book) came in the late 1980s and early 1990s, with the emergence of 'new populism' in Western Europe and 'neopopulism' in Latin America. The former term was used to refer to figures such as Jörg Haider, Jean-Marie Le Pen, Umberto Bossi and Christoph Blocher (Taggart 1995, 1996), while the latter referred to figures like Alberto Fujimori, Carlos Menem and Fernando Collor, who combined populism with neoliberal economic policies (Roberts 1995; Weyland 1999).

This 'wave' of populism—which has continued ever since—has produced a rich explosion of literature on populism, bringing the concept into the domain of mainstream political science, and fuelling renewed debates about how to define the concept. This literature has been particularly pronounced from the mid-1990s onwards, when Betz's *Radical Right-Wing Populism in Western Europe* (1994), Kazin's *The Populist Persuasion* (1995), the journal *Telos*'s special issues on populism (1995a, 1995b), and Taggart's (1995, 1996) and Roberts's (1995) work on populism in Europe and Latin America, respectively, kicked off contemporary debates about the conceptual status of populism. It is to these debates that the remainder of this chapter turns.

In this contemporary literature, there are four central approaches to populism—as ideology, strategy, discourse and political logic.[2] This section outlines the features of each of these approaches, identifies their key arguments, and interrogates their strengths and weaknesses. It shows that while most of these approaches tend to agree on a number of the *features* of populism in their definitions—for example, reference to 'the people'—there are challenges presented by the terms that are used to *categorise* the phenomenon.

Ideology

Building on the legacy of Shils (1956), there is little doubt that the conceptualisation of populism as an ideology has become the dominant position in the literature over the past decade. Much of this success, particularly within European political science, can be attributed to the contribution of Mudde (2004, 2007), whose writings on populism have set the agenda for comparativists in the field. Mudde (2007, 23) puts forward a minimal definition of populism as "a thin-centred ideology that considers society to be ultimately separated into two homogeneous and antagonistic groups, 'the pure people' and 'the corrupt elite', and which argues that politics should be an expression of the *volonté general* (general will) of the people". For Mudde, the strength of a minimal definition of populism as an ideology lies in its applicability to comparative empirical research—particularly its ability to transcend regional bias—as well as its ability to jettison any normative baggage with which conceptions of populism have often been burdened. He further argues that by conceptualising it as a 'thin-centred' ideology, we can understand that populism does not exist in any 'pure' form, but rather that it is always present in mixed forms with other ideologies. Other writers who have developed the idea of populism as a thin-centred ideology include Abts and Rummens (2007), Fieschi (2004b), Stanley (2008) and Rovira Kaltwasser (2012, 2013), while Akkerman (2012), March (2007), Rooduijn et al. (2014), Rooduijn and Pauwels (2010) and Učeň (2010) have applied the concept to particular case studies.

Underlying this notion of populism is the morphological approach to ideology developed by Freeden (1996). As opposed to a 'full' or 'thick' ideology (such as liberalism or socialism), which is understood as a "wide-ranging structural arrangement that attributes *decontested* meanings to a range of mutually defining political concepts" (Freeden 2003, 54, emphasis in original), thin ideologies have a much more restricted core, and focus on only a limited number of key concepts. As such, they do not attempt to provide the ideational roadmap for the wide range of questions that a full ideology would. So while populism as a thin ideology may be able to provide the resources to argue forcefully for the sovereignty of 'the people', as Freeden (2003, 98) puts it: "The point is that it does little else". In this view, populism is thus not a fully formed Weltanschauung but rather a limited set of concepts that is always combined with other thick ideologies.

It is certainly understandable why the ideological definition of populism has become popular in recent years. In Mudde's minimal definition, the literature has found a succinct and basic description of the concept that can be used to classify which politicians and parties can be described as populist—and perhaps more usefully, who *is not* a populist. For specialists in comparative politics this has been a positive development, as this semiconsensus in the definition wars has allowed a break from heated theoretical debates about the status of populism, and given comparativists the ability to set their sights on a wider range of cases for analysis. This has been a fruitful move, with some important cross-regional analyses now beginning to emerge (Mudde and Rovira Kaltwasser 2012b).

Despite these positive developments, there are a number of issues with classifying populism as a thin-centred ideology. The primary issue with this approach is that the term 'ideology' is used relatively unproblematically throughout the literature on populism, and often ends up serving as a catch-all term that implicitly swallows up other approaches along the way—particularly the discursive approach discussed later in this chapter—thus losing its initial apparent clarity. Whether purposely or not, many of the authors working within this approach add tacit criteria to their definitions of populism in order to make them operationalisable for political analysis (for example, moving towards a discursive approach in order to 'measure' the level of populism, or mistaking features of the 'host' ideology for features of populism—something that is particularly noticeable in work on radical right populism in Europe), suggesting that the ideological minimal approach may not be enough to sustain a nuanced account of populism.

Another question that needs to be raised is whether a thin ideology can become so thin as to lose its conceptual validity and usefulness. Freeden (1996, 486) notes that thin ideologies such as ecologism or feminism, although starting from a restricted conceptual core, "have since made strenuous efforts to accumulate a range of conceptual furniture that will thicken their ideational density and sophistication and extend their appeal and viability". It is difficult to say the same for populism, and as a result, one must have doubts about whether it can really be classified in the same category as other thin ideologies. While not calling for a return to Marxist, or even Gramscian conceptualisations of ideology as a tool of repression or all-encompassing worldview, there is reason to be concerned about just how far the concept of ideology can be stretched in this situation. Even adherents of the ideological approach acknowledge the difficulty of the lack of 'thickness' when it comes to the populist ideology, with one noting that:

> whilst many prominent ideologies have 'left record' of themselves in the shape of philosophical-political institutions that transcend individual parties, movements or leaders, there is little evidence of institutional elements indicating a common purpose or unity amongst populists: there is no Populist International; no canon of key populist texts or calendar of significant moments; and the icons of populism are of local rather than universal appeal. (Stanley 2008, 100)

In other words, populism, unlike other 'thin ideologies', has made no attempt to become 'thicker'. As such, the very 'thinness' of the concept of populism as an ideology, combined with its lack of a common historical or genealogical refer-ent beyond the People's Party of the 1890s, can make it difficult to conceptualise populism as a distinct ideology.

Strategy

Authors working within the ideological approach are not the only ones who have aimed to develop a minimal definition of populism. Those who see pop-ulism as a strategy have also attempted to present a minimal definition, with Weyland's (2001, 14) definition of populism as "a political strategy through which a personalistic leader seeks or exercises government power based on di-rect, unmediated, uninstitutionalized support from large numbers of mostly unorganized followers" proving popular as a starting point for empirical anal-yses, particularly in the literature on Latin American populism (Ellner 2003; Roberts 2003, 2006). Others working within this approach have focused on populism's organisational features, examining populist movements' plebiscita-rian linkages (Barr 2009) or modes of election campaigning (Conniff 1999). In these strategic approaches, populism is thus not defined by the political values of the political actor, nor by the way that they communicate, but by their rela-tionship (which is supposedly 'direct') with their followers.

While those working with these kinds of definitions are correct to highlight the important position of the leader within populism, the primary difficulty with them is that they identify strategies or 'direct' modes of organisation that appear across the political spectrum in many different manifestations that we would ordinarily never consider calling 'populist'; indeed, a number of social movements (such as religious or millenarian movements) or forms of com-munity politics could easily fall under such a definition (Hawkins 2010, 168). Equally, there is no reason to believe that populism thrives only in instances of low institutionalism or organisation—the fortunes of Le Pen's Front National or Wilder's Partij voor de Vrijheid prove that populism can certainly thrive in an environment of tight party discipline and organisation. This is even the case in the Latin American context, where there are actually a number of different types of organisational linkages used by populists—Roberts (2006) identifies at least four subtypes of Latin American populism on this basis (organic, labor, parti-san, and electoral). Indeed, the legacy of the classic literature on Latin American populism as multiclass urban alliances under charismatic leaders casts a long shadow here (see Di Tella 1965; Smith 1969), and it is telling that such definitions have not travelled well to other regional contexts, although some authors (Phongpaichit and Baker 2009b; Rocamora 2009) have used it in the Southeast Asian context. Such definitions also miss both the stylistic and ideational elements of populism: as Hawkins (2010, 39) has pointed out, these "conceptualizations of populism emphasize largely material aspects of politics, that is, coalitions, historical preconditions and policies. This is an incomplete account".

Additionally, this approach can sometimes leave out the classic referent in discussions of populism: 'the people'.[3] To do so not only abandons the one central feature that all the other approaches agree upon but also ignores the etymological roots of the term, which are primarily based on the Latin *populus*. While tracing the etymology of terms is not always a primary reason to discard concepts, Knight (1998, 226) notes that when it comes to populism: "[T]he etymology is sufficiently clear, recent, and compelling for us to take it seriously".

Discourse

An approach that has proven popular in recent times in the literatures on populism in Europe and Latin America views populism as a discourse that pits 'the people' against 'the elite' (Hawkins 2009) or 'the oligarchy' (de la Torre 2010). Here, rather than being a feature of a set of political beliefs, populism is seen as a particular mode of political expression, usually evident in speech or text. An important difference between the two approaches described above and the discursive approach is that while those who subscribe to the ideological or strategic view of populism tend to see it as an 'either/or' category, those who view it as a discourse tend to see it as "a gradational property of specific instances of political expression" (Gidron and Bonikowski 2013, 8). As such, according to the discursive view, a political actor can be 'more or less' populist at different times depending on how and when they use populist discourse, whereas for the ideological or strategic views, one 'is' or 'is not' populist. In his work on populism as a discourse, Hawkins (2010, 30–31) further explains the difference between these approaches by arguing that a discourse "lacks the official texts and vocabulary that accompany an ideology, and must be discerned through more diffuse linguistic elements such as tone and metaphor and by a search for broad themes". So while an ideology has a normative programme for political action, Hawkins claims that a discourse does not. As such, he argues that while a figure like Chávez may have a *populist discourse*, his ideology is not populism, but socialism.

To discern where and when these populist discourses are being used, authors such as Hawkins (2009, 2010) and Koopmans and Muis (2009) have used classical content analysis, typically developing a qualitative coding scheme that attempts to measure the 'level' of populism in a certain set of discursive texts.[4] These studies have provided some interesting—and at times, unexpected—results, showing that actors who are commonly accepted as populist may not have used a particularly populist discourse at all, while actors who are usually not included in the populist pantheon have been shown to utilise populist discourse quite frequently. However, as Pauwels (2011, 102) acknowledges, classical content analyses such as these can suffer from questionable reliability, irregular sampling and possible coding bias. Furthermore, there is little agreement on what sources should be measured, from speeches to party manifestos to party broadcasts. Others (Armony and Armony 2005; Pauwels 2011; Reungoat 2010) have used computer-based quantitative content analysis to measure populist discourse, but this method has its own issues—it is difficult to see how charting the percentages of how often certain keywords appear in party material can really do much more than supplement already existing theoretical assumptions. As Hawkins (2010, 71) puts it: "[W]e cannot gauge a broad, latent set of meanings in a text—a discourse—simply by counting words. . . . [T]he ideas that constitute the underlying worldview are held subconsciously and conveyed as much by the tone and style of language as the actual words". So while this is certainly a promising method for *measuring* populism, it does not provide us with an overarching conceptual approach for *understanding* populism.

Nonetheless, the discursive approach is on the right track, and its appreciation of the gradational quality of populism, as well as the primacy of speech acts and rhetoric, is encouraging. However, it may not go far enough in taking account of what else is vital to populism's appeal: focus on primarily linguistic or text-based materials means that elements beyond what is recorded on the page are missed. These include visual, performative and aesthetic elements— those features that contribute to the affective or passionate dimension of populism that numerous significant researchers on the topic of populism (Canovan 1999; Mouffe 2005a; Stavrakakis 2004) have stressed. For a subject notorious for its prevalence of allegedly charismatic leaders and stylistic flourishes, this presents a problem, as we are only getting half the picture by focusing on written or spoken discourse. As shall be argued, the political style approach that is developed in the next chapter allows us to take the performative and aesthetic elements into account *as well as* speech and text.

Political Logic

While the ideological, discursive and strategic approaches have primarily been developed with empirical analysis as the end goal, it is Laclau's conceptualisation of populism as a political logic that has had the biggest impact in the area of political and social theory. Simultaneously building on and moving beyond his earlier efforts that saw populism as a discourse (1977, 1980), Laclau argued over a series of articles (2005c, 2006) and his book *On Populist Reason* (2005b) that prior attempts to define populism have necessarily failed, as they have been concerned with locating populism's ontic content, rather than capturing the ontological status of the concept. By moving away from the specific concrete contents of 'politics'—that is, the empirical practices of what we usually see as 'conventional politics'—and to the more abstract level of 'the political'—that is, the broader ways in which society is instituted (Mouffe 2005b, 8–9)—Laclau put forward his case for populism as a particular structuring logic of political life, evident wherever equivalence triumphs over difference.

However, populism is not just any political logic: Laclau argued that it is *the* logic of the political (2005b, 154). Why is this? Laclau claimed that any political project is premised on the division between two competing antagonistic groups (us/them, underdog/system, 'the people'/'the elite' and so forth). The way in which these groups are formed stems from what he posits as the minimal unit of politicosocial analysis: the demand. To put it briefly, when a demand is unsatisfied within any system, and then comes into contact with other unsatisfied demands, they can form an equivalential chain with one another, as they share the common antagonism/enemy of the system. A frontier is thus created between this equivalential chain (the underdogs) and the system. From here, the loose equivalential chain between demands is interpellated and finds expression as 'the people' through a leader. 'The people' then demand change to, or of, the system.

'The people' in Laclau's formulation thus become the possibility of any renewed and effective political project, and indeed, the very subject of the political. And if 'the people' are the subject of the political, then populism is the logic of the political. In this sense, Laclau (2005b, 47) basically argues that all politics are populist: "If populism consists in postulating a radical alternative within the communitarian space, a choice in the crossroads on which the future of a given society hinges, does not populism become synonymous with politics? The answer can only be affirmative".

The true theoretical innovation that sets Laclau's approach apart from those outlined earlier is that it sees populism as something that is *done*. Whether in his earlier work, where he focused on the role of interpellation in populism (1977, 1980), or his later work, which focused more on the role of performance and naming (2005b, 2005c), the political *practice* of populism remains key: as Laclau put it in formal terms, "political practices do not *express* the nature of social agents but, instead, *constitute* the latter" (2005c, 33, emphasis in original). To put it in more concrete terms, Laclau's formulation of populism acknowledges that populists do not speak to or for some pre-existing 'people' but arguably bring the subject known as 'the people' into being through the process of naming, performance or articulation. This very process is what Laclau saw as populism. The next chapter discusses this performative aspect in more detail, particularly focusing on the problematic distinction between populist style and content.

Beyond this innovation, Laclau also offered a number of other important contributions to conceptualising populism. First, he added much-needed nuance to the analysis of populism by not seeing it automatically as something dangerous and thus as a phenomenon to be rejected—a move that he sees as "the denigration of the masses" (2005b, 1) and "the dismissal of politics *tout court*" (2005b, x)—but rather as an ubiquitous feature of political life that should not be ignored. Second, his concept of populism takes account of both the linguistic *and* nonlinguistic aspects of the phenomenon.[5] Third, his attempt to map the processes at play in speaking for 'the people' acknowledges not only the radical indeterminacy that marks the subject of 'the people but also the crucial role of representation in this process.

However, despite these strengths, there are three serious issues with Laclau's approach that need addressing—all of which relate to an overreach in terms of the status of populism as a political phenomenon. The first is the slippage of concepts. While Laclau and Mouffe (1985, 193) once argued that the name of the game that takes place in the field of the political is hegemony, Laclau later argued that "populism is the royal road to understanding something about the ontological constitution of the political as such" (2005b, 67). This results in a conflation of Laclau's key concepts, most aptly put in the title of a review article on Laclau's work: "Populism Is Hegemony Is Politics?" (Arditi 2010). When both critics (Žižek 2006a, 2006b) and former acolytes (Howarth 2008; Stavrakakis 2004) put forward similar critiques, there is cause for concern about the conceptual slippage at play within one's claims.

The second is that there are empirical counterexamples that challenge Laclau's thesis about the universality of populist logic. A number of political movements in the contemporary political landscape, such as the Zapatistas as well as the alter-globalisation, Occupy and *indignados* movements self-consciously seek to distance themselves from populist modes of discourse, organisation and representation by refusing to articulate demands through a leader, or not articulating concrete demands at all. They therefore attempt to disavow the 'populist logic' that Laclau sees as universal.[6] There are clearly ways of doing politics that lie outside the populist model, thus challenging Laclau's claim that all politics is populism.

The third issue is that from a methodological point of view, Laclau's conceptualisation is potentially too broad to allow meaningful application of his theory. A clear illustration of this is the collection of essays that make up Panizza's edited volume, *Populism and the Mirror of Democracy* (2005b), in which the majority of the contributions attempt to apply a version of Laclau's theory of populism to a broad range of empirical cases. The problem here is that the empirical examples chosen all correspond to the allegedly problematic 'ontic' content that Laclau attempts to jettison in his theory. However, one cannot blame the authors for grasping at those political manifestations that revolve around concrete appeals to 'the people'; if we are to take Laclau's theory of populism seriously, it should be able to be applied to absolutely *any* political case study. One can see, however, how this level of generality begins to lead to vagueness and banality in the choice of concrete cases for empirical analysis if followed to its logical conclusion. Overall, the sense one gets from Laclau's approach is that while it is perhaps the most innovative—and not to mention, most formally developed—theory of populism that has yet been attempted, if it is to be used for empirical analysis, it must be 'brought down to earth' in some regards.

Conclusion

As can be seen, populism has been a contested concept throughout its history. From its beginnings on the prairies of the Midwestern United States (or alternatively, the villages of rural Russia), populism has undergone wide conceptual travels and has been applied to a dizzying array of political phenomena. However, despite significant conceptual advancement in the literature, particularly over the past two decades or so whereby distinct schools of thought on populism have emerged with their own central arguments, theorists, key texts and even favoured case studies, *how* to understand populism—whether as an ideology, strategy, discourse or political logic—still remains an open question. While there is some uniformity in the *features* ascribed to populism by each of the key approaches—for example, it is clear that nearly all approaches speak of a divide between 'the people' and 'the elite' or an Other—more thought needs to be given to the consequences of choosing certain social science *categories* to describe populism. This is reflected in critiques of the different approaches that have been made throughout this chapter, as well as the fact that some of the key authors themselves slip between the categories at times.

Let us take the example of those who subscribe to the ideological or discursive views of populism. Although ideology and discourse are clearly different types of political phenomena, Hawkins, Riding and Mudde (2012, 2–3, emphasis mine) "refer to populism as a *discourse* or what some scholars call a *thin-centered ideology*: a coherent set of basic assumptions about the world and the language that unwittingly expresses them". Similarly, Hawkins (2009, 1043) elsewhere claims that authors as varied as Knight (1998), Kazin (1995), Canovan (1999) and Mudde (2004) all "define populism discursively", despite their using clearly different terms for the phenomenon, ranging from style, language, appeal or thin ideology. The muddling of such categories does not provide any clarity in trying to conceptualise populism—instead, it blurs the divisions between the distinct approaches, which is a real problem given that "these two traditions give different ontological status to populism and, consequently, favour different analytical strategies for operationalizing and measuring the phenomenon" (Gidron and Bonikowski 2013, 15).

Moreover, although there might be a mild consensus on which political actors can be labelled as 'populist' in the contemporary literature—this can be seen in the familiarity of the same leaders that are repeatedly invoked within the populist literature—there is actually a wide disparity in these populist actors' ideologies, discourses and political and organisational strategies if we use the definitions provided by the approaches to populism identified in this chapter. For example, populists can appear across the ideological spectrum, from those traditionally identified as being on the far left (Evo Morales) to the far right (Marine Le Pen). Populists can incorporate different discourses into their populism, as in the cases of ethnopopulists in Latin America (Madrid 2008) or Africa (Cheeseman and Larmer 2015), or hardly use populist discourse at all, as in the case of Carlos Menem (Hawkins 2010, 80–81). Finally, in terms of political organisation, populists can build loose networks (Hugo Chávez) as well as enforce tight party discipline (Geert Wilders). In other words, current ideological, discursive and strategic conceptions of populism leave one in the strange position of arguing that some of the 'usual suspects' or archetypal cases of contemporary populism are not actually populist at all.

What should be done in such a position? One possibility is to try to create an *Ur-definition* that combines the different approaches to populism, as well as accounts for all the usual cases of populism in the literature. Yet even if this were possible, it would be likely that we would return to the kinds of unwieldy lists of features that marked the 1969 Ionescu and Gellner collection mentioned earlier, which would be very unhelpful. Instead, it is useful to acknowledge that there is no single definition of populism waiting to be 'discovered' if the 'right words' can simply be found to describe it. To believe this is to subscribe to correspondence theory—a problematic epistemological standpoint when theorising social and political phenomena, to say the least.

Instead, the conceptual deadlock of the literature suggests another possible path: building on elements of the most promising approaches to populism, whilst acknowledging that populism today may have shifted and evolved from its previous iterations and thus needs new thinking to reconsider it, redescribe it, and bring it up to date in a way that is sensitive to its time and space context. This is especially pertinent and pressing given that the contemporary political landscape that populism finds itself within is increasingly mediatised and 'stylised'—something that the approaches to populism identified in this chapter tend to overlook.

In an attempt to provide this renewed perspective on the topic of populism, the next chapter introduces a different approach to populism—the notion of populism as a political style. While other authors have used the term 'political style' to describe the phenomenon, it has remained underdeveloped. It develops this approach by examining leaders that are commonly accepted as populist in the contemporary literature, and identifies the points of similarity and difference of this approach from the approaches identified in this chapter. Seeking to 'thicken' our conceptual understanding of the important role of style and performance within contemporary politics, it offers a way to bring the populist literature into the twenty-first century, to present a nuanced gradational approach to the phenomenon, and to locate populism firmly within the context of the contemporary mediatised political landscape.

3   Understanding Contemporary Populism: Populism as a Political Style

> *The political theorist avoiding the notion of political style because he thinks the notion too difficult or too cumbersome to use is like somebody who decides that it would be too much of an effort to learn the language which is used by the people among whom he lives.*
>
> —Ankersmit (2002, 159)

If populism is not quite an ideology, strategy, discourse or political logic, then what kind of phenomenon is it? This chapter argues that the best way to understand contemporary populism is as a *political style* that is used by a wide range of actors across the world today. This approach stresses the performative aspects of populism, moving beyond the approaches discussed in the previous chapter, and contextualises populism's position in the heavily mediatised and 'stylised' milieu of contemporary politics.

The term 'political style' is not new to the literature on populism, with a number of authors having used it to understand the political communication of populist actors (Canovan 1999; Jagers and Walgrave 2007; Taguieff 1995). However, the term has remained underdeveloped, and has tended to be used synonymously with discourse or rhetoric. Perhaps as a result of this underdevelopment and conceptual slippage, it has not expanded into its own distinct approach to populism to the extent of those laid out in the previous chapter, despite its promise and potential to shine a new light on the phenomenon. This chapter seeks to change this situation by developing and defending the concept of political style, explaining why it is different from other approaches to populism, and how it can be put to use to understand contemporary populism in a novel way.

It does this over four sections. The first section briefly examines the previous usage of the term in the literature on populism, demonstrating that clear definitions have thus far been hard to discern. To remedy this, the second section takes a step back and develops the general concept of political style, which is defined as *the repertoires of embodied, symbolically mediated performance made to audiences that are used to create and navigate the fields of power that comprise the political, stretching from the domain of government through to everyday life.* It does this by drawing on previous work on the notion of political style in the fields of rhetoric, political philosophy and political sociology, and it outlines the reasons why this new notion of political style is an important and useful concept for contemporary political analysis. Having developed this new understanding of political style, the third part of the chapter seeks to discern the key features of *populism* as a political style. This is done inductively, by examining the cases of a number of populist leaders from around the world and determining what links them in terms of political style. The three key features of populism thought of in this way are: *appeal to 'the people' versus 'the elite'; 'bad manners'; and crisis, breakdown or threat.* The fourth section then explains the advantages of utilising this new conception of populism, including its ability to transcend a number of different contexts, its nuanced gradational view of populism, its characterisation of populism's 'thinness' or 'emptiness' and its engagement with questions of political representation.

Political Style in the Literature on Populism

When the term 'political style' has been used previously by scholars who are trying to conceptualise populism, what have they actually meant by it? What aspects of the phenomenon have they tried to grasp and get at by employing 'political style' as a category for understanding populism? The term has been used by a number of influential authors working across different regional literatures. In the European literature, two key authors stand out for their early work using the concept: Taguieff and Canovan. In his seminal 1995 article "Political Science Confronts Populism: From a Conceptual Mirage to a Real Problem", Taguieff follows a path set out earlier by Worsley (1969), arguing that populism "does not embody a particular type of political regime, nor does it define a particular ideological content. It is a political style applicable to various ideological frameworks" (1995, 9). However, in ascribing meaning to the concept of political style, he argues that "populism can only be conceptualized as a type of social and political *mobilization*, which means that the term can only designate a *dimension* of political action or discourse" (1995, 9, emphasis in original), thus conflating elements of a number of definitions presented in the previous chapter—strategy and discourse—with political style. While Taguieff does fill out his conception of populism—identifying five central traits of the concept on the basis of utilising the nationalist populism of Jean-Marie Le Pen as an ideal type, as well identifying two poles of populism (protest/social and identitary/national)—we are still left with a somewhat unclear idea of what a political style actually *is*, beyond some sort of discursive or rhetorical appeal that mobilises 'the people'.

As noted, another key theorist of populism as a political style is Canovan. A common thread running through Canovan's work across three decades of writing on populism is a focus on the phenomenon's communicative dimension. Indeed, from as early as 1984, Canovan argued that the only feature that links populist actors is their "rhetorical style which relies heavily upon appeals to the people" (1984, 313), arguing that populism is "a matter of style rather than substance" (1984, 314). A concerted focus on a rhetorical appeal to 'the people', like that of Taguieff's, continues throughout her work, with Canovan (1999, 3) later arguing that "populism in modern democratic societies is best seen as an appeal to 'the people' against both the established structure of power and the dominant ideas and values of the society", arguing that this feature "in turn dictates populism's characteristic legitimating framework, *political style and mood*" (1999, 3, emphasis mine). Here, focusing on populism's political style means moving beyond the simple framing of 'the people' against those in power, and additionally taking into consideration the *way* that this appeal is shaped and delivered—according to Canovan: "Populist appeals to the people are characteristically couched in a *style* that is 'democratic' in the sense of being aimed at ordinary people" (1999, 5, emphasis in original). This style relies on directness and simplicity, in terms of not only the language it is delivered in but also the kind of analyses and solutions it offers.[1] Canovan's conception of populism provides the inspiration for one of the few stringent empirical applications of populism as a political style: Jagers and Walgrave's (2007) content analysis of political party television broadcasts in Belgium, which develops a measurable concept of populist style, delineating between a 'thin' concept of populism as *"a political communication style of political actors that refers to the people"* (2007, 322, emphasis in original), while a 'thick' concept of populism also adds "an explicit anti-establishment position *and* an exclusion of certain population categories" (2007, 323, emphasis in original). Unsurprisingly, the authors find that on both of these definitions, the Belgian populist party par excellence at the time of their study—Vlaams Blok—had a far more populist communication style than other parties.

As can be seen, it is difficult to delineate these definitions of populism as a political style from the discursive approaches discussed in the previous chapter, as all remain primarily concerned with populism's linguistic or rhetorical dimension. This is also the case for one of the most influential accounts of populism as a political style in the American literature on populism: Kazin's (1995) examination of the 'populist persuasion' in American political history. Kazin refers to populism as "a persistent yet mutable style of political rhetoric with roots deep in the nineteenth century" (1995, 5), elsewhere claiming that it is "a language whose speakers conceive of ordinary people as a notable assemblage not bounded narrowly by class, view their elite as self-serving and undemocratic, and seek to mobilize the former against the latter" (1995, 1). Yet again we remain on the level of discourse or rhetoric here. Despite the sophistication of each of these approaches, the fact remains that the slippage between language, discourse, rhetoric and style make political style a hard concept to get a grasp upon in Taguieff, Canovan and Kazin's work.

It is Knight's (1998) work on populism in Latin America that most clearly articulates what the notion of political style has to offer beyond the rival approaches presented in the previous chapter. Unimpressed with the Latin American literature's tendency to conflate populism with certain social bases, modes of organisation or linkages, Knight argues that populism is a "political *style* characteristically involving a proclaimed rapport with 'the people', a 'them-and-us' mentality, and (often, though not necessarily) a period of crisis and mobilization" (Knight 1998, 223, emphasis in original). We also get a better sense of what *political style* actually is from Knight than from other authors— as he puts it simply, it is "the way of doing politics" (1998, 234). While this is a vague categorisation, Knight illustrates what he means by moving beyond the formally discursive and rhetorical level of analysis provided by Taguieff, Canovan and Kazin and gesturing towards the more performative and affective dimensions of politics—hence the 'doing' part of politics, not just the words that are delivered. Drawing on examples from throughout Mexican history, he refers to President Álvaro Obregón's "bluff, gregarious, wisecracking manner, and a talent for populist gestures" (1998, 236), such as his tendency to wear pyjamas when greeting foreign dignitaries; President Lázaro Cárdenas's public refusal to be associated with elite tastes by eschewing a buffet prepared in his honour in order to eat a chocolate bar and drink water from an old lady's food stall in a plaza; and the image of President Carlos Salinas "marching down dusty streets in casual shirtsleeves or leather jacket" (Knight 1998, 245). Here, fashion, cultural tastes and modes of public performance and self-presentation become important to consider as part of the central appeal to 'the people' in populism. In this case, it is not just enough to speak on behalf of 'the people' to be populist—one must *do populism* and perform for 'the people' as well. The benefit of this approach, according to Knight, is that it has "the virtue of flexibility and—perhaps most important—historical fidelity" (1998, 233) in terms of understanding a broad swath of 'populist' cases across different institutional and ideological contexts. De la Torre's work on Ecuadorian populism has also taken notice of this performative dimensions, moving beyond rhetoric in his examination of Abdalá Bucaram's "actions, words and performances" (de la Torre 2007, 391) and Rafael Correa's demonstrative public spectacles as evidence of their populism (de la Torre 2012).

These authors' distinct contributions to understanding populism as a political style cannot be underestimated: they have each tried to push beyond dominant approaches to populism by highlighting the centrality of its communicative (and at times, performative) appeal. Yet despite their conceptual innovations, Weyland's (2001, 12) critique of the approach still remains potent: "Political style denotes the forms of political performance and emphasizes populism's expressive aspects, including its discourse. But political style is a broad not clearly delimited concept". It is worth noting the specific target of Weyland's critique: it is not that the *features* of populism as a political style laid out by these authors are problematic—indeed, those varying features are relatively uncontroversial and appear throughout the literature in different forms. It is the concept of *political style itself* that remains "broad [and] not clearly delimited". The problem here may be that unlike ideology, political strategy, discourse or political logic, there is no wider literature on 'political style' in general to fall back upon for those authors who wish to utilise the concept to analyse populism.[2] This essentially means the following: if we want to take the notion of populism as a political style seriously, then it is necessary to take a step back, and make clear what we mean by political style first. This involves moving beyond Knight's helpful, but overly suggestive and vague "way of doing politics" (1998, 234), and building political style as a serious social scientific concept useful for empirical analysis.

The Roots of Political Style

The first step, then, for making sense of the term 'political style' is to consider its usage in the wider academic literature. While the term is used indiscriminately throughout the political science and political communication literatures, it is almost never explained or qualified. Rather, it is often utilised whenever the phenomenon at hand does not easily fit into another established conceptual category. In this way, 'political style' often exists as a kind of academic place-holder to group certain phenomena together, or as shorthand for a political 'something' that is ephemeral and difficult to pin down. Such indeterminacy has led to the situation in which it can be put to use to describe anything from "the political style of the Soviet elite" (Burant 1987, 273) to "noir realism as a political style" (Nelson 2008, 1). Much of this terminological slippage stems from the root of the phrase—'style'—and its association with aesthetics, theatre and fashion. As such, it has failed to gain a substantial foothold in the political science literature. Given its rhetorical, performative and visual connotations, it is relegated to the 'outside' of mainstream political science as a 'surface level' feature of politics—something for media scholars, cultural theorists or rhetoricians to study rather than 'serious' political scientists.

Despite the term's slipperiness, two central usages of the term 'style' can be discerned. The first basically equates style with patterns—here, style is a way in which we order or bring together disparate objects or phenomena with similar characteristics so to schematise them in a comprehensible fashion. Ackerman (1962, 227) exemplifies this approach when speaking of style in art history, arguing that it is "a way of characterizing relationships among works of art that were made at the same time and/or place, or by the same person or group". The second usage of the term opposes style to content: for example, Goodman (1975, 799) has argued that "subject is what is said, style is how". Both of these meanings of style are valid, and are often intertwined with one another when the term is put to practical use. For example, when we refer to the Expressionist style in art, we are actually undertaking two tasks: we are first carrying out a grouping activity (in this case, of artists and artistic works), and second, we are basing our judgement on what we are choosing to include (and exclude) within our grouping category on the basis of *how* a work has been painted (style) rather than *what* has been painted (subject).

Although this distinction may be relatively clear-cut when it comes to classifying works of art, the line between style and content is a little more blurry when it comes to politics. In his work on political representation, Ankersmit (2002, 135, emphasis in original) argues that although we might keep the terms 'style' and 'content' apart for reasons of conceptual neatness, "aspects of *political reality itself*, as denoted or referred to by the notions of 'content' and 'style', tend to interfere and interact with one another. . . . [S]tyle sometimes generates content, and vice versa". While Ankersmit does not reference them explicitly, earlier authors who used similar terms to 'political style' also grappled with this important dualism between style and content: Lasswell (1949, 38) argued that "style is not to be dismissed as ornamentation", and claimed that studying style might be useful in interpreting political trends. Later, Verba (1965, 545) linked political style to the "informal norms of political interaction that regulate the way in which beliefs are held", and made links between the expressive communicative styles of politicians and the kinds of policies they might advocate. One should also note the seminal work of Hofstadter, whose *The Paranoid Style in American Politics* (1965) traced a tendency of "heated exaggeration, suspiciousness and conspiratorial fantasy" (1965, 3) in American political history, touching on prairie populism, McCarthyism, Illuminism and Masonry amongst others phenomena. Unable to quite label this tendency an ideology or discourse, 'style' served as the most suitable term for Hofstadter to explore this phenomenon.

Hariman's Political Style

More recently, Hariman (1995), Ankersmit (2002) and Pels (2003) have each attempted to put forward political style as a viable and useful concept for political analysis in the fields of rhetoric, political philosophy and political sociology, respectively. In *Political Style: The Artistry of Power,* Hariman (1995, 2) argues that although political experience is always negotiated through elements of style—"speech, gesture, ornament, decor and other means for modulating perception", there exists no sufficient vocabulary to describe this collection of skills. As such, his theory of political style attempts to fill this lacuna, and to develop the necessary concepts to grasp these important but elusive elements of political life. Hariman (1995, 187) defines political style as

> (1) a set of rules for speech and conduct guiding the alignment of signs and situations, or texts and acts, or behaviour and place; (2) informing practices of communication and display; (3) operating through a repertoire of rhetorical conventions depending on aesthetic reactions; and (4) determining individual identity, providing social cohesion, and distributing power.

Utilising this definition, Hariman identifies four main political styles—realist, courtly, republican and bureaucratic—and explains them by applying a hermeneutic close reading of a text that he argues is indicative of the style, before briefly applying it to contemporary political situations. These are noted in Table 3.1.

TABLE 3.1: Hariman's Political Styles

Style	Characteristics	Text
Realist	Sees the political realm as the state of nature; agents as rational actors; is indicative of the 'common-sense' of modern politics.	*The Prince*—Machiavelli
Courtly	Locates authority in the body of the sovereign; preferences gestural conduct.	*The Emperor: Downfall of an Aristocrat*—Kapuściński
Republican	Preferences verbal and oratorical skill; civic virtue.	Cicero's letters to Atticus
Bureaucratic	Preferences clear definitions; technicality; seen in writing and 'office culture'.	*The Castle*—Kafka

(Adapted from Hariman 1995)

The strong influence of Weber is clear here. Hariman develops political styles as ideal types, arguing that political styles and their related texts are not 'mirrors of nature' per se, but rather act to capture a 'political moment' for critical analysis. Accordingly, "style becomes an analytical category for understanding a social reality" (Hariman 1995, 9). In true Weberian fashion, he further notes that the bureaucratic style is the most powerful of the political styles that he identifies, as "once it gets a toehold . . . [it] can absorb all others" (1995, 173). He is also sure to note that his rubric is merely a starting point, and that there may be other political styles that exist—in fact, how we might conceptualise a 'democratic style' was the topic of a recent issue of *Rhetoric and Public Affairs* (see Engels 2008).

Ankersmit's Political Style

While Hariman's conceptual framework is rooted in the study of rhetoric, Ankersmit (1996) develops his notion of political style from the viewpoint of political philosophy, and in particular, aesthetic theories of representation. Ankersmit argues that the concept of political style offers the most accurate way for theorising how citizens most commonly relate to the fractured, fragmented and postmodern nature of contemporary political reality. This is due to the complicated technocratic nature of modern politics, whereby the complex technical details of policy, governance and political processes are often incomprehensible to the general public. If this is the hard-to-grasp 'inside' of modern politics, then political style for Ankersmit (1996, 158) represents the means by "which citizens can regain their grip on a complex political reality" by engaging with its more easily accessible 'outside' or periphery. He likens this to our experience of art, whereby we can appreciate the 'stylistic' elements of a painting for example, without necessarily understanding its 'technical' aspects, which we can leave to connoisseurs and experts. Similarly, to vote for a certain representative, one need not understand every technical detail of how the candidate is elected, how she was pre-selected, how she voted in previous caucus meetings, nor the precise details of her proposed policies—one might simply feel an affective bond to the candidate or might like the way she carries herself. According to Ankersmit's argument, political style is thus a central aspect of political reality, as it is the very domain or space where mass politics occurs, where politicians most often relate to the electorate, and citizens to the state.

Although this concept of political style may be criticised for being 'unscientific' or 'superficial', Ankersmit (2002, 151, emphasis in original) argues that these are its actual strengths:

> [T]he notion of style *is* unscientific and 'superficial' in the proper sense of that word, but this is precisely why we need it so much: for in our dealings with other human beings we are interested in what goes on *between* us, so in what is on the *surface* of the behaviour of the other, so to speak.

Political style, then, does not reveal "some deep, psychological truth about the other" (Ankersmit 2002, 151) but is located at the level of the most common and mundane everyday experience of politics. In constructing this concept, Ankersmit correctly rejects the clichéd and elitist notion of the 'informed citizen' who has access to all the information needed to make 'rational' political decisions—a kind of *homo politicus*—and acknowledges more realistically how people *actually* interact with politics on an everyday level. The further importance of identifying political styles come in their historicity: Ankersmit (2002, 159) argues that new developments in political reality will always bring about the development of new political styles. Consequently, to ignore political style is to overlook an important stratum of political experience, as well as fail to notice the constantly shifting terrain of contemporary politics.

Pels's Political Style

The work of Pels, both on his own (2003) and with coauthors (Corner and Pels 2003a; Pels and te Velde 2000) represents a sociological 'thickening' of Ankersmit's theoretical work. Pels links the increasing importance of political style in contemporary politics to broad changes in the mediatic landscape, pointing to trends like the increased media coverage of politicians, the emergence of the 'cultural economy' and the cult of celebrity as bringing about an increased 'stylisation' of politics more generally. According to Pels (2003, 45):

"'Style' refers to an heterogeneous ensemble of ways of speaking, acting, looking, displaying, and handling things, which merge into a symbolic whole that immediately fuses matter and manner, message and package, argument and ritual". Pels sees this notion of political style as both positive and negative for democratic politics: on one hand, it can help bridge the 'aesthetic gap' between representative and represented by offering more affective 'intimacy' with political actors (particularly through media channels). On the other, Pels worries about political style's ability to empty politics of its 'content', and turn citizens into simple voyeurs who are happy to watch politics at a distance, rather than actively participating.

In a telling example, Pels uses the murdered Dutch populist politician Pim Fortuyn as a paradigmatic illustration of a political actor who keenly understood the power of political style, combining political spectacle and media technologies to great effect. Here was a politician who made politics 'fun' and accessible, who "embodied a politics of stylish individuality and personalised trust", and who "capitalised on his personality as a brand, radically blurring the boundaries between private life and public showtime" (Pels 2003, 42). Importantly, Pels notes that Fortuyn could not have emerged without a media landscape that encouraged and fostered such performances: Fortuyn's success "would have been unthinkable without the expanded visibility afforded by media technologies" (2003, 43).

Hariman's, Ankersmit's and Pels's three conceptions of political style can be broadly linked back to the two interrelated views of style mentioned earlier in this chapter. While Hariman's conception of political style is primarily a typological exercise, drawing together political communicative practices into ideal-type analytical categories, Ankersmit's and Pels's conceptions are concerned with the second, aesthetically based meaning of style—that is, style as opposed to content (although they both succeed in complicating that simplistic binary). What links all of these authors is that they take seriously the often-ignored 'shallow' elements of political style and imbue the concept with analytical substance; and relatedly, that they acknowledge the importance of the communicative and aesthetic dimensions of political activity. So while Hariman provides the classificatory schema needed to think through political styles in the plural, Ankersmit and Pels provide the theoretical sophistication necessary to capture political style's implications for contemporary political analysis. Taken together, their insights provide a strong conceptual basis from which to synthesise and develop a new understanding of political style.

A New Definition of Political Style

In this light, political style can be understood as *the repertoires of embodied, symbolically mediated performance made to audiences that are used to create and navigate the fields of power that comprise the political, stretching from the domain of government through to everyday life.*[3] This new definition bridges the divide between Hariman's definition on one hand and Ankersmit's and Pel's definitions on the other, in that it takes in both the rhetorical (including spoken and written language, argumentation and associated modes of delivery, including tone, gestures and body language), as well as the aesthetic (including images, fashion, self-presentation, design and 'staging'). Framing these elements under the notion of performance shows that these two fields are interrelated, and also stresses that decisions are made about how to present oneself politically—that is, it recognises that political performances are *constructed*. Furthermore, the focus on performance acknowledges that there is always an ever-present power dimension regarding who is able to perform, the audiences that performances are aimed at, and who is able to distribute or broadcast political performances (Alexander and Mast 2006). Finally, the shift towards focusing on performance resonates with recent developments in a number of other academic fields: the 'constructivist turn' in studies of political representation (de Wilde 2013; Disch 2011, 2012; Saward 2010; Severs 2010), whereby it is argued that "representing is performing, is action by actors, and the performance contains or adds up to a claim that someone is or can be representative" (Saward 2010, 66); the 'performative turn' in cultural sociology (see Alexander 2011; Alexander, Giesen and Mast 2006), which has made a forceful argument for the importance of focusing on symbolically mediated action in contemporary social and political analysis; and the turn towards social action in political sociology (Jansen 2011; Tilly 2008).

While there are various antecedents for focusing on performance in the analysis of social or political phenomena, including Burke's (1957 [1941], 1965) dramatism and approach to symbolic action, Goffman's (1959) dramaturgical analysis, Austin's (1975) speech act theory and Butler's (1990) work on performativity, political style's focus on the performative is given particular significance by empirical shifts in how politics operates in the contemporary world. The shape of the political has undoubtedly changed under conditions of reflexive modernity (Beck 2006) and the age of communicative abundance (Keane 2013). The sustained challenge to the legitimacy of 'mainstream' or 'traditional' politics—characterised by the decline of ideological cleavages, the displacement of the class character of politics and the alienation of ordinary citizens from traditional party politics amongst other factors (Crouch 2004; Mair 2006; Tormey 2015; van Biezen, Mair and Poguntke 2012)—have seen 'styles' and 'repertoires' take on much greater resonance as markers of political experience, rather than party affiliation or other markers of 'formal' political activity. Combined with the increased mediatisation of politics, this has meant that the political has become more 'stylised' and 'spectacular' in both the precise (Debord 1994; Vaneigem 1994) and ordinary usage of term. The point here is not to argue that all politics is now purely 'surface' (as per Baudrillard 1994), nor on the other hand that the 'superficiality' of contemporary politics conceals a much more important, obfuscated Real (as per Žižek 1999), but simply to acknowledge and highlight the fact that contemporary politics are intensely mediatised and 'stylised', and as such the so-called 'aesthetic' and 'performative' features of politics are particularly (and increasingly) important. In such a state, style and performance become central to political experience and analysis, whereby political actors must perform, project and make themselves visible through mediatic channels across public, private and institutional spheres (Corner 2003) in order to achieve political success.

With its focus on symbolically mediated performance, it is clear that the notion of political style developed in this chapter differs substantially from other central approaches to labelling populism explored in the previous chapter, such as ideology or discourse. While ideological approaches are generally concerned with analysing sets of beliefs, ideas and values (Freeden 2003), or exploring the reproduction and maintenance of certain Weltanschauungen, they do not emphasise performative elements. Ideological 'content' is their focus, which, as has been argued, is only one part of the picture. So while we can accurately speak of liberalism and socialism as ideologies, the political styles associated with them are not necessarily functions *of* the ideology: the ideology of communism, for example, has spurred very different political styles, from the grandiose displays associated with Stalin to the more modest styles associated with communists like Luxemburg. In other words, ideology and political style are not mutually reliant on each other, nor are they one and the same. As such, in our particular case, populism does not need to be understood as an ideology to examine it as a political style.

There is some overlap between the political style approach and discursive approach, in that political style's focus on the performative folds in a number of discursive features, such as use of language, speech, written texts and so forth. However, political style also moves *beyond* these features, taking in aesthetic and performative elements that the discursive approach does not take into account, including images, self-presentation, body language, design and 'staging'. There is a clear distinction here: while discursive approaches focus primarily on discursive 'content' and have a tendency to sideline the ways in which this 'content' is presented, framed, performed, enacted or broadcast, the political style approach is sensitive to both features. It recognises that 'style' and 'content' are linked, and that both need to be acknowledged. More so, there is a split between the discursive and political style approaches when it comes to the question of ideas versus action: while Jansen (2011, 80) notes that "the discursive approach assumed that ideas and subjectivities translate unproblematically into political action", the political style approach flips the equation, and rather sees political performance and action as *constitutive* of identities in the first place.

In this regard, the political style approach finds much consonance with Laclau's political logic approach discussed in the previous chapter. The central reason for this is that Laclau also highlights the constitutive effect of political action on political identity, and puts the notion of *performance* at the core of this operation. Indeed, Laclau draws on the performative throughout his theory of populism, claiming that "our approach to the question of popular identities is grounded, precisely, in the performative dimension of naming" (2005b, 103), that populism "tries to operate performatively within a social reality" (2005b, 118) and most important, making clear that the constitution of 'the people' relies on "a *performative* operation" (2005b, 97, emphasis mine), rather than 'the people' being some already existing group that awaits a representative to speak on their behalf. His approach also makes clear the central role of the leader in carrying out this performative operation—something that will be discussed in detail in the next chapter. Finally, both the political style and political logic approaches share the view that style and content are intricately linked, and that style is a category that is worthy of serious consideration: while Laclau did not use the terms exactly, he indicated towards the link when he argued that "we could say that a movement is not populist because in its politics or ideology it presents actual contents identifiable as populistic, but because it shows a particular logic of articulation of those contents—whatever those contents are" (2005c, 33). In other words, it is not just about the 'what' of populism—content—but also importantly the 'how'—the style.

Yet while there might be similarities between Laclau's approach and the political style approach outlined here, there also remain central differences. Specifically, the political style approach has a more focused and clearly delineated field of analysis. While the approach associated with Laclau argues that "all objects are objects of discourse" (Howarth and Stavrakakis 2000, 3), and thus takes potentially *anything* as its focus for analysis given that nothing can be 'outside' discourse, the political style approach narrows its focus to the embodied, symbolically mediated performative elements of politics (taking in rhetoric, aesthetics and performance). As such, while the key conceptual tools of Laclauian analysis are empty signifiers, dislocation, nodal points and antagonism, the political style approach utilises conceptual tools from dramaturgical approaches to politics that are arguably more 'concrete' and useful for empirical analysis—performance, actors, audiences, stages, scripts and mise-en-scène. This is particularly useful for the empirical analysis of populism, refocusing on its *ontic* content rather than the phenomenon's ontological structure. Finally, the political style approach arguably remains more open and versatile in its ability to be combined with other theoretical approaches than the political logic approach: if one wishes to use Laclau's approach to populism, one must also essentially accept Laclau's overall theoretical schema, his theory of hegemony and his ontology. However, this ontology of 'constitutive lack' has been criticised for being problematically essentialist and stultifying (Robinson 2005), while his theory of hegemony has been critiqued for its self-validating theoretical structure and its universal claims (Arditi 2007b; Beasley-Murray 2010). In comparison, the political style approach is not rooted in a set ahistorical ontological framework, but instead is sensitive to the time and space-bound contours of contemporary politics, which are intensely mediatised and 'stylised'. Accordingly, one does not need to subscribe to a distinct political theoretical framework to utilise the concept of political style.

Populism as a Political Style

Having outlined the concept of political style, we can now move onto the pertinent question of how *populism* can be thought of as a distinct political style. This section outlines the features of populism as a political style, explaining how this definition was developed, describing each of these features, and outlining the advantages of thinking of populism in this way.

How have the features of populism as a political style been discerned? This was done on an inductive basis,[4] in which a review of the literature on contemporary populism (from the 1990s onwards) was undertaken, and twenty-eight cases of leaders who were generally accepted as examples of populists were identified. To be 'generally accepted' as populists, the leaders had to be labelled as populists by at least six authors within the literature. While this selection criterion may be at risk at being academically introspective, it was undertaken with the assumption that the best place to start when considering populism is the scientific literature on the subject. More so, while there is wide disparity in the literature as to how to conceptualise populism (as demonstrated in the previous chapter), there is at least some (mild) consensus regarding the actual cases of actors that are usually called 'populist'.[5] In other words, while authors may not agree on what populism *'is'*, they tend to agree more on who populists *are,* and have a habit of drawing on the same cases throughout the literature. As such, in selecting cases on which to base the notion of populism as a political style, any 'borderline' cases, where the categorisation of the actor as populist is a matter of significant and sustained debate (examples include Viktor Orbán and Alexis Tsipras), were ignored. So while mild consensus may not be an ideal starting point for the inductive redefinition of a concept, it is the best—or perhaps more precisely, 'least worst'—place to begin when dealing with such a contested concept.

In order to ensure geographical coverage of populism across the world, populists were included from a number of regions. These included eight populist leaders each from Europe and Latin America, and four from North America, Africa and the Asia-Pacific regions. The reason for the increased number of leaders examined from Europe and Latin America is twofold: first, these are the most-covered regions in the literature on populism, and second, these regions have the most populist leaders in the period covered in this book. To reduce them to the number of populist leaders from the other regions would be to ignore some of the most important empirical cases of populism in recent times. The leaders were then examined to find out what linked them in terms of political style. The table in Appendix I outlines the leaders examined, the country that they are from, and key authors who have classified the leader as populist. While the list is not exhaustive—and some more 'recent' populists whose stature grew as the writing of the book progressed, such as Nigel Farage, Timo Soini, Jimmie Åkesson, Donald Trump and Clive Palmer, were unfortunately not included because of time and geographical limits—it is broadly representative of the academic consensus as it currently stands.

Populist leaders, rather than populist movements or parties, have been focused upon, because they are most clearly the central performers and 'embodiments' of populism as a distinct political style. As shall be outlined in the next chapter, leaders hold a central position in all contemporary theories of populism, and popular discussion and concern about populism often focuses on the personalities and performances of populist leaders, over and above the parties or movements to which they are attached.[6]

It is important to note that this is not an attempt to capture the very 'essence' of populism, nor is it an ideal-type (as per Hariman's approach to political style). Rather, this approach allows us to chart, as a baseline, what links a number of disparate cases of contemporary populism across the world—very much in line with Canovan's and Knight's original usages of political style—and construct a minimal concept (in line with the approaches advocated by those working within the ideological and strategic approaches to populism) that outlines the three necessary and sufficient characteristics to be considered as utilising the populist style. The features of the concept should thus not be considered in isolation from one another—each feature is not 'in itself' populist. Like the approaches to populism considered in the previous chapter, the concept should thus be considered as the sum of its parts. So what are the features of the populist style?

Features of Populism as a Political Style

Appeal to 'the People' versus 'the Elite'

'The people' is both the central audience of populists, as well as the subject that populists attempt to 'render-present' (Arditi 2007a) through their performance. 'The people' are also presented as the true holders of sovereignty. This appeal to 'the people' can take many forms, from invocations of 'the people', 'the mainstream', 'the heartland' or other related signifiers, to performative gestures meant to demonstrate populists' affinity with 'the people'.

Connected to the appeal to 'the people' is the dichotomic division of society between 'the people' and 'the elite' (or other related signifiers, such as 'the Establishment' or 'the system')—a divide that is acknowledged throughout the majority of contemporary definitions of populism.[7] Populists may also target particular Others—such as asylum seekers, immigrant workers or particular minority groups—as enemies of 'the people', but these Others will be linked to 'the elite'. For example, it might be argued that 'liberal elites' have allowed increased immigration, which has led to an influx of migrants, which has threatened 'the people's' livelihood. In such cases, it is 'the elite' or 'the Establishment' that is the source of crisis, breakdown, corruption or dysfunctionality, as opposed to 'the people' who in turn have been 'let down', 'ripped off', 'fleeced', rendered powerless, or badly governed.

The appeal to 'the people' can also include claims against the 'political correctness' of the system/elite, which are used to demonstrate that the populist 'really knows' what people are thinking as well as prove their exteriority from such entities (Barr 2009). This often takes the form of the denial of expert knowledge, and the championing of 'common sense' against the bureaucrats, technocrats, representatives or 'guardians of our interests'. This was particularly evident in the language of Preston Manning's Reform Party of Canada, whose charter declared that "we believe in the common sense of the common people" (Reform Party of Canada 1993, 2), as well as figures like Evo Morales's or Pauline Hanson's valorisation of the wisdom of ordinary citizens.[8]

'Bad Manners'

A function of the appeal to 'the people' as the arbiters of 'common sense', the 'way forward' and of the urgency of the matters that populist actors present is a coarsening of political rhetoric, and a disregard for 'appropriate' modes of acting in the political realm. Canovan (1999, 5) has identified this as the 'tabloid style' of populism, while Ostiguy (2009b) has identified this as the 'low' of a high-low axis that runs orthogonal to the traditional left-right axis. Such elements of this 'low' include use of slang, swearing, political incorrectness, and being overly demonstrative and 'colourful', as opposed to the 'high' behaviours of rigidness, rationality, composure and use of technocratic language. An American example of this high-low distinction would be to compare the refined manner of Al Gore to the populist manner of Sarah Palin. Gore's virtues are those of the establishment: seriousness, earnestness, gravitas, intelligence and sensitivity to the positions of others. Palin's are those of the 'outsider': directness, playfulness, a certain disregard for hierarchy and tradition, ready resort to anecdote as 'evidence', and a studied ignorance of that which does not interest her or which does not go to 'the heart of the matter'. What constitutes the 'bad manners' of populism may differ from one cultural context to another: as Ostiguy (2009b, 5–6) makes clear in his conceptualisation of populism: "[I]ssues of accents, level of language, body language, gestures, ways of dressing, etc. . . . link deeply with a society's history, existing group differences, identities, and resentments", meaning that such divisions are often culturally specific, yet have great political and cultural resonance.

Crisis, Breakdown, Threat

Populism gets its impetus from the perception of crisis, breakdown or threat (Taggart 2000), and at the same time aims to induce crisis through drama-tisation and performance. This in turn leads to the demand to act decisively and immediately. Crises are often related to the breakdown between citizens and their representatives, but can also be related to immigration, economic difficulties, perceived injustice, military threat, social change or other issues. The effect of the evocation of emergency in this fashion is to radically simplify the terms and terrain of political debate. For example, Hugo Chávez ramped up his populist style in the light of a perceived crisis regarding an imperialist conspiracy perpetrated by the United States, while Geert Wilders has posited the increasing Islamisation of the Netherlands as an imminent threat to social and economic well-being.

This performance of crisis, breakdown or threat relates to a more general distrust of the complex machinery of modern governance and the complicat-ed nature of policy solutions, which in contemporary settings often require consultations, reviews, reports, lengthy iterative design and implementation. In contrast, populists favour short-term and swift action rather than the 'slow politics' (Saward 2011) of negotiation and deliberation. Politics thus becomes highly instrumentalised and utilitarian. That which gets in the way of address-ing 'the issue' or the 'crisis' has to be ignored, supplanted or removed.

Implications

Contemporary populism can thus be defined as *a political style that features an appeal to 'the people' versus 'the elite', 'bad manners' and the performance of crisis, breakdown or threat.* Thinking of populism in this way has four central repercussions for the analysis of populism.

The first is that the notion of populism as a political style allows us to un-derstand populism's ability to appear across a number of contexts. As a political style, there is little difficulty in understanding why populism can travel across the ideological spectrum, from left to right, as well as making sense of populist actors who are more difficult to map on the traditional left-right divide, such as Beppe Grillo (Corbetta and Vignati 2013). It also delinks populism from cer-tain modes of organisation, allowing us to see that populism can rely on loose or 'grassroots' structures, as well as highly organised structures of tight party discipline.

Second, the political style approach moves away from the dominant view of seeing populism as a binary category towards conceptualising it as a gradational concept. Binary approaches (such as the ideological and strategic approaches outlined in the previous chapter) view the category as a simple populism vs. nonpopulism binary, whereas the political style approach acknowledges that political actors can be *more or less populist* at certain times. Put in another way, while binary approaches see populism in a 'black-and-white' fashion, the political style approach accounts for the 'gray area' between the two extremes. Focusing on this gray area acknowledges that "the degree of populism that a given political actor employs may vary across contexts and over time" (Gidron and Bonikowski 2013, 9), and in this regard, the political style approach shares ground with the discursive and political logic approaches outlined in the previous chapter.

However, if we are to see populism as a gradational property, then it is important to identify what is on the 'other end' of the spectrum: what is the opposite of populism? While Mudde and Rovira Kaltwasser (2013b) have argued that populist ideology is the opposite of pluralist and elitist ideologies, and Hawkins (2012) has presented populist discourse as the opposite of pluralist discourse, when it comes to political style, populism should be opposed to technocratic political style.[9] This spectrum is illustrated in Figure 3.1.

Each of the features of the technocratic style are directly opposed to the features of populist political style. While populists appeal to 'the people' versus 'the elite' and argue that we should trust 'common sense' or the wisdom of 'the people', technocrats place their faith in expertise and specialist training, and by and large do not concern themselves with 'the people'. While populists utilise 'bad manners' in terms of their language and aesthetic self-presentation, technocrats have 'good manners', acting in a 'proper' manner in the political realm, utilising 'dry' scientific language, dressing formally and presenting themselves in an 'official' fashion. This divide is also marked by the role of affect and emotion: while populists rely on emotional and passionate performances, technocrats aim for emotional neutrality and 'rationality'. Finally, while populists aim

Technocratic Political Style		Populist Political Style
Appeal to expertise		Appeal to 'the people' vs. 'the elite'
'Good manners'		'Bad manners'
Stability and progress		Crisis, breakdown, threat

FIGURE 3.1: Technocratic-Populist Political Style Spectrum

to invoke and perform crisis, breakdown or threat, technocrats aim for and perform stability or measured progress.[10] Here, the 'proper' functioning of society is presented as being able to be delivered by those with the requisite knowledge, training and standing.

The divide between technocracy and populism has been put forward by a number of prominent thinkers on populism, including Laclau (2005b), Mouffe (2005a,b) and Žižek (2006a, 2008), and has also been invoked in recent policy and popular debates about populism in Europe (Freeland 2012; Leonard 2011) and the United States (Kenneally 2009; C. Williams 2010). It is important to stress that the difference between populism and technocracy here does not refer to modes of governance or ideological dispositions, but to *distinct embodied, performative political styles*. We are interested in the way that political actors *present themselves* along this technocratic-populist scale, not in the models of government they might present or advocate. Leonard (2011, 2) sketches the performative differences between populism and technocracy as such: "Technocracy and populism are mirror images: one is managerial, the other charismatic; one seeks incremental change, the other is attracted by grandiose rhetoric; one is about problem solving, the other about the politics of identity".

Plotting political actors along this scale rather than seeing populism as a simple either/or proposition has a number of benefits. As noted above, it is more nuanced than a binary approach. Second, it avoids implicit normative views overshadowing the categorisation of political actors. While seeing populism as a binary category may allow comparativists to put political actors and parties in neat boxes for categorisation, too often is it the case that these researchers are not clear about where the blurry line between the categories is actually drawn, thus allowing them (either purposefully or not) to impose their own normative views on populism on their cases. The populism/nonpopulism binary too often echoes its usage in media debates, becoming shorthand for 'political actors I dislike/political actors I like'. The gradational approach does not leave this division up to the researcher's implicit normative views, and instead acknowledges that some of those actors who are commonly labelled as 'populist' may not actually be as populist as we think when scrutinised carefully, while other actors, especially those usually subsumed under the vague notion of 'mainstream' political actors, might actually utilise the populist style in some form.

Indeed, such 'mainstream' actors as Tony Blair (Mair 2002), George W. Bush (Shogan 2007), Nicolas Sarkozy (Mondon 2013) and John Howard (Wear 2008) have all been accused of being populists by scholars who work in the field. While we should not necessarily take these labels on face value, the binary approach leaves us with no way to deal with such claims with any sensitivity or nuance: you 'are' populist or you are not. On the other hand, the gradational perspective offered by the political style approach allows us to see that such figures may have oscillated around the centre of the populist-technocrat spectrum, perhaps stressing one style more than the other at different periods of time. As such, while we might not be able to call these figures truly 'populist' as they have not used the populist style in a consistent or overt manner, we can understand how they have appropriated elements of the populist toolbox.[11]

Other figures that might fall into gray area include political media actors that utilise the populist style, but have thus far been broadly ignored in the populist literature, as they are not elected officials, running for office, or official members of a political party. Examples of such figures include former US Fox News host Glenn Beck and Australian radio host Alan Jones, whose inflammatory remarks, aggressive manners and self-appointed 'voice of the people' personas map clearly onto the definition of populism presented. Despite officially being 'media actors', these figures have been heavily involved in populist politics, with Krämer (2014, 50) going so far as to call such talkback radio hosts and associated print media editorialists "often downright leaders of nonbureaucratic populist movements". For example, Beck created the '9/12 Project', which is a self-described "volunteer based, non-partisan movement focusing on building and uniting our communities back to the place we were on 9/12/2001" (9/12 Project 2010), and organised the "Restoring Honor" rally in Washington D.C. in August 2010, which was promoted by the Tea Party (Leibovich 2010). Meanwhile, Jones played an active role in promoting and acting as the master of ceremony at the antigovernment 'Convoy of No Confidence' in Canberra in 2011, which Wear (2014) has identified as a populist 'astroturf' event.[12] With such "unelected representatives" (Keane 2009b, 2013; Saward 2009, 2010) who claim to speak for 'the people' becoming increasingly common, these figures deserve further attention in the populist literature as users of the populist style.

The third implication of seeing populism as a political style is that we can now make sense of what other approaches to populism have seen as the phenomenon's lack of 'substance'. Taggart (2000, 4) has referred to populism's "empty heart"; Mény and Surel (2002, 4) have called it an "empty shell"; while as seen in the previous chapter, others have referred to it as a 'thin' or 'thin-centred' ideology (Abts and Rummens 2007; Mudde and Rovira Kaltwasser 2013b;

Stanley 2008). Critics of populism have also noted the phenomenon's apparent 'emptiness'—former Mexican foreign minister Jorge Castañeda (2006, 38) has claimed that "rhetoric is more important than substance" for populist leaders in Latin America today; while the former president of the European Council, Herman Van Rompuy, has attacked Italian populist Beppe Grillo for lacking 'substance', claiming that he "has votes but he doesn't have policies" (in Carroll 2013). The explanation of populism as a 'thin ideology' does not quite capture what is going on here, and does not explain how or why populism interacts in the way that it does with so-called thicker 'host ideologies'. The notion of populism offered in this chapter offers an alternative explanation of populism's 'thinness' or lack of 'substance' by emphasising populism's primarily *stylistic characteristics*—that is, what is ostensibly 'on the surface' of populist politics— as of great analytical importance. This does not mean, however, that populism is 'superficial', and we should not underestimate it on these grounds. Style and content are interrelated, and style can generate, affect and interact with content in quite complex ways.

Fourth, the political style approach gives us a new conceptual vocabulary to work with when trying to make sense of populism. Focusing on performers, audiences, stages, performative repertoires and mise-en-scène not only speaks to the inherent theatricality involved in populism but also brings the issue of how *populist representation* operates to the forefront of any discussion of the phenomenon. By conceptualising populism as a political style, the question is not only *who* 'the people' are, but also *how* the activity of interpellating or 'rendering-present' (Arditi 2007a) 'the people' actually occurs. This means that it is not enough just to analyse the 'content' of the signifiers of 'the people' and 'the elite' (for example, are 'the people' perceived to be a nation, or perhaps an underclass? Are 'the elite' financial oligarchs, or the government?), but that we should also ask the following questions: *how* are these categories constituted through performance? What do populist leaders actually *do* when they claim to speak for and embody 'the people'? Who are the audiences for these performances? What stages do they take place upon? And why are some performances made in the name of 'the people' received well, while others are perceived as insincere and unsuccessful? The emphasis on performance shifts the focus from *forms* of representation to the actual *mechanisms* of representation—mediated enactments, televisual performances, rallies, speeches, riots, use of certain dress, vernacular and so forth—and in doing so, stresses the very important (and sometimes forgotten) role of presentation in re-*presentation*. The following chapters use these concepts to map out a picture of how populism is *'done'* as a performed political style across the globe today.

Conclusion

In the famous 1969 Ionescu and Gellner collection on populism, Worsley (1969, 245) argued that populism needs to be understood as an "emphasis, a dimension of political culture in general, not simply a particular kind of over-all ideological system or type of organization". The same still holds, but this 'emphasis' is best expressed in the idea of political style, the repertoires of embodied, symbolically mediated performance made to audiences that are used to create and navigate the fields of power that comprise the political. While the term 'political style' has been used somewhat haphazardly in the existing literature, it has been the aim of this chapter to give the term substance, to make it less slippery and more useful for political analysis—both in the empirical study of populist leaders, and in the development of theory around populism.

This chapter has made clear that the concept of populism as a political style is sensitive to the contours of the contemporary politics, as politics becomes increasingly more 'stylised', mediatised and spectacular. In this context, it is little wonder that populism has established itself as a permanent feature of the political landscape over the past twenty years or so. The concept of political style allows us to rethink populism by placing its performative dimensions at front and centre, and gives us a chance to reflect on the complex relationship between style and content. For all these reasons, thinking about populism as a political style opens up a timely and important new dimension from which to explore the phenomenon.

4   The Performer: Populism and the Leader

I AM the people–the mob–the crowd–the mass.
Do you know that all the great work of the world is done through me?
I am the workingman, the inventor, the maker of the world's food and clothes.
I am the audience that witnesses history. The Napoleons come from me
    and the Lincolns. They die. And then I send forth more Napoleons and
    Lincolns.
                   "I Am the People, the Mob"—Carl Sandburg (1970, 71)

    I am not an individual, I am the people.
    —Chávez in AFP (2010)

A set of important questions begin to emerge when we view populism as a political style: who actually 'performs' populism? What do these performances look like? Who are these performances aimed towards? And where do these performances take place? In order to answer these questions, the next four chapters of the book seek to unpick the constituent parts of the performative relationships at the heart of contemporary populism: the performers, the audiences, the mise-en-scène and the stages that these relationships play out upon. Examining each of these elements of contemporary populism helps to provide an understanding of how populism operates in the contemporary mediatised political landscape. The following chapters each follow a similar structure, introducing the particular aspect of populism to be examined, outlining how it is presented in the contemporary literature on populism (as per the approaches identified in Chapter 2), and explaining what the political style approach adds to our knowledge of the phenomenon of populism today. Weaving together conceptual insights with empirical illustrative examples, they give a fuller and richer picture of the shape of contemporary populism.

    This chapter focuses on the first element of this relationship: the leader as the *performer* of populism. While those who study populism are often split on what agent to focus upon—leaders, parties or movements—this chapter makes the argument that in these mediatised times, it is the leader that should be our main focus when studying the phenomenon, given that they are the figures that ultimately 'do' populism. The reasons for doing this are numerous: the leader is the figure that performs and renders-present 'the people' within populism; the leader is the central figure of affective focus from populist followers *as well as* the central target of derision or hatred from opponents; and because populist leaders' links to political parties and movements vary widely across regional contexts. More broadly, it is clear that for audiences beyond the ivory towers of academia, it is the leader that is generally the focus when it comes to populism: Geert Wilders, Thaksin Shinawatra and Hugo Chávez are the household names, not necessarily the parties attached to them.

In making this argument, the chapter examines how populist leaders must strike a balance between appearing as both ordinary and extraordinary to appeal to 'the people'. In doing so, they must ostensibly be of 'the people' *as well as* simultaneously beyond 'the people'. They attempt to achieve this balance in a number of central ways. The chapter outlines how populists appear as ordinary by utilising 'bad manners' to distance themselves from other political actors in terms of legitimacy and authenticity, often breaking the unwritten rules about how politicians are 'supposed' to conduct themselves. On the other hand, it demonstrates how populist leaders appear as extraordinary by positioning themselves as the embodiment of 'the people', and examines how this can take a more literal form in terms of how the leader's performance of health, strength, sexuality and strong corporeal presence links with notions of a strong 'people'. The chapter demonstrates that the tightrope walk between ordinariness and extraordinariness can be a difficult balancing act, with the populist performance often at risk of being disrupted.

The Role of the Populist Leader

But let us get down to basics: what does the leader actually *do* when it comes to populism? While there is a general consensus in the populist literature that the leader is *important* to populism, current approaches to understanding populism differ in regards as to what they see as the actual role of the leader: are they 'organisers' of populist followers, 'articulators' of populist discourse or ideology or just representative figureheads who happen to lead populist parties or movements? Should we even focus on leaders, or are parties and movements more important when it comes to populism?

A number of authors place the leader at the centre of their analysis of populism, seeing the leader as vital to the phenomenon in that they are responsible for bringing 'the people' together. However, they tend to differ in regards to *how* they think 'the people' are brought together by the leader. Those who subscribe to the view of populism as a strategy often view the leader as *literally* bringing 'the people' together, acting as the figure who unites an unorganised mass of followers through noninstitutional means. For example, Weyland's (2001, 14) influential definition of populism portrays the leader as the key figure responsible for mobilizing the masses, while Roberts has argued that "personalistic and paternalistic . . . leadership" (1995, 88) is a core feature of populism, and has developed four subtypes of populism based on the mode of linkage between the populist leader and followers (2006).

Others take a less literal approach, viewing the leader as the central figure in populism in that they bring 'the people' together on a *symbolic* level. For Laclau (2005b, 100), who sees populism as a political logic, 'the people' simply cannot emerge without a leader, as "the symbolic unification of the group around an individuality—and here I agree with Freud—is inherent to the formation of a 'people'". According to Laclau's account, under populism, the name of the leader begins to act as an empty signifier in which 'the people' can lay their various demands and complaints about the system. Because of their shared opposition to the system, these demands become linked in what Laclau calls an 'equivalential chain' under the name of the leader, and thus it is through the leader that disparate identities become symbolically linked together as a new political subject—'the people'.

However, not all authors who write on populism are as certain about the role of the leader, particularly those who see populism as an ideology or discourse. Although at times the authors working within the ideological approach depict the leader as the articulator (Stanley 2008, 103) or "main protagonist" (Mudde and Rovira Kaltwasser 2011, 6) of populism, in that the leader is the figure that delivers the 'content' of the populist ideology, they also tend to focus at least as much (if not more) on populist parties (for example, Albertazzi and McDonnell 2008; de Lange and Art 2011; Mudde 2007). A similar ambivalence marks the literature on populism as a discourse. While a number of authors within this tradition see the leader as the key articulator of populist discourse (Barros 2005; Hawkins 2010), others place their focus on the party as their key unit of analysis, focusing on party literature or manifestoes (Pauwels 2011; Rooduijn and Pauwels 2010).

What is clear across each of these approaches is that the choice of whether one decides to focus on the leader, party or movement when it comes to studying populism is heavily influenced by the case or region that one is writing about. Those who place central focus on the leader have tended to be situated within the literature on Latin American, African or Asian-Pacific populism, whereas those who focus on parties have tended to study European populism. In many ways, this makes sense, with numerous Latin American populist leaders (including Hugo Chávez, Alberto Fujimori and Fernando Collor), African populist leaders (including Michael Sata and Raila Odinga) and Asian-Pacific populist leaders (including Thaksin Shinawatra and Pauline Hanson) cycling through different party affiliations and organisations, while European populist parties have arguably been more stable and long lasting. This trend also reflects a broader divide between the predominantly presidential systems of Latin America and the predominantly parliamentary systems of Europe, whereby leaders are more prominent and powerful in the former case (see the chapters in Mudde and Rovira Kaltwasser 2012b). However, this divide creates some problems when it comes to cross-regional comparisons: how do you compare a leader with a party if you want to study populism? This tension can be seen in the work of Mudde, whose earlier work on European populism (Mudde 2007, 36–38) noted the methodological pitfalls involved in focusing on populist leaders rather than political parties, but whose recent comparative work on European and Latin American populism with Rovira Kaltwasser has focused on both leaders *and* parties, claiming that "the two are deeply interlinked, which often makes it difficult to differentiate between the ideas of the former and the latter" (Mudde and Rovira Kaltwasser 2013a, 156). While understandable, this is not the most convincing argument for a comparativist to make, given that identifying a common unit of analysis across cases is a basic requirement of comparative research (Lijphart 1971).

With these tensions in mind, there are a number of important reasons for choosing to focus on the leader as the key actor or 'performer' of contemporary populism. First, individual leaders are undoubtedly the most visible and prominent symbols of populism today, with much academic and popular discussion of populism hinging on their personalities and performances. The devotion of followers—and indeed, the hatred of detractors—similarly hangs on the leader in many cases rather than the party. Second, a significant number of populist parties function as little more than 'personal parties'[1] (McDonnell 2013) that prop up the political careers of the leader, and a number of prominent populist figures—Berlusconi, Hanson, Thaksin, Chávez and Wilders—have shifted through a number of party affiliations to suit their personal political ambitions and needs, suggesting that the leader is more pertinent than the party in populism. Third, and perhaps most important, leadership is relatively constant across a number of regional contexts when it comes to contemporary populism, whereas party or movement forms are not.[2]

None of this is to say, however, that contemporary populist movements must always *begin* with a leader, and nor should we assume that populist movements must always develop and coalesce into formal political parties with a distinct leader. The US Tea Party arguably does not fulfil either of these criteria. It is fair to say, however, that populist movements almost always *end up* with a clear leader, as do populist parties. Given the populist combination of the desire for quick action and distaste for complexity, it makes sense that the demands or messages of a populist movement will find unification, representation and voice in a strong figure.[3] This process can also work in the opposite way, in which a leader with an appealing political message or style can emerge and rally enough followers who identify with their characterisation of 'the people' to attempt to develop a movement around them. In either process, it is the leader that ultimately 'performs' populism, and should thus be seen as the key actor of populism. To put it simply: while we can imagine populism without a party (such as the Tea Party), or populism without a movement (that is, a politician who claims to speak in the name of 'the people' but without a popular base behind them), it is rather difficult to imagine contemporary populism *without leadership at all.*[4]

Balancing Extraordinariness and Ordinariness

Yet the populist leader is stuck with a difficult dilemma in being the central performer of populism: how can you be of 'the people' as well as transcend 'the people' at the same time? How can a leader be "exactly like you are", as Chávez (in Zúquete 2008, 100) once claimed, yet also be special or talented enough to rise above 'the people' as their leader and representative? In order to do this effectively, populist leaders must negotiate the precarious balance between appearing as ordinary on one hand, and extraordinary on the other. This combination between extraordinariness and ordinariness is not easy to achieve.

On one hand, the perceived extraordinariness and remarkability of populist leaders are most evident in the way that they are often raised to a celebrity or even messiah-like status in the eyes of their audiences. This perceived centrality and special nature of the leaders within populism is clear in the title of many populist parties that bear the leaders' name—examples include Pauline Hanson's One Nation, Pauline's United Australian Party, Lijst Pim Fortuyn and Groep Wilders—as well as the different forms of populism that are stamped with their name—Berlusconismo, Chavismo, Grillismo, Hansonism and Thaksinomics, among others. Populism in this regard is inextricably tied to the personalities of the 'extraordinary leaders' who are seen as able to channel 'the people's' will and desires, rising above them as their representative.

Positioning the leader as the singular redemptive or extraordinary figure who rises above 'the people' is obviously not a new phenomenon: there are historical precedents in totalitarianism, in which the leader functions as the embodiment of a unified society (Arendt 2004 [1951]), as well as in *caudillismo*, which Krauze (2011, 289–90, emphasis in original) describes as "the concentration of power into the hands of a single man. ... When the *caudillo* takes over, the strictly *personal* passions of a leader (traumas, obsessions, whims) are transferred to the history of the nation, converting history into a kind of 'biography of power'". Some commentators have noted the links between these forms of politics and populism, with a number of authors seeing populism as a kind of 'proto-totalitarianism' (Abts and Rummens 2007; Panizza 2005a), while others have investigated the parallels between *caudillismo* and populism (de la Torre 2010; Mudde and Rovira Kaltwasser 2014).

Yet the perception of the extraordinariness of contemporary populist leaders has been served by two distinctly modern trends—the increasing 'presidentialisation' and 'celebritisation' of contemporary politics. The presidentialisation literature (for example, Helms 2005; Maddens and Fiers 2004; Mughan 2000) describes a situation in which leaders have become as important as—if not *more* important than—policies and platforms in influencing how people vote. Authors point to trends like the increasing concentration of power within the hands of single leaders, the increasing autonomy of leaders and the personalisation of electoral processes as some of the key markers of this process.[5] Meanwhile, the celebritisation literature (for example, Corner and Pels 2003b; Couldry and Markham 2007; Marsh, 't Hart, and Tindall 2010; van Zoonen 2005; Wheeler 2011) has tracked an increased focus on singular, attention-grabbing politicians and their personal lives, relationships and passions in contemporary politics. Taken together, these two modern trends mean that a particular aura is granted to those leaders who can perform successfully for 'the people' by combining strong leadership with interesting, 'accessible' and entertaining personas—in other words, the recipe for so-called extraordinary populist leaders.

Yet unlike its historical precedents, in which the extraordinary nature of the leader need not have any limits, when it comes to populism, this extraordinariness must be tempered with ordinariness. After all, populism is ultimately about 'the people', so populist leaders must be able to present themselves as possessing outstanding leadership qualities—that is, extraordinary—as well as being of 'the people'—that is, ordinary. In describing the rise of "the ultimate celebrity politician" in the twenty-first century, van Zoonen (2005, 84) unwittingly hits on this contradictory performance required by populist leaders: "He or she projects a persona that has inside experience with politics but is still an outsider; his (or in some cases, her) performance builds on a unique mixture of ordinariness and exceptionality". In other words, populists must have one foot in and one foot out at all times—they must 'know' politics while remaining an 'outsider', and must be 'salt of the earth' while rising above those they represent.

Performing Ordinariness: 'Bad Manners'

What forms do these performances of ordinariness take? While most leaders in the contemporary political setting have to play the game of making themselves seem regular or ordinary to some extent—witness Barack Obama's professed love of beer, basketball and hip-hop (McDonald and King 2012), or former Australian prime minister John Howard's much-publicised love of cricket (Hutchins 2005)—populists can take this role to an extreme. Examples of these performances abound: Sarah Palin (2008) has gone to great lengths to prove her ordinary nature, calling herself "just your average hockey mom" and a "mama grizzly" to prove her maternal credentials, and has displayed her 'regular' family at every possible moment to back up these claims. Chávez (2005) presented himself as a "farm kid . . . from a very poor family", and used a folksy and common language on his television show, *Aló Presidente,* to display his ordinary roots. Zambia's Michael Sata often played up his lack of education and mocked his central opponent, a former accountant, as a 'calculator boy' to demonstrate the difference between them (Resnick 2010), while South Africa's Jacob Zuma used a similar tactic against his rival, Thabo Mbeki (Vincent 2011). Meanwhile, Pauline Hanson (2007, 59–60) has made much of her regular nature as an owner of a takeaway fast food shop in suburban Queensland, claiming that "the fish and chip shop put me directly in touch with the average Australian". Fashion and aesthetic self-presentation can also be another important resource in signifying one's ordinariness: Evo Morales's *chompa* (an alpaca wool sweater) signifies a tie to rural areas and the land, as does Yoweri Museveni's ever-present broad-brimmed hat, which associates him with the farming sector of Uganda (Muth 2011).

These performances of ordinariness seek to distance populist leaders from other politicians, who are portrayed as being removed from the experience of everyday citizens, and consequently not 'in touch' with 'the people'. The performances thus seek to bolster the 'outsider' credentials of populist leaders. However, whether they are *actually* 'outsiders' or not does not seem to matter too much if the performance is suitably convincing. Indeed, many populist leaders are objectively *not* outsiders when it comes to occupying the halls of power: to name but a few examples, Geert Wilders had been in politics for twenty years before launching his own party, beginning his career as a parliamentary assistant; Hugo Chávez had a long and storied career in the military before his political success; Thaksin Shinawatra was a millionaire and member of the business elite before joining politics; Silvio Berlusconi owned a media empire; and Ross Perot was a billionaire businessman. Yet these figures have all been able to present themselves as 'outsiders', even if in some cases this has taken some creative rewriting of personal biographies. Populist leaders' status as 'outsiders' is thus a matter of their rhetorical or aesthetic 'location' and perceived distance from mainstream politics (Barr 2009), rather their actual experience as or with 'the elite'. The further that they can dissociate themselves from the technocratic style of 'politics as usual', the better.

Yet claiming to be ordinary goes only so far. Any politician can 'talk the talk', but 'walking the walk' and actually demonstrating that you are not a 'regular politician' is more valuable in proving your populist credentials. The most pertinent way that populist leaders do this is through using 'bad manners'. This concept refers to populist leaders' apparent disregard for 'appropriate' ways of acting in the political realm, and the deliberate flouting of such expectations and practices. The looseness of the term is deliberate, given that these performances of 'bad manners' may manifest in a number of different ways, including self-presentation, use of slang, political incorrectness, fashion or other displays of contempt for 'usual' practices of 'respectable' politics. The term also reflects the fact that considerations of what constitutes appropriate behaviour are themselves culturally specific—bad manners in one political arena may not be considered bad manners in another.

The notion of 'bad manners' is based on the innovative work of Pierre Ostiguy (2009b). Ostiguy outlines the distinction between the 'high' and 'low' in politics, which relate to ways of acting (or in our terms, performing) in politics.[6] As he notes:

> High and low have to do with ways of relating to people; as such, they go beyond "discourses" as mere words, and they include issues of accents, level of language, body language, gestures, ways of dressing, etc. As a way of relating to people, they also encompass the way of making decisions. (Ostiguy 2009b, 5)

This high-low axis runs orthogonal to the left-right axis, and as such is not tied to traditional ideological distinctions. Dividing the high-low axis into two subdimensions (social-cultural and political-cultural), Ostiguy presents his distinction between high and low as noted in Table 4.1.

The attributes of the social-cultural 'low' of Ostiguy's axis partly make up the 'bad manners' that can be ascribed to populist leaders. Indeed, Ostiguy claims that his high-low distinction mirrors the distinction between antipopulism and populism. This is of course correct, but the key difference between Ostiguy's position and the one put forward in this book is that Ostiguy does not stress the binary between 'the people' and 'the elite' as strongly or explicitly as put forward in the previous chapter—a binary that is acknowledged throughout the majority of the literature on populism. More so, while Ostiguy correctly argues that populists often resort to 'coarse' and culturally vulgar appeals, this is not *always* the case—see here the cases of Geert Wilders or Ross Perot, who are relatively 'slick' and can come off as aloof or even border on 'snobby' at times.

TABLE 4.1: Ostiguy's High-Low Spectrum

	Social-cultural	Political-cultural
High	Well behaved Well mannered Composed Rationalist Ethical Stiff/rigid/boring	Impersonal Procedure-driven Formal, impersonal Legalistic/rational Institution-mediated Restrained
Low	Slang/swearing Demonstrative Raw/popular tastes More colourful	Personalistic Strong leadership Closer to 'the people' Decisive action Immediate

(Adapted from Ostiguy 2009b: 7)

Instead, populists like these can often simply seek to distance themselves from other political actors by acting quite *differently* to them; drawing on Arditi's (2007a, 78) metaphor of populism being the 'drunken dinner guest' of contemporary democratic politics, we might simply say that populists disregard the appropriate social cues and 'table manners' in the usually "gentrified domain of political performances". The different methods of upsetting this "gentrified domain" are outlined in more detail below under the rubric of 'bad manners'. Nonetheless, what Ostiguy does offer is a novel consideration of what is appealing about the way that populist leaders *act* as opposed to other kinds of leaders, and how political and sociocultural ways of performing are linked. More so, Ostiguy's high-low distinction adds credence to the position that the divide between populism and its 'opposite'—whether technocracy or antipopulism—is a *gradational* divide, rather than a strict binary. As he notes, the high-low distinction is a "spectrum" (2009, 7) or a "scale" (2009, 24) on which a broad range of political actors can be plotted.

Let us look at a few concrete examples of how 'bad manners' are performed by populist leaders. One way is by lowering the level of political discourse through swearing, taunts or over-the-top claims. For example, Hugo Chávez would often make crude and overly offensive remarks about his opponents; Marine Le Pen has accused political rivals of being paedophiles (Warren 2011); while Beppe Grillo held 'V-Day' rallies against Italian politicians and the mass media—the V standing for *Vaffanculo,* an Italian expletive. Zambian populist Michael Sata was so well known for his venomous attacks on the opposition and his enemies that he was nicknamed 'King Cobra'. Another way is through the *type* of language that is used. Sarah Palin has employed so many non sequiturs and malapropisms—from claims about nonexistent "death panels" (Nyhan 2010) to made-up words such as "refudiate" (Weaver 2010)—that her garbled sayings have earned their own label, 'Palinisms', while Pauline Hanson became similarly well known for her misuse of the English language.

More broadly, 'bad manners' can simply mean acting or presenting oneself in more 'colourful' ways than we usually expect from politicians or representatives: Chávez would sing and dance on his television show *Aló Presidente;* Raila Odinga has sung parodic songs and improvised riddles to mock the opposition in Kenya (Resnick 2010); Pauline Hanson has appeared as a contestant on numerous Australian reality television shows; and Herman Cain released a series of bizarre campaign videos in 2012 showing a rabbit being shot after being catapulted in the air, a goldfish being killed and a man being pecked to death by chickens to apparently characterise the problems of small business in the United States (Cain 2012a, 2012b, 2012c). Needless to say, none of these examples represent 'traditional' behaviour—the social-cultural 'high' of Ostiguy's spectrum, which we associate with typical 'mainstream' party politics—and therein may lay their appeal, or at very least their attention-grabbing qualities.

Populist leaders' 'bad manners' can also take the form of political incorrectness. Often presenting political correctness as a project of elites, populists tend to 'mention the unmentionable', and merely claim to be presenting 'what everyone thinks'—hence the constant references to 'common sense' or 'the silent majority'. This political incorrectness frequently takes the form of claims of favouritism or slurs against minority groups. For example, Hanson continuously rallied against Asian immigrants and Aboriginal rights, and more recently claimed that she would not sell her house to a Muslim (Hirst 2010). Wilders compares the Koran to *Mein Kampf*, and has called the prophet Muhammad a paedophile (Wilders 2010b), while Uganda's Yoweri Museveni has consistently targeted homosexuals, accusing them of "recruiting normal people" and being "mercenaries" and "prostitutes" (in Monitor 2014). Chávez constantly taunted his rivals as *pitiyanquis* ('little Yankees') (Romero 2008), and declared disgraced Libyan dictator Muammar Gaddafi a "martyr" (in Romo 2011). Sarah Palin (in Smith 2009) summed up the populist approach: "Screw the political correctness". Whether such statements are sincere does not matter. Instead, the aim is to get a reaction—often negative—which allows populist leaders to receive media coverage, and further position themselves as being outside 'the elite' or the establishment, who would not dare to utter such things.

The central point is that it is populists' performances—not *just* their policies, ideology, discourse or so-called content of their populism—that are disruptive to 'mainstream' politics. In these technocratic times we usually expect our political representatives, if not necessarily acting honourably, to make at least an effort to appear on the social-cultural 'high' of Ostiguy's schema. We assume that they should be polished, professional, composed and 'play the game' correctly. In short, we expect them to have 'good manners'. As such, the unpolished, seemingly off-the-cuff 'bad manners' of populist leaders can appeal in an era when political performances often seem homogenous, circumscribed, stage-managed and predictable across the political spectrum.

The notion of 'bad manners' can act as a supplement to a concept that is often used and abused in the literature on populism in explaining populist leaders' appeal: charisma. Charisma has long held a privileged position in the literature on populist leadership (Conniff 1999; Taggart 2000; Weyland 2001), but it has a number of problems. Conceptualised by Weber (1978, 241) as "a certain quality of an individual personality by virtue of which he is considered extraordinary and treated as endowed with supernatural, superhuman, or at least specifically exceptional powers or qualities", charisma has often been attributed to populist leaders in order to explain the seemingly mystical grip that they have on their followers. However, there are two central challenges in using the concept, and the notion of 'bad manners' may prove useful in addressing these challenges.

The first challenge is simple: some populists are not 'charismatic' leaders in the traditional sense of the term. Alberto Fujimori, Preston Manning and Pauline Hanson are good examples in this regard. They do not demonstrate particularly impressive oratorical skills, they hold themselves stiffly in the public domain, and they are not generally considered to display inspiring leadership skills overall. Equally, charisma is not just the domain of populists—many 'nonpopulist' leaders throughout history have been considered charismatic. As such, charisma may be useful for attracting popular support for populists—Hawkins (2010, 42, emphasis in original) calls it "an important *facilitator* of populist movements"—but it is not a necessary characteristic of populism.

The second challenge is methodological: charisma is incredibly difficult to operationalise, and authors too often overlook its inherently relational nature. As Mudde (2007, 262) argues, many authors use charisma in an absolute rather than a relative sense, forgetting that the concept is actually reliant on the *perception* of followers (that is, the leader being *seen as* charismatic), rather than any intrinsic personal qualities that the leader may hold (that is, being *inherently* charismatic). Perceptions of charisma thus rely heavily on political culture—and some political cultures are less susceptible to charisma than others. Lending credence to this position is Mizuno and Phongpaichit's (2009, 10) claim that the concept of charisma "never translated well into the Asian environment" because of the political culture of the region. Nevertheless, numerous populist leaders have done well in Asia, indicating that something other than charisma may be at play when it comes to populist success. Beyond this, the term is so poorly defined in the literature that claims about charismatic leadership are difficult to falsify, making the concept particularly problematic for empirical research (van der Brug and Mughan 2007).

The concept of 'bad manners' offers a way to partly overcome these issues by operationalising what it inherent in many theories of charisma—the *appeal* of the populist leader. So while we may not be able to understand all populist leaders' appeal by way of charisma because of certain political cultures' aversion to it, we can at least understand how the flouting of 'appropriate' behaviour can appeal in very different contexts. *All* political cultures have certain rules about what constitutes appropriate behaviour or decorum, and what populists share is an ability and willingness to flout those rules. 'Bad manners', in this light, are easily operationalisable, can travel across a number of political and cultural contexts, and are applicable to a wide number of cases. More so, the concept of 'bad manners' helps us avoid guesswork about either the leader's 'inherent' qualities or how devoted their followers 'really' are—two elements that are often invoked in talk of populist charisma—and instead, we can simply analyse the perceived 'appropriateness' of the populist performance. By focusing on the *stylistic methods* that populists use to perform—the allure of 'bad manners', appealing to the social-cultural low, and 'pulling the rug' on mainstream politics are all key here—we can better explain how populist leaders set themselves apart from other types of political actors.

Performing Extraordinariness:
The Leader's Body and the Body Politic

Yet it is not enough just to be ordinary and one of 'the people' by flaunting one's 'bad manners'. To truly rise above and represent 'the people', populists must also prove their extraordinariness. Populist leaders use a number of techniques to do this, including presenting themselves as the singular figure who can fix 'the people's' problems, as in the case of Thaksin (in Phongpaichit and Baker 2009a, 282), who claimed in 2006: "I am the major force in government and everyone else is just my helper". Sometimes this goes so far as presenting oneself in a divine light: Berlusconi (in BBC News 2006) declared in the same year: "I am the Jesus Christ of politics. I am a patient victim, I put up with everyone, I sacrifice myself for everyone", while Hugo Chávez presented himself as the reincarnation of Simón Bolívar and claimed that Jesus Christ was his "commander-in-chief" (quoted in Zúquete 2008, 109). Indeed, this presentation of the populist leader as the figure of salvation has led Zúquete (2007, 2013) to see a number of cases of populism in Latin America and Western Europe as examples of 'missionary politics', which combine populist leadership with a salvationist appeal, ritualisation, mythology and millennial visions.

Populist leaders ultimately present themselves as the voice of 'the people'.

Such leaders are extraordinary in that they are able to understand what 'the people' think and ultimately articulate their needs and desires. Yet the leader's extraordinary symbolic function goes beyond mere articulation—in populism, the leader does not simply represent 'the people' but is actually seen as *embodying* 'the people'. This embodiment has been significantly undertheorised in the literature, which is problematic, given that populism needs to be understood as something that is performed and 'done', rather than just as a set of ideas or way of organising followers. In 'doing' populism, populist leaders attempt to present themselves as strong, virile and healthy in order in order to present 'the people' as strong and unified. This is because within populism, 'the people' are a homogenous and united collective body who ultimately find their voice through the populist leader, as "the leader perceives himself not as an ordinary politician elected in a succession of temporarily elected officials. He rather sees himself as the incarnation of the people" (de la Torre 2013a, 19). This incarnation of 'the people' extends to 'the people' being present in the leader's physical body.

The link between the body of the leader and the unified political subject is not new—metaphors of the body politic and its literal interpretation within the bodies of actual living leaders have a relatively long history in political thought (de Baecque 1997; Kantorowicz 1957; Protevi 2001). However, talk of the body politic has largely disappeared from our political vocabulary following the rise of liberal democratic politics (Neoclaus 2003). While under monarchy, the king had 'two bodies' that were inseparable from each other (Kantorowicz 1957)— the 'body natural', which was his physical body, and the 'body politic', which was the invisible and divine body that symbolised the unity of the people; under democracy, the body politic is ostensibly 'disembodied', as democracy is conceptualised as an 'empty place' of power. As Critchley (1993, 80), following Lefort (1986), puts it: "In democracy power is not occupied by a king, a party leader, an egocrat or a *Führer,* rather it is ultimately empty; no one holds the place of power. Democracy entails a disincorporation of the body politic, which begins with a literal or metaphorical act of decapitation". Populism, then, can be read as attempt to 're-embody' the body politic, to suture the head back on the corpse, and provide unity in the name of 'the people' through the leader. Such metaphors certainly fit with the general characterisation of the extraordinary and singular leader spoken about throughout this chapter.

Indeed, Lefort saw totalitarianism in the same light—an attempt to fill the empty place of power with the materialisation of the "People-as-one"—usually in the body of the Great Leader. Keane (2009a) has pointed to the embalming and display of Lenin's corpse, as well as the construction of the Memorial Hall in Tiananmen Square in memory of Mao, as material evidence of such tendencies.[7] Here, even in death, the great leader remains present and pure, as a testament to 'the people's' unity. While populism is obviously not the same as totalitarianism, they share a tendency in this regard. In both, the leader is the figure that represents 'the people', bringing together and uniting them against enemies. The health of their bodies then is symbolically linked to the health of the body politic—a sagging, ill body is not a sign of a tough, united people. A strong one, however, is. In this light, what are the different ways that populist leaders use their bodies to prove the link between themselves and 'the people'?

Congruent with the previously explained concept of 'bad manners' as a central feature of populism, populist leaders are often keen to draw attention to their bodies to prove or demonstrate their potency and strength through crude banter, politically incorrect statements or boasts. Indeed, while Ostiguy (2009b, 38) has noted that one of the appeals of populist leaders is that they metaphorically 'have balls'—that is, they are tough, daring and decisive—some populist leaders seem to take this in a literal sense, with former Ecuadorian president Abdalá Bucaram claiming to have 'big balls' and poking fun at the 'watery sperm' of his key opponent, while using "an effeminate tone of voice and gestures" when referring to other 'oligarchical' politicians (de la Torre 1997, 16) to cast doubt on their sexuality and masculinity. The well-publicised bedroom antics of Silvio Berlusconi also speak to this obsession with proving the virility of the leader's body: Berlusconi has boasted of having sex with up to eight women a night (Squires 2011) and has been embroiled in a number of scandals involving 'bunga bunga' parties with prostitutes. This obsession with sex was underlined when Berlusconi made suggestions to change the name of his party, Forza Italia to Forza Gnocca (Kington 2011)—that is, from 'Go Italy' to a crude term for female genitalia. As Mancini (2011, 26) has argued in his study of Berlusconi's 'lifestyle politics', this intermingling of sexual performance and politics has meant that "the very body of Berlusconi has become a site of political, as well as erotic, power"—the two types of power intimately connected to each other.

Although the examples of Bucaram and Berlusconi might seem extreme, they are not outliers. There are numerous examples of populist leaders keen to prove their virility and masculinity. When on trial for rape charges, South African president Jacob Zuma asserted that he knew that his accuser was "clearly aroused" from the dress that she was wearing and the way that she sat, and claimed that it was his duty as a Zulu warrior to have sex with her: "In the Zulu culture, you cannot leave a woman if she is ready. ... To deny her sex, that would be tantamount to rape" (in Vincent 2009, 216). Hugo Chávez highlighted his sexual potency on numerous occasions, telling his wife on live television on Valentine's Day eve, "Marisabel, tomorrow I'm giving you yours" (in Guillermoprieto 2005). He also made crude sexual jokes about former US secretary of state Condoleezza Rice, suggesting that she had erotic dreams about him, and claiming that "I can invite her on a date with me to see what happens to her with me" (in *Washington Times* 2005). Elsewhere, Norocel (2011, 2012) and Azzarello (2011) have outlined the links between populism and demonstrations of masculinity and heteronormativity in Romania, Sweden and Italy. Even if sexual prowess is not stressed, it is often the case that the leader's strength and machismo are highlighted, as in the case of former Philippines president (and current mayor of Manila) Joseph 'Erap' Estrada, whose image as a former action film star has been central to his political appeal and success (Hedman 2001; Rocamora 2009), or Ecuadorian president Rafael Correa, whose toughguy antics included brandishing a belt while campaigning (ostensibly to whip opponents with) and aggressively ripping open his shirt and daring rioters to kill him while trying to quell a police uprising (Conaghan and de la Torre 2008; de la Torre 2012).

As such, it would seem that Weyland's (2010, viii) claim that "populist leaders deliberately project a very masculine image" rings true. In these cases, extraordinariness is related to displays of machismo, linking the populist's bodily strength or virility with the strength of 'the people'. However, the obvious rebuttal to this remark is—what about female populists? While female populist leaders like Pauline Hanson and Sarah Palin have stressed their toughness and strength, they have typically combined these allegedly 'masculine' traits with attributes traditionally associated with femininity, including caring, empathy and maternalism—a phenomenon that has also been noted in the female leadership of populist parties in Scandinavia (Meret 2015; Mudde and Kaltwasser 2015). Mason (2010, 190) argues that these can be understood as performances of "frontier femininity", claiming that Hanson and Palin "both portrayed an alluring physicality as working mothers, and used their sexual appeal to reinforce an image of themselves as vessels of national renewal". This sexual appeal—Hanson appearing in a swimsuit while washing cars on the reality television show *Celebrity Apprentice,* Palin coquettishly winking during speeches—was balanced with constant reference to their roles as mothers: Hanson went so far as to claim that "I care so passionately about this country, it's like I'm its mother. Australia is my home and the Australian people are my children" (in Saunders and McConnel 2002, 232). Indeed, it seems that this combination of sexuality and maternalism worked to some extent: Hanson's former media advisor, John Pasquarelli (1998, 281–82), claimed that Hanson received many gifts, letters, photographs and even marriage proposals from ardent male admirers, writing that "these Sir Galahads saw Pauline as a classical damsel in distress—feisty and strong, yet vulnerable and almost girlish as she stood alone against her assorted foes". However, it has often been the case that the sexual appeal of these female populists has not necessarily been performed by them, but has been forced in an exploitative manner upon them. For example, footage of Palin in a swimsuit from a 1984 Miss Alaska has been uploaded on YouTube and received more than 4 million views; a series of pornographic films have been produced by Hustler Videos titled *Who's Nailin' Paylin* that feature a Palin impersonator as the main protagonist; and in 2009 there was a 'leak' of fake nude photos in the Australian press purporting to be of Hanson. However, other female populist leaders (such as Marine Le Pen) have managed to avoid such sexualisation, meaning that this is not an iron rule for all female populists across the board.

Performances of strength and health to prove the leader's extraordinariness can go beyond concerns about sex, machismo and virility. They can simply take the form of attempting to deny the weaknesses of an aging body and the natural pitfalls that affect all of us at some point in our lives—to use Kantorowicz's (1957) term, the denial of the 'body natural'. These denials are perhaps most aptly illustrated in the figures of Silvio Berlusconi and Hugo Chávez. Berlusconi has undergone numerous rounds of hair transplants and plastic surgery in an attempt to preserve his dwindling youth, which together with the sexual exploits noted earlier, indicate a certain denial of the reality of his aging (Mancini 2011). Chávez attempted to deny the mortality of the natural body in a different way. Before his death, Chávez speculated that the United States may have developed a secret weapon to cause leftist Latin American leaders to get cancer, including himself (Phillips 2011), a claim that was reiterated by his successor, Nicolás Maduro, who blamed "historical enemies" (Lopez and Watts 2013) for Chávez's death. The same paranoia about foreign enemies was mirrored in Chávez's obsession with trying to prove that his hero, Simon Bolívar, had died not of tuberculosis—a rather common disease of the time—but of poisoning from the Colombian 'oligarchy' (Halvorssen 2010). This obsession went as far as ordering, by presidential decree, all television stations in the country to show the live exhumation of Bolívar's remains in mid-2010. In these examples, it is as if the actual frailty of the physical body and the mortality of the populist leader are too problematic to deal with given what they represent (the dissolution of 'the people'), so the illness is blamed on external enemies—not pathological viruses, *but actual physical enemies.*

Indeed, the threat or fantasy of death via the hands of the enemy is a common trope amongst populist leaders. Examples of this tendency are numerous. Wilders lives under constant security protection after a number of attempts on his life, and as a result is moved to a new location every evening (Wilders 2012), while Hanson filmed a much-ridiculed 'death video'—after receiving threats on her life—in which she claimed, "If you are seeing me now, it means I have been murdered. . . . You must fight on" (Hanson 2004). The point here is not to trivialise the very real threats that populist leaders can face—the assassination of Pim Fortuyn looms large here—but rather to highlight the importance of the leader's body, and to stress that *external threats* are treated as the real danger rather than anything natural or as mundane as aging. Paradoxically, while populist leaders must appear to be of 'the people', they must also transcend 'the people' by being immune to disease or physical frailty. In a strange case of doubling, the threat to 'the people' and the leader are thus one and the same—the foreign or pathological enemy—tying the body politic and the leader's body together in an existential bond. Overall, the contemporary populist leader is stuck with a modern, secularised version of Kantorowicz's (1957) characterisation of the king's two bodies. Following the perceived dissolution of the unified body politic and the loss of God-given sovereignty, the populist leader's 'natural body' takes on a far more substantial role in legitimising the leader's position as the figure that embodies the vox populi: 'the people' as unified, strong, tough and long-living.

Conclusion

This chapter has argued that the populist leader should be seen as the key 'performer' of populism. While populist parties and movements are undoubtedly important and worthy of our attention, it is the populist leader who inspires hope in followers, anxiety and panic in detractors, and who attracts the attention of the all-important media through which they broadcast their appeal to 'the people'. More than this, it is the performances of the populist leader that seek to bring together and render-present 'the people' under populism. As can be seen, these performances involve a great deal of skill—the balance between presenting oneself as both ordinary and extraordinary takes much work, as does maintaining the illusion of health, strength and virility in order to reflect and embody a strong 'people'. Similarly, the line between using 'bad manners' to appeal to 'the people' and not going so far as to lose credibility with 'the people' can be quite a thin one.

Yet populist leaders are particularly well positioned in the contemporary political landscape, which in the midst of presidentialisation and celebritisation tends to focus on remarkable and entertaining personalities. In this context, it becomes clear that in order to understand contemporary populist leadership, we must move from a focus on just the 'content' of populist party platforms, organisational strategies or ideologies towards the performative repertoires that populist leaders use to represent 'the people'. The notion of populism as a political style allows us to do this, tracking the balance between extraordinariness and ordinariness that populist leaders negotiate to appeal to this nebulous political subject.

However, it is important to realise that these performances are not *just* the product of singular leaders. Although the limelight is shone on the unique and remarkable leader as way of creating the most affective (and effective) bonds between leaders and 'the people', populist leaders' performances are often actually the result of careful planning, staging and scripting reliant on a team of professionals and an array of media resources: presenting oneself as ordinary and extraordinary does not occur in a vacuum. How do populists perform on the 'stage' of the contemporary media landscape? Who is involved in these performances? How do they use different forms of media, and how have changes in the media landscape affected contemporary populism? The next chapter turns to such questions, as it continues to unfold the relationships at the heart of contemporary populism.

5

The Stage I: Populism and the Media

The survival of populism as a 'political style' cannot be understood without an examination of contemporary media politics.

—Waisbord (2003, 201)

It often assumed that populism and the media make good bedfellows.[1] Claims are frequently made about populists actors' savvy manipulation of media channels, the media's thirst for the salacious and entertaining headlines and soundbites that populist actors provide, and the general cosiness between the two. Yet despite this 'common wisdom', it is a surprise to find that literature that actually examines the relationship between populism and the media is rather piecemeal, with little systematic theoretical or empirical work having been undertaken.[2] This is problematic in a time when media touches upon all aspects of political life, when "communicative abundance" (Keane 2013) is the new norm, and when new digital media tools see networked information flow globally at astonishing speeds. In this new media landscape, how does populism operate, how has it changed, and how can we understand the relationship between contemporary populism and media?

This chapter argues that the media should be seen as one of the central 'stages' on which contemporary populism plays out upon, and as such, argues that media processes need to put at the centre of our thinking about contemporary populism. It contends that the rise of contemporary populism is intimately related to shifts in the media landscape that have not been examined in depth in the literature on populism. It examines these shifts from three angles. First, it considers how *mediatisation,* which can be broadly understood as the process "whereby social and cultural institutions and modes of interaction are changed as a consequence of the growth of the media's influence" (Hjarvard 2008, 114), has affected the shape of populism, and how populism adapts elements of 'media logic' to politics in increasingly effective ways. Second, it examines the ways that populist actors concretely relate to *mass media,*[3] focusing on two central tactics utilised by populists: control (in regards to muzzling or attempting to own elements of the media) and celebrity (in regards to blurring the line between politics and entertainment). Third, it considers what the rise of *new media*—such as social networks, blogs, YouTube and LiveLeak—has meant for contemporary populism, both from the perspective of populist leaders and audiences. Overall, the chapter stresses the importance of considering the role of media in the creation, distribution and promotion of the performances that comprise contemporary populism as a distinct political style.

Current Approaches to Populism and Media

Why focus on the relationship between populism and media? Although the extant literature on populism certainly gives *some* consideration to the media's role in shaping and affecting contemporary populism, it is fair to say that the media has not been at the centre of the literature's analysis. As it stands, the literature has focused on two central aspects of the relationship between populism and media in recent years: the first being the effect that mass media coverage has on populist success, and the second being the ways in which populist actors use (usually traditional) media.

The former question has mainly been taken up by those utilising discursive or ideological conceptions of populism. Those working within the discourse approach have attempted to examine how mass-media coverage affects the electoral chances of those who use a populist discourse, but have failed to come up with conclusive results. Some have linked the increased visibility and 'discursive opportunities' that mass media channels afford populist actors to electoral success, but there is disagreement over if it matters whether that coverage is positive or negative (Curran 2004; Koopmans and Muis 2009, 659). Others have argued that media coverage should be seen as just one of a number of possible explanatory factors for the success of populist actors: for example, in the Belgian context, it has been argued that "the media had a catalytic effect rather than providing an independent explanation" (Pauwels 2010, 1022) and that "the media could be considered co-responsible" (Walgrave and de Swert 2004, 479) for support for the electoral success of the populist parties. However, it is likely that such findings apply not only to populist actors but to all political actors in general.

Working within the ideological approach to populism, Mudde (2007, 249) has captured this double-edged nature of media coverage for populists by characterising the media as both a 'friend' and 'foe' of populists. It can be a 'friend', in that it can set out a sympathetic public agenda for populists and 'prime' the public with issues on which populists can capitalise (such as immigration or law and order); and 'foe', as the media can also often be openly hostile to populists. Akkerman (2011) has tested this notion by analysing newspapers in the UK and Netherlands, finding mixed results in terms of how tabloid and 'quality' newspapers cover populist politicians and parties.

On the other hand, the second question—how populist leaders use the media—has been addressed mainly by those working within the strategic approach. Authors using this approach tend to posit mass media as the central vehicle by which populist leaders are able to bring together unorganised masses through allegedly 'direct' means. For example, Roberts (2006, 135–36) has acknowledged that the emergence of the mass media has enabled "populist figures to appeal directly to mass constituencies and demonstrate popular support without any sort of institutional intermediation". He cites the examples of Fernando Collor, who did not need the backing of the usual party apparatus to attain political success in Brazil because of his strong media support, and Alberto Fujimori, who relied on state controlled media rather than his party's support in order to run for president in Peru. Conniff (1999) and Weyland (2001) have made similar arguments, claiming that if radio was the key medium by which classical populists reached millions of followers in the early to mid-twentieth century in Latin America, television has played the same role, only more powerfully, for contemporary populists in the region.

Finally, those who follow the political logic approach to populism have only begun to touch on the role of media when it comes to populism. For example, Brading (2013) has explored the battles over media ownership in Venezuela under Chávez, while Griggs and Howarth (2008; Howarth and Griggs 2006) have acknowledged the ways that populism demands engagement with the media sphere. However, Laclau's (2005b, 2005c, 2006) work on populism as a political logic overall tends to overlook the important role of different forms of media in populism.[4]

As can be seen, there is *some* consideration given to the relationship between populism and media throughout all of the main approaches to contemporary populism identified in this book. We have a reasonably cohesive empirical picture of how the mass media covers populist leaders and parties, and relatedly, how this can both help and hinder populists. We also have some sense of how populist leaders use different (older) forms of media to appeal to 'the people'.

But there are a number of key elements still missing from the literature that demand further exploration: analysis of how processes of mediatisation affect populism; consideration of the growing sophistication of political communication practices used by populists; and an understanding of how populists use *new* media. These are outlined below.

First, there is a distinct lack of consideration of how the wider trend of mediatisation has come to affect the shape of the political in these 'spectacular' times,[5] and more specifically, how this has affected contemporary populism. In one sense, this theoretical gap is understandable, given that most of the recent literature on populism and media has been firmly case study based, and thus not particularly interested in broader historical shifts. Nonetheless, it is necessary to take a step back and get a sense of the wider situation if we want to comprehensively understand and contextualise the changing shape of contemporary populism. The only authors within the broader populist literature who have sufficiently dealt with these wider trends are those sympathetic to stylistic approaches, such as Arditi (2007a), Filc (2011), Pels (2003) and Peri (2004), and those from the political communications literature (Mazzoleni 2008, 2014; Waisbord 2011, 2012), who have all sought to contextualise and account for these media transformations in some manner.

The second concern is a lack of engagement with the growing sophistication of the political communication practices used by populist actors. While it is one thing to discursively analyse the different communiques and speeches of populist actors, as is often done in the literature, we need a clearer understanding of what is going on 'behind the scenes' of these communicative practices. This means understanding the mise-en-scène of populist performances, and questioning the organisation, makeup and behaviour of the increasingly professionalised media and public relations teams behind populist actors. Who is 'directing' the performances of populism? What tools are they using? And how are they blurring the boundaries between politics and entertainment for the benefit of populists?

A final concern is the lack of consideration of the role of *new* media—particularly social-networking and other online media associated with Web 2.0—in populism, both in regards to top-down communications as well as the mobilisation of populist supporters. This may be a case of the published literature simply not catching up to empirical developments as they happen: the recent popular attention bestowed upon the MoVimento 5 Stelle and the Tea Party's online exploits may very well change this. However, the populist literature is still firmly set in its analysis of old media. This is evident in the frequent references to '*the* media' and the failure to differentiate between distinct types of media. Research that takes account of the impact of Web 2.0, the shift from centralised to decentralised networks and the social nature of new media is sorely needed.

Mediatisation and Populism

Let us address the first lacuna: the link between populism and mediatisation. There certainly seems to be some affinity between the increasing mediatisation of politics and contemporary populism. This is evident in the names of various subtypes of populism that have appeared in the literature in recent years: tele-populism (Peri 2004; Taguieff 1995), newsroom populism (Plasser and Ulram 2003, 27) and media populism (Krämer 2014; Mazzoleni 2008) amongst them. Each of these terms links changes in the media communication landscape to the increased prominence of populism—Peri (2004, 6), for example, argues that telepopulism is "the embodiment of populism in the era of mediapolitik and is the most concrete expression of the new symbiosis between media and politics". Yet there are problems with such neologisms—namely, their inherent technological determinism. One gets a picture from such terms that the changes in the shape and character of populism are a *direct* result of mediatic-technological shifts.

Even if this is correct, proving these ties are difficult—as noted earlier, we can see from both the ideological and discursive approaches to populism that mass media can certainly 'set the scene' for populism or 'diffuse' sentiments that populists can capitalise on, but proving direct causation is near impossible. It is more fruitful (and less controversial) to look at the bigger picture, and claim that the increasing mediatisation of the political has led to the rise of populism as a distinct political style. Such a claim does not automatically mean that the changes in the media landscape have *caused* populism's rise, but rather, that mediatisation has *encouraged* and *buttressed* the rise of contemporary populism in its current form. As Mazzoleni (2008, 62) correctly claims: "[T]here are close ties between media-centered processes and the political phenomenon of populism".

What kind of changes and processes are we talking about when we refer to mediatisation, and when exactly did they begin? Although it is admittedly difficult to discern the exact historical moment when this gestalt switch 'went off' when it comes to mediatisation, Keane (2013) traces such changes to the first live international satellite broadcast in 1967. From there, we have seen the rapid and exponential growth and spread of communication technologies, from fax machines, pagers and mainframe computers, to today's on-demand television, cloud computing, social networking, mobile technologies and wearable computing. According to Hjarvard (2008, 113), although mediatisation has been a gradual process, it has accelerated quickly from the last years of twentieth century onwards, predominantly in highly industrialised societies. The repercussions of these changes are hard to overstate. Flows of information are now networked globally, meaning that time and space barriers are overcome in terms of the distribution of information and communication; content is cheap, portable and easily reproduced; and for perhaps the first time ever, text, sound, image and form are now brought together into a seamless whole, enveloping three senses—sight, hearing and touch—all at once. Perhaps most important, the extent of these mediatic changes has led to the situation whereby media touches almost every aspect of everyday life, from banking, shopping and work to socialising and relationships. Politics has certainly not been immune to such changes.

Within this historical context, mediatisation can be viewed as a process by which certain spheres of life (politics, culture, family and so on) are "to an increasing degree . . . submitted to, or [become] dependent on, the media and their logic" (Hjarvard 2008, 113).[6] Media logic in this context can broadly be understood as "the dominance in societal processes of the news values and the storytelling techniques the media make use of to take advantage of their own medium and its format, and to be competitive in the ongoing struggle to capture people's attention" (Strömbäck 2008, 233).

To draw on examples from the political communications literature, these values and techniques include:

- "simplification, polarization, intensification, personalization, visualization and stereotypization" (Strömbäck 2008, 233);
- "emotionalization and an anti-establishment attitude" (Bos, van der Brug and de Vreese 2011, 185);
- negativism, sports-based dramatisation and the triumph of 'style' over 'substance' (Plasser and Ulram 2003, 27);
- the prioritisation of conflict (McManus 1994);
- focus on scandals (Sabato, Stencel, and Linchter 2000); and
- the privileging of the visual over other senses (Bucy and Grabe 2007).

To speak of the 'mediatisation of politics' is thus to claim these types of techniques, trends and narrative logics increasingly shape contemporary politics—a claim not particularly surprising or controversial to any political observer today. In such a situation 'media logic' colonises 'political logic', which according to Meyer (2002) involves both a policy dimension—finding solutions to political issues—and a process dimension—the efforts to get others to accept your solution. Under mediatisation, such policy and process dimensions become increasingly beholden to the rhythms, demands and processes of media logic as noted above. Recent literature in the field of political communications has set about analysing how this has occurred in different countries around the world (Kriesi et al. 2013; Lundby 2009; Strömbäck and Esser 2014).

Populism can be seen as being located at the nexus of these logics, combining elements of media logic with the policy and process dimensions of political logic. Indeed, the table below demonstrates that many of the attributes of media logic are roughly analogous with (or at least complementary to) the features of populism as a political style as laid out in Chapter 3.

If we accept the premise of the mediatisation hypothesis—that politics is increasingly influenced, shaped and colonised by media logic—then we can see from this table that populism is particularly well suited to the contours of the contemporary political and media landscapes. While all forms of politics are obviously affected by these processes and are mediatised in one form or another, it is populism that most effectively marries the tendencies of media logic with the central processes of political representation and decision-making at present. Its appeal to 'the people' versus 'the elite' and associated Others plays

TABLE 5.1: Populism as Political Style versus Media Logic

Populism as Political Style	Corresponding Aspects of Media Logic
Appeal to 'the people'	
Dichotomy between 'the people' and 'the elite'	Sports based-dramatisation and polarisation
Antielite/establishment/system	Prioritisation of conflict
Denial of expert knowledge	Antiestablishment attitude
'Bad manners'	
Disregard for 'appropriateness'	Personalisation
Political incorrectness	Stereotypisation
'Colourfulness'	Emotionalisation
Crisis, breakdown, threat	
Demand to act decisively	Intensification
Distaste for complexity	Simplification
Instrumentalisation of politics	Focus on scandals

into media logic's dramatisation, polarisation and prioritisation of conflict; its 'bad manners' line up with media logic's personalisation, stereotypisation and emotionalisation; while its focus on crisis plays into media logic's tendency towards intensification and simplification. In this situation, populism can thus potentially be considered the media-political form par excellence at this particular historical juncture. This might help explain why populism currently seems to be more widespread and successful across the globe than any other time in its history.

What are the repercussions of this positioning of populism? The first repercussion is that a growing number of political actors who wish to enter and succeed in the political arena seem increasingly compelled to adopt *some* version of the populist style in order to gain media coverage and obtain political success. Given that politics is increasingly mediatised, and that mediatisation tends to favour those styles of politics that are closest to its own internal logic, this drive towards populism as a more widespread phenomenon makes sense. So on one hand we have a clearly populist politician like Pim Fortuyn, who received a great amount of media attention as a result of his skilful melding of media logic and political performance—so much so that he was labelled "Holland's first mediacrat" (Pels 2003, 43). On the other hand, we have those politicians who might not usually be labelled 'populists' adopting some form of populism in order to play by the (new) rules of the arena of mediatised politics. While we should not necessarily go so far as to lump leaders like Tony Blair (Mair 2002), Stephen Harper (Sawer and Laycock 2009) or John Howard (Wear 2008) together with the Wilders, Hansons and Correas of the world, it is important to acknowledge that they have, at times, drawn on the populist playbook to some extent.

If populism is indeed so closely aligned to the logic that drives the seemingly unstoppable mediatisation of politics, a central question that must be asked is whether one can avoid capitulating to populism at all: can one escape what Žižek (2006a) has labelled "the populist temptation"? The answer is that of course one can, as the examples of Occupy, the *indignados*, the Zapatistas and other forms of postrepresentative politics (Tormey 2012, 2015) show us—not all politics is populism, despite what Laclau has argued. However, it is perhaps fair to say that it is becoming *increasingly difficult* to ignore the pull of populism, with a number of otherwise nonpopulist leaders attempting to tap into the "populist Zeitgeist" (Mudde 2004) to gain political attention and success.

The tactic of adopting the populist style, however, is by no means a *guar-*

antee of political success—a poor performance, where the populism on offer seems inauthentic, can be disastrous. This can be seen in the examples of former opposition leader Michael Ignatieff in Canada (2008–11) and the 2012 presidential candidate Mitt Romney in the United States. Both are undoubtedly members of 'the elite', with Ignatieff being a human rights professor and public intellectual, and Romney a wealthy businessman. Although both of these men are clearly more at home utilising the technocratic style outlined in Chapter 3—with their appeal to expertise, 'good manners' and sense of stability—they nonetheless attempted to adopt the populist style in highly publicised media performances. Ignatieff undertook a bus tour across regional Canada to take him to 'the people' (Martin 2010; Murphy 2010), while Romney's awkward attempts to present himself as 'salt-of-the-earth'—including attending NASCAR races and making false claims about his hunting prowess—fell flat (T. Stanley 2012). Both struck an inauthentic note with the electorate, who did not 'buy' their performances, which were widely mocked.

The point here is that although these men were not 'traditional' populists by any real measure—they are so clearly members of the privileged upper class, with the dress, accent, education, diction and overall 'style' and habitus to match—it appears that they felt compelled to try to *adopt* the populist style. However, in each case, it simply did not work: as van Zoonen (2005, 75) notes: "[P]erformance must be consistent ... because if anything will devastate a good performance, it is its detection as a performance". If the audience knows that the actor is not a good fit for the role, and the performance becomes obvious, the proscenium arch collapses, and the show is over. Populism, then, to be used effectively, requires mastery and skill over the medium that is being utilised. It is not merely a 'base' form of politics, but a repertoire of embodied, symbolically mediated performance that even with its increased purchase in the contemporary mediatised setting, requires mastery and careful skill to be adopted successfully. The fact that ostensibly nonpopulist politicians have felt compelled to adopt elements of populism tells us something about its increased political purchase today.

The flipside of more 'mainstream' political actors attempting to adopt elements of populism is that populist actors have increasingly adopted the slicker political communication strategies of 'mainstream' politics to legitimise themselves. This has been evident in the increasing sophistication of populist media performances as well as the usage of professional public relations managers and media liaison teams by populist actors and parties. However, as it stands, our view of this important aspect—essentially, who is responsible for setting the mise-en-scène—of populist performances remains somewhat blinkered. In many ways, this 'blind spot' is understandable: populists are not particularly keen to reveal the artifice behind their own media performances, nor the professional machinery behind them, given that much of their appeal stems from appearing to connect with 'the people' in an unmediated way that is different from 'politics as usual'.

Yet the small literature on the topic unsurprisingly suggests that many populists indeed do have professional media teams and organisations behind them. Beyond the more obvious cases (Berlusconi with his broadcast media empire and Thaksin with his telecommunications empire), there are a number of other examples within the literature that give us some clues of the key role of media and public relations advisors within populist politics. The role of publicists and the changing media strategies of the *Front National* in moving towards the mainstream have been outlined by Birenbaum and Villa (2003, 59), while Ellinas (2010) has produced perhaps the most comprehensive overview of the media tactics of the far right in Western Europe, with a focus on a number of populist parties. Stewart, Mazzoleni and Horsfield (2003, 229) have further related the media management skills of populists to their political successes.

Perhaps the most pertinent recent example of the core relationship between populism and media expertise can be seen in the case of Gianroberto Casaleggio, the so-called web guru behind Beppe Grillo and his MoVimento 5 Stelle (M5S) in Italy. Casaleggio is the president and founder of his own web and marketing strategy company, and is alleged to be the "'overlord' . . . spin doctor, ideologist, and in some people's view, the man at the helm behind the MoVimento" (Bordignon and Ceccarini 2013, 438–39). Casaleggio does not shy away from such allegations, claiming that he is "the cofounder of this movement" (in Bordignon and Ceccarini 2013, 439), having designed Grillo's blog, proposed the Meetup model used by the M5S, helped organise the V-Day rallies and meetings central to M5S's growth, and coauthored the party's 'nonstatute'. Accusations of maintaining a tight grip on the media relations of the party have certainly not been helped by charges from within the party itself, with one councillor going so far as to publicly criticise the lack of democracy within M5S, claiming that Casaleggio makes all the decisions for Grillo and that he prevents other party representatives from appearing in the mass media in order to control the party's official narrative (Favia in Ruggiero 2012, 316).

Elsewhere, Skocpol and Williamson (2012, 92) have outlined how partisan external bodies assist populist movements and actors with their media relations. They explain the key role that nonprofit advocacy organisations such as FreedomWorks and Americans for Prosperity have played in the mobilisation and media promotion of the Tea Party, including dispatching staff to organise and promote events, and even writing a manifesto to give the movement the appearance of ideological coherence (Armey and Kibbe 2010). While local Tea Party groups certainly did pop up without these organisations' help, it was "FreedomWorks and other professionally run advocacy organisations [who] were thinking in terms of rallies with television camera and sign-up sheets to capture new adherents and donors" (Skocpol and Williamson 2012, 92), thus giving the Tea Party media visibility and adding a level of expertise and professionalism to their organisation.

However, just as some 'mainstream' politicians cannot quite adopt the populist style in a convincing manner, some populist actors cannot quite manage with dealing with communication professionals. A number of populist actors have fallen out with said advisors in quite public circumstances, demonstrating the tension between attempting to speak 'authentically' for 'the people' and keeping up with the demands of contemporary mediatised politics. In his tell-all book, Pauline Hanson's former media advisor John Pasquarelli (1998, 304) colourfully noted that "the media and Pauline Hanson are like two unwilling, brawling participants in a shotgun wedding", and outlined Hanson's lack of media guile and nous, as well as her refusal to take guidance from her public relations advisors. This familiar situation was repeated a decade later in the case of Sarah Palin, whose constant clashes with advisors inspired the title of her first book, *Going Rogue,* a phrase used by one of John McCain's aides to describe Palin's tendency to ignore her advisors and go 'off-message' (Palin 2009, 328). Indeed, in the book, Palin is keen to put a distance between herself and her advisors, whom she tars as part of 'the elite'. She claims: "I was in the hands of 'campaign professionals', and it was my first encounter with the unique way of thinking that characterises this elite and highly specialised guild. In Alaska, we don't really have these kinds of people—they are a feature of national politics" (2009, 231). The claim that the former governor of Alaska had not been involved with campaign professionals seems rather dubious, yet it illustrates the lengths that some populist actors will go to in order to deny the professionalisation of elements of their operations.

None of this is to say that populist actors are any different from their more mainstream brethren when it comes to having professionalised media and public relations expertise behind them—such expertise is now a permanent fixture of contemporary politics. What makes things difficult for populists is that 'spin' or the dilution of their message by communications professionals is anathema to the core populist notions of authenticity and directness. Accordingly, populists must negotiate a delicate balance between utilising such expertise and still constructing their performances as immediate and authentic.

Populist Approaches to Traditional Media: Control and Celebrity

While the process of mediatisation may be pushing populism increasingly towards the mainstream, in practice, populist actors themselves demonstrate a dichotomic love/hate relationship with the media. On one hand, populists tend to target the media as a tool of 'the elite' that is used to discredit them, marginalise 'common sense' opinions and mislead 'the people'. On the other hand, populists are often very opportunistic about their media opportunities, willing to align themselves with tabloid and 'low' forms of media to reach 'the people', blurring the line between politics and entertainment in the process. These two positions manifest in two very different ways, both used by populist leaders: control and celebrity. These strategies are situated in a time when 'mass audiences' have ostensibly dispersed into more segmented niche audiences (Castells 2010; Iyengar and Hahn 2009; Napoli 2010), where these audiences are faced with 'communicative abundance' (Keane 2013) in terms of a vast choice of information and communication sources, and where traditional media organisations face significant financial challenges (and sometimes disappear as a result). They represent two ways of dealing with these shifts: the first attempting to stem some changes, the second adapting to them.

Control

Although populist actors often claim to hate the media—indeed, Jagers and Walgrave (2007) go so far as to code for it in their measurement of populism as a style—we know empirically that this is not true. Some of the most successful cases of populism in recent years have come from leaders who literally *own or control* parts of the mass media. Thaksin Shinawatra and Silvio Berlusconi are the most instructive examples here. Both are media magnates who have successfully blurred the line between political and media success, utilising their media empires to deliver them favourable coverage, exposure and political influence, and both have utilised populism to bring them to the highest office in their respective countries. Thaksin's empire was built on telecommunications—computers, pagers, cable television, satellites, television stations and Thailand's biggest mobile phone company—while Berlusconi made his fortune in cable television. Ginsborg (2004, 10) has called Berlusconi's project "the most ambitious attempt to date to combine media control and political power", while Keane (2009b, 765) groups the two leaders together as worrying examples of "pathological reactions to monitory democracy"—arguing that their "vital priority is executive control of political communication" (2009b, 766).

The hatred of the media that populist leaders often profess is thus perhaps better acknowledged as hatred of media that opposes them or is critical of them. This can be seen in the usual populist complaints about the 'mainstream media', 'elite media', 'liberal media', and Sarah Palin's trademark phrase, the "lame-stream media" (Larson and Porpora 2011, 756). While rhetorical attacks on the media are one thing, sometimes this hatred takes the more serious form of media interference. Waisbord's (2012) work on populism's 'media activism' in Latin America in instructive in this regard. He claims that populists attempt to change media systems in their countries by doing three central things: "strengthening the media power of the President, bolstering community media, and exercising tighter control of the press through legislation and judicial decisions". These aim to contribute to a 'media statism', whereby the state has a large degree of control over media matters. Examples include Chávez framing the curbing of media freedom as a matter of ensuring that the opposition media is "truthful" (Hawkins 2010, 67), his closure of opposition television stations and the introduction of legislation regarding "press crimes" (Committee to Protect Journalists 2009). Rafael Correa has also demonstrated a high degree of 'media activism', using libel laws to deter criticism from journalists, whom he has called "*mafiosos*, journalistic pornography, human wretchedness, savage beasts, and idiots who publish trash" (in Conaghan and de la Torre 2008, 278).

This 'media statism' is not a problem just in Latin America. In South Africa, Jacob Zuma toyed with the idea of introducing a Media Appeals Tribunal to regulate private media, which was accused of being "'politically and ideologically' out of sync with the society in which they operated" (Gumede 2008, 269). In Thailand, numerous complaints were made about Thaksin's meddling with election coverage; mysterious 'technical difficulties' occurred when anti-Thaksin interviews took place; and licenses were revoked from previously somewhat-independent television stations. Television stations were instructed to "cut down on negative news and bring out more positive news to boost businessmen's morale" (Phongpaichit and Baker 2009a, 150). Thaksin pursued a number of defamation cases, and even opinion pollsters were harassed and intimidated. Indeed, the ferociousness and sustained nature of Thaksin's attack on media outlets led one academic (Chongkittavorn 2001) to predict 'media apartheid' in Thailand, whereby only pro-Thaksin coverage would prosper.[7] In Italy, Berlusconi (who via his company, Mediaset, owns three of the seven major national television stations) was accused of interference with the national broadcaster Radiotelevisione Italiana (RAI) when he was prime minister, and has been criticised by Reporters Without Borders on numerous occasions for such meddling (Reporters Without Borders 2005, 2009). It is worth making the obvious point that what links all of these populists who have had some success in controlling or stifling the media is that they have achieved high office, and as such, are in a far better position to restrict the press than populists who have not enjoyed similar positions of power.

These attempts to own, control or stifle media channels suggest that the relationship between populism and media is more complicated than it may first seem: just because the populist style corresponds so closely to media logic does not mean that all media automatically support populists. Indeed, populist actors often play certain parts of the mass media against each other—the Tea Party's Fox News versus the 'liberal elite's' MSNBC; Morales's and Chávez's community media versus private media (Waisbord 2012)—or even different *types* of media against one another. For example, various populist figures in Australia have favoured talkback radio over television interviews as a way of appearing familiar and accessible to a sympathetic audience (Faine 2005; Pasquarelli 1998). Furthermore, when it comes to populism, not all press is good press, a view occasionally raised in the populist literature[8]—if this was the case, there would little need for populist leaders like Chávez, Berlusconi and Thaksin to attempt to shape their own coverage by the mass media to such an extent. It does suggest, however, that populist actors do see the line between media and political logics as either blurry or artificial, and in their disregard for respecting the independence of media, seek to combine the two arenas.

Celebrity

However, the vast majority of populist actors do not have the political position, resources or finances necessary for launching such major attempts to control or own elements of the media. As such, for many populists, a key tactic in dealing with the media is simply being incredibly opportunistic about media appearances, particularly those that ostensibly bring them closer to 'the people', whether through the appearance of 'directness' or through their association with tabloid or 'low'—that is, not 'elite'—media. Of those populist leaders noted above, this can include using state television to broadcast their own television programs: for example, Chávez was infamous for his long-running weekly television show, *Aló Presidente* (Hello President), which often ran for six hours or more every Sunday, while Correa has his own version, *Enlace Ciudadano* (Citizen's Connection), which runs for the slightly more modest three hours every Saturday morning. In Thailand, Thaksin had his own television special, *Backstage Show: The Prime Minister,* which followed him around poor rural areas of Thailand as he met 'the people', as well as a weekly radio show, *Premier Thaksin Talks with the People.* These efforts at least have the façade of being related to accountable democratic representation—in each, so-called ordinary people are either in the audience or call in to ask questions of their leaders.

However, sometimes populist leaders do not even bother with political forms of media at all and instead simply aim for media fame and self-promotion, blurring the lines between politics and entertainment. Indeed, what is striking about these performances is the ease with which a number of these figures slip between political and media roles. Sarah Palin is perhaps the prime example of this: she has two documentary series, *Sarah Palin's Alaska* and *Amazing America with Sarah Palin;* is a Fox News political commentator; has appeared on *Saturday Night Live*; has written three best-selling books (2009, 2010, 2013); maintains an active online presence; while her family is their own small media cottage industry, with their own reality television shows, books and media profiles.[9] Palin even went so far as to launch an online television station, the Sarah Palin Channel, in July 2014. A more undignified example is Pauline Hanson, who has appeared as a contestant on reality television shows *Dancing with the Stars* and *The Celebrity Apprentice,* has been a reporter on tabloid news show *A Current Affair* and morning talkshow *Sunrise,* has appeared in a television advertisement for an Australian donut franchise, and has recorded an ill-fated cover of 'What a Wonderful World' with a country star.

This slippage between media and politics can also operate the other way around, as there are a number of media figures who have moved quite easily into populist politics. For example, Glenn Beck—former Fox News host, now host of his own radio and television shows—was an early figurehead for the Tea Party, and began his own political campaign (the '9/12 project') as well as having organised the 'Restoring Honor' rally that was an important catalysing event for the Tea Party movement (Burack and Snyder-Hall 2012). As Skocpol and Williamson (2012, 133) argue: "Glenn Beck deserves special credit for his role in building and shaping the Tea Party as an organized force". Another example is former Philippines president and current mayor of Manila, Joseph 'Erap' Estrada, who utilised his position as one of the Philippines's most famous movie stars to launch his successful political career. There is also the case of Sweden's Bert Karlsson, who moved from being a record company owner and manager in the 1980s, to populist politician in the 1990s, and back again to entertainment, being a host and judge on light entertainment shows *Fame Factory* and *Sweden's Got Talent (Talang Sverige)* in the late 2000s.

As touched upon in the previous chapter, the effect of such performative acts is that populist leaders can become quasi-celebrities, known as much—or sometimes more—for their media performances and stylistic outbursts than for the 'content' of their politics. Indeed, the rise of the 'celebrity politician'— those politicians who court celebrity as a form of political capital—has been documented by a number of authors (Higgins and Drake 2006; Street 2004; t' Hart and Tindall 2009b). A potential underside of this 'celebritisation' of politicians is that it "thrives by virtue of the public behaving as admiring fans rather than discriminating citizens" (t' Hart and Tindall 2009b, 274). As politicians become media identities and celebrity heroes, this situation allows them to get away with things that they might not have otherwise been able to get away with, avoiding scrutiny because of the media glow and star aura that surround them.

While some authors have bemoaned these kinds of developments, claiming that the 'populistisation' of politics has seen a dumbing-down of politics, and the emergence of increasing cynicism and apathy towards politics more generally (for examples, see the 'media malaise' thesis in Norris 2003), there is a minor view in the literature that sees it as a potentially positive phenomenon. Here, it is argued that the melding of media and political logics has actually benefited political constituents and 'everyday citizens', in that it makes politics more relatable, relevant and accessible. For example, Corner and Pels (2003a, 7) describe:

> new forms of visual and emotional literacy, which allow audiences to 'read' political characters and 'taste' their style. . . . The continuous media exposure of political personae lends them a strange familiarity which, despite the sharp asymmetry that separates the visible few from the invisible many, still to some extent bridges the gap between them.

They further note that while there might be increasing political apathy when it comes to traditional parties and political professionals, this may be at least counterbalanced by interest in political celebrity and infotainment. This is precisely what Ankersmit (2002) means when he argues that most citizens today, isolated from the complex machinery of contemporary politics, primarily access politics through political style. Van Zoonen (2005, 151) also sees this intersection of popular culture and politics in a positive light, arguing that it can provide "a resource that produces comprehension and respect for popular political voices and that allows for more people to perform as citizens; a resource that can make citizenship more pleasurable, more engaging, and more inclusive".

In this regard, populists' canny understanding of celebrity, politics and the power of 'low' forms of media—reality television, gossip magazines, talkback radio, the Italian *veline* tradition—can help to provide an effective and simple "availability heuristic" (Sunstein 2007, 534) for citizens, which is a mental shortcut and roadmap for organising and managing political issues in an increasingly complex world. By simplifying issues, treating the political as dichotomic, emphasising big personalities and utilising many of the same tactics that audiences are familiar with as a result of their exposure to the mass media, populism can make politics easier to grasp for those who may not have the time, patience or civic education to understand complicated policy debates or ideological differences amongst their representatives. In this sense, those leaders who are "able to communicate with ordinary people, and who might be said to be truly 'populist' in style" (Stewart, Mazzoleni, and Horsfield 2003, 228) could potentially be viewed as quite 'democratic', in that they are opening up the political sphere for all to access though clever and accessible usage of media and adaption of media logic.

However, while it is possible that populist use of media could render the political world more accessible, it is unclear whether pure accessibility should be the primary goal of political representation or media coverage of politics. It is obviously important that people feel enfranchised and part of their political system. There is clearly a need to ensure that political knowledge is not rarefied and only accessible to those with the requisite education or training. But there are limits to this accessibility: as shown, populists have a tendency to simplify issues to such an extent that nuance and detail can often disappear from political discussion, dividing society in a dichotomic fashion. These tendencies are problematic: social and political life *is* complex, and as such, social and political knowledge will likely be complex as well—and populism's position at the nexus of media and political logics does not sit well with complexity.

What is striking about the media strategies noted above—control and celebrity—is that they both have a strong focus on televisual modes of mass media communication above and beyond other media forms: those populists who have attempted to own or muzzle the media have primarily focused their efforts on television stations, while those who take the other approach of seeking celebrity have attempted to do so mainly through television programs (whether they are current affairs shows, reality television or advertisements). As Mancini (2008, 15) puts it, for populists, "television is more important than the printed word". He argues that this is the case as television still reaches the largest number of people versus other modes of communication, even in the age of the proliferation of varied media channels. Indeed, television remains a potent source of engendering support for populists (Mazzoleni, Stewart, and Horsfield 2003), with a number of authors demonstrating that links exist between television consumption habits and electoral choice (Iyengar and Hahn 2009; Mancini 2011; Stroud 2008).

We could add one more reason that television is so important to contemporary populism: populism is inherently a performative style that goes beyond mere words or ideology, and thus finds its best expression through communication channels that allow the visual *and* aural aspects of political performance to be transmitted. As will be discussed in the next chapter, performances of 'the people' in contemporary populism rely on spectacle, and television has played an important role in broadcasting and reinforcing these spectacles. Indeed, populism's embodied nature is perhaps best expressed on television, and the populist tendency towards speaking in attention-grabbing soundbites lends itself to television coverage.

Yet while television remains important to contemporary populism, changes afoot in the media landscape have meant that other modes of media communication have become increasingly important to populist success. While the 1990s and early 2000s bore witness to a number of populist leaders whose political rise was inextricably linked to television—Perot, Collor, Fujimori and Berlusconi among them (Boas 2005; Laurence 2003)—this era seems to be in its dying days, with a number of new populist figures such as Grillo, Vona and Wilders harnessing the power of new media and opportunities brought about by the emergence of the Internet and social networking to great effect. The next section looks at these changes, and how they have affected contemporary populism.

Populism and New Media

New media has opened up many performative opportunities for populist actors. Indeed, a number of populists have taken great advantage of the Internet's turn to Web 2.0, social networking and the ubiquity of mobile devices in order to speak 'directly' to and for 'the people', harnessing new media's reach, connectivity, user-interactivity and relative affordability in particularly effective and novel ways. This situation, of course, has not emerged ex nihilo: there is a historical precedent of populists adopting new technologies and using innovative techniques to spread their message. In the 1930s, American populist Huey Long allied with radio broadcaster Father Coughlin to use radio broadcasts to appeal to 'the people', standing as an early example of the populist style (Kazin 1995). As mentioned earlier, in the latter part of the century, a number of prominent populist leaders utilised television for similar purposes (Boas 2005; Laurence 2003). However, the novelty of the current situation stems from the proliferation of 'stages' on which claims to represent 'the people' can be made, and how these stages intensify the sense of immediacy that enables strong identification between the populist leader and 'the people'. While there has been substantial commentary about how social media and Web 2.0 technologies have been utilised by social movements (Bennett and Segerberg 2013; Gerbaudo 2012; Loader 2008; Shirky 2011; van de Donk et al. 2004), less has been said about the opportunities it presents populists. There are two key changes at play here: populist leaders are no longer as reliant on traditional media outlets to provide a stage for their performances; and the geographical limits of their performances and associated representative claims have become far more permeable and flexible.

In regards to the first point, populist actors can now circumvent traditional media by contacting their audiences (and vice versa) via social networks like Twitter, Facebook or Weibo; publishing blogs and websites; and uploading You-Tube videos to address 'the people'. For example, since his forced exile from Thailand, Thaksin has used YouTube to speak 'directly' to his followers, and has maintained an (at times) very active Twitter account—indeed, at one point he even had to use Twitter to deny media rumours that he had been killed in a car accident (Bangkok Post 2013). Even in the very recent past, this kind of broadcast of populist performances would not have been possible: given that there is often government control around radio, television and print media, it would have been difficult for any addresses by Thaksin to be broadcast in

Thailand. In fact, when he did call into a community radio station in May 2007 from exile, the government threatened to close the station down (Phongpaichit and Baker 2009a, 295). If the government (or government-aligned) media in the past wanted to deprive populists of 'the oxygen of publicity', the situation has now changed: there are almost always platforms by which the populist can gain more and more oxygen. You cannot suffocate a populist in the age of blogs, YouTube and social networks.

A number of newer populist actors have used the Internet and new media as a central instrument for political organisation and mobilisation, including Beppe Grillo and his MoVimento 5 Stelle in Italy and Jobbik, headed by Gábor Vona in Hungary. Grillo has used different online tools to great efficacy, including his very popular blog (beppegrillo.it); online voting for candidates as well as which group to join in the European Parliament; and perhaps most important, the website meetup.com to organise local (offline) group meetings to build the M5S. Jobbik, on the other hand, has built up a well-organised online presence utilising Facebook, iWiW (a now-defunct Hungarian social network) and their own official websites to appeal to young voters (Barlai 2012; Bartlett, Birdwell, Krekó et al. 2012). One Jobbik MP sums up their approach as such: "The internet has been and remains very important to us . . . not only on account of our limited access to the traditional media, but also because a major part of our supporters and voters are young people who we can best reach via new media" (Gyöngyösi in Verseck 2012). To a lesser extent, Geert Wilder's Partij voor de Vrijheid has used the Internet to increase hostility towards the alleged enemy of 'the people' by creating a website that invites Dutch citizens to write in with their complaints about Central and Eastern European migrants, ranging from losing a job to a migrant, to drunkenness, double parking and pollution caused by migrants (BBC News 2012). Such sites and platforms allow populist leaders and parties not only to distribute their messages more easily and freely but also to portray a sense of immediacy, closeness and intimacy with their followers, giving the appearance of direct accountability and representation.

Equally, content that simply would not be published or broadcast by traditional media can be easily uploaded and disseminated via the Internet by populists. For example, Wilders's anti-Islam film *Fitna*, which caused a large uproar in the Netherlands, was released via video-sharing website LiveLeak. Even though it has been taken down numerous times, it has been easily reuploaded and hosted by numerous websites. This would be unimaginable without the proliferation of decentralised networks and the viral, immediate and low-cost nature of information distribution enabled by the Internet.

The second related shift is that geographical boundaries have become far less important in the distribution of populist performances. While many traditional media broadcasts were geographically limited (in terms of broadcast area or the locations where such media was distributed) or temporally limited (in that the broadcaster or publisher had control over when political content was released or broadcast), recent media-technological changes have meant that the audiences of any populist representative claim can be more dispersed, and these audiences can often access content whenever they might wish. For example, a person in Johannesburg can now write to Winston Peters on his Facebook page, while a Kenyan immigrant in London can follow Raila Odinga on Twitter. A person in Stockholm was able to watch a livestream of Chávez's *Aló Presidente*, while Beppe Grillo and M5S Meetup Groups have sprung up in places as far-flung as London, Washington, Melbourne and Singapore. Such technological changes present a number of opportunities for those populists who might wish to spread their message—and perhaps their conception of 'the people'—more widely.

This point seems to be understood by a number of populist figures. For example, Wilders has travelled to a number of countries, including Australia, Canada, England and the United States, to great fanfare and controversy, in order to warn 'the people' of the 'dangers' of Islamisation and multiculturalism (Wilders 2010a, 2013a,b); in Australia he has even inspired and helped launch a new political party, the Australian Liberty Alliance. Before his death, Chávez made efforts to act as the spokesman not only of 'the people' of Venezuela but of Latin America more generally, suggesting a new kind of 'Bolivarian populism' for the region (Castañeda 2006; Edwards 2010). And in late 2013, Grillo's M5S held its third European meeting in London with the explicit aim of determining the "next steps for [t]he 5 Star MoVement in Italy *and Europe*" (Londra 5 Stelle 2013, emphasis mine). These examples suggest that mediatic changes may be prompting a gradual rethinking about who can be included in populist conceptions of 'the people'. Such developments are consistent with recent discussion in the literature on political representation, particularly about nonelected representatives (Saward 2010) and representation beyond the nation-state (Zürn and Walter-Drop 2011).

What about the other side of the screen? How has the rise of new media affected audiences and followers of populist leaders? Beyond the issues of mobilisation and organisation as discussed above, these shifts have only recently begun to be explored in the literature on populism. This research has come from a number of different regional contexts, suggesting that these changes are relatively widespread. For example, Kim (2008) has looked at the rise of "digital populism" in South Korea following the approval of a free-trade agreement with the United States and a panic about mad cow disease. In the US, the important role of email lists, conservative blogs, Twitter and YouTube have been documented in regards to the quick spread and growth of the Tea Party movement (Skocpol and Williamson 2012). Meanwhile, under the 'Populism in Europe' project run by the UK think-tank Demos, Bartlett et al. (2011, 2012, 2013) have looked into the online world of the European populist right, focusing on Facebook fans of populist parties. They have found that many digital populists' political activism is not purely online but extends 'IRL' too—that is, in real life—in the form of more traditional repertoires of political action.

Indeed, the user-generated media associated with Web 2.0, such as blogs, social networks and YouTube, have allowed followers of populist leaders to move from being consumers of media to become digital *prosumers*—those who both produce and consume political content (Ritzer and Jurgenson 2010). This has shifted models of media consumption from traditional top-down processes to a far more dynamic model that works between populist leaders, parties and 'the people'. Such changes have made political mobilisation and organisation far easier and less expensive among populist followers, in that all that is needed to participate actively in a political movement today is a smartphone or Internet connection.

Kim (2008) sees three main effects of these changes to the electronic media landscape for populist politics. First, these changes allow less expensive recruitment of populist followers: a viral video, which usually costs very little, can possibly garner more attention than an expensive and time-consuming mailout campaign or television advertising spot. This was demonstrated in the case of the Tea Party, whereby a clip of CNBC host Rick Santelli's tirade against Obama's bailouts on the floor of the Chicago Mercantile Exchange (CNBC 2009) spread quickly and memetically though these electronic media forms—blogs, Twitter, partisan news sites—and is now acknowledged as a key 'catalyst' for the Tea Party's formation (Lo 2012; Skocpol and Williamson 2012, 7). Second, Web 2.0 technologies give 'the people' more of a voice in that they are able to respond to events or performances in real time, but this immediacy also discourages reflection, fact-checking or the gathering of information. Third, the anonymity of online formats allows 'witch-hunting' and online 'flame wars' to escalate rapidly: one only need look at the comments section of any mainstream news site today to witness this.

Populism is particularly suited to the contours of this "new media galaxy" (Keane 2013) in at least three central ways. First, populism's dichotomisation of the political space suits the antagonistic sphere of the world of blogs, comment sections and the Web 2.0 Internet more generally, where discussions often take on a Schmittian 'us' versus 'them' hue, and as per the well-known Godwin's Law, comparisons of your interlocutors to Hitler are only ever a couple of comment section entries away. Second, the 'bad manners' of populism are evident in the often crude nature of discussions on online message boards and blogs, as well as the kinds of memes that tend to gain a viral quality on the Internet. Third, in the valorisation of commentary from 'nonelites' in the forms of blogs, mailing lists and the like, we see both a glorification of 'the people' and 'common sense', and an associated dismissal of expert knowledge—what has been called "epistemological populism" (Saurette and Gunster 2011). While there are definitely some positive ramifications to this trend—particularly in regards to questioning the status quo and uncovering corruption and wrongdoing—it can also be a negative development, in that 'echo chambers' or 'feedback loops' can develop, in which opposing views can be shut out of conversations, creating "self-protective enclave[s]" (Hall Jamieson and Cappella 2010, x) where ideological unity is more important than matters of truth. In such situations, conspiracy theories can gain far more traction than they might have otherwise: the 'Birther' campaign associated with the Tea Party, which had its beginnings on email lists, is evidence of this, whereby Barack Obama's citizenship has been continually brought into question, despite the matter being settled many times over.

It is clear that the emergence of new media has been of benefit to the spread of populism. Populist actors have benefited from the ability to reach 'the people' in a low-cost and efficient manner that sidesteps traditional media channels, while at the same time appearing as more 'direct', 'immediate' and accountable to their 'people'. Populism is also suited to the contours of the digital media landscape, whereby ideological division, virality and immediacy are favoured over the qualities of 'slow politics' (Saward 2011)—listening, understanding, modesty and discussion. This does not mean, of course, that *all* populists are helped by these developments: new media can be a double-edged sword for populist actors, in that it can also be used to attack or discredit them. This was illustrated in the 2013 federal election campaign in Australia, when Stephanie Banister, a candidate for Pauline Hanson's One Nation Party, was forced to withdraw her candidacy after a video of her claiming that "I don't oppose Islam as a country" (in Olding 2013) went viral on social networks to much ridicule and derision. Similar online derision followed Sarah Palin anytime she made a gaffe when running as the vice presidential candidate in 2008. The rise of new media also presents a potential threat to those populist actors who have made their mark via traditional media. For example, in Italy, we can see a clear divide between the televisual broadcast populism of Berlusconi, which is looking somewhat old and worn, and the new media populism of Beppe Grillo, which appears to be increasingly prescient and timely. While it is doubtful that the former variety will disappear anytime soon, it is the latter variety that we are likely to be seeing more of in the future.

Conclusion

The relationship between contemporary populism and media is only going to become more important as the process of mediatisation continues apace and different media forms become even more entrenched in our personal and political lives. This chapter has shown the centrality of media for understanding contemporary populism, demonstrating the multifaceted way that it acts as the 'stage' on which contemporary populist actors perform. From traditional media to new media, we can see not only that populist actors have used media in novel and effective ways but also that populism itself is particularly suited to the wider process of mediatisation. As has been argued, this manifests itself in increased political success by populist actors, the succumbing to the 'populist temptation' by mainstream political actors and an increasing professionalisation of populist communications. These trends are not likely to dissipate anytime soon, and populist usage of new media technologies will likely continue to be on the cutting edge of the intersection of media and politics. To reiterate the point made throughout this chapter, it is not that these tendencies are necessarily exclusive to populism—indeed, as has been discussed, many politicians feel forced to follow the populist example—but rather that these tendencies are *most pronounced* within contemporary populism. This is why it is no surprise to see populist figures like Sarah Palin, Pauline Hanson and Bert Karlsson on reality television shows, but it would be peculiar to see more mainstream politicians on the political 'high' do the same—the likelihood of Barack Obama or Angela Merkel appearing on *Dancing with the Stars* anytime soon is rather small. It may also explain why figures like Berlusconi, Thaksin and Chávez have attempted to buy up or control the media in a fashion more akin to autocrats than democrats.

While all contemporary politics are mediatised to some extent, it is ultimately populism that hews closest to the process of mediatisation. The collision between media logic and political logic finds its most pure expression in contemporary populism. As such, media can no longer be treated as a 'side issue' when it comes to understanding contemporary populism. It must be put at the centre of our analysis, so that we can make sense of the relationship between the stages and performances of populism as a distinct political style. As Blumler (2003, xvi) presciently argues: "[A]ny future attempt to analyze populism without taking into account . . . "the media factor" will be severely incomplete". We must heed his warning.

6   The Audience:
Populism and 'The People'

Appealing to the people means constructing a fictitious entity: since the people as such do not exist, populists are those who create a virtual image of the popular will. . . . A populist identifies his plan with the will of the people and then, if he can manage it (and he often can), he takes a goodly number of citizens—who are so fascinated by this virtual image of themselves that they end up identifying with it—and transforms them into the very people he has invented.

—Eco (2007, 130)

As we have seen thus far, populism is one of the most controversial concepts in contemporary political science. Scholars still remain divided on how to define populism, as well as the concept's distinct features. Thankfully, there is at least one feature that the vast majority of those studying the phenomenon *do* agree on: populism's key reference to 'the people'. Canovan (1981, 294) noted over three decades ago that "all forms of populism without exception involve some kind of exaltation and appeal to 'the people'", and this has been the case from the earliest forms of agrarian populism in the villages of rural Russia and the American Midwest to the different manifestations of populism existing around the world today.

Yet while there may be a consensus on the centrality of 'the people' when it comes to populism, we still know little about the actual *ways* in which 'the people' are represented and "rendered-present" (Arditi 2007a) in contemporary populism. We have an understanding of *who* 'the people' are—empirical case studies have shown us who votes for populist candidates, as well as identifying the ways that populists tend to characterise 'the people' in different regions of the world—but not about *how* these populist constructions and representations of 'the people' operate.[1] To put it another way: we understand the *content* of populist representations of 'the people', but we do not know as much about the *processes* involved in speaking to and for 'the people'. So how do these processes operate? Who are the audiences that these populist performances are actually aimed towards? And why do some characterisations of 'the people' gain traction, while others fail?

This chapter introduces the concept of mediation to help us answer these questions about 'the people'. Its key contention is that contemporary populism is never just a 'direct' or 'unmediated' phenomenon that occurs only between the populist leader and 'the people' (as is sometimes implicitly assumed), but rather that populist representations of 'the people' rely on a complex process of mediated claim-making between populist leaders, audiences, constituencies and media. It maps out this process over four steps, demonstrating that the audience for populism is never as simple as we might initially assume.

The first part of the chapter sets the scene by showing that talk of 'directness' with 'the people' when it comes to populism is misleading, and demonstrating that the concept of mediation has been underexplored in the contemporary literature on populism. The second section examines *why* 'the people' have to be mediated as opposed to other political subjects, and uses Arditi's (2007a) concept of "rendering-present" 'the people' to examine the context in which these mediated representations take place. The third section then turns to the important question of *how* 'the people' are constituted within contemporary populism. It does this by utilising the work of Debord (1994) to highlight the role of mediated 'spectacle' inherent in speaking for 'the people', and by employing Saward's (2010) concept of 'the representative claim' to explain the difference between populist audiences (those who are spoken *to* by populists) and populist constituencies (those who are spoken *for* by populists), showing that successful representations of 'the people' rely on both of these groups. It explains these concepts by drawing on the illustrative examples of Silvio Berlusconi's advertising campaigns and the 2002 Venezuelan coup against Hugo Chávez. The final section then turns to the role of media in this process, showing that the media are never just neutral 'loudspeakers' for populist performances but are actually active participants, often presenting themselves as proxies for 'the people' and answering claims on their behalf. As such, the chapter closes by considering the media's self-appointed role as the voice of 'the people'. This chapter thus reveals that speaking for 'the people' is far from a simple and direct process—rather, it relies on a complex cycle of mediation.

Mediation in Contemporary Theories of Populism

What does it mean to speak of mediation? Put broadly, mediation can be understood as "communication via a medium, the intervention of which can affect both the message and the relationship between sender and recipient" (Hjarvard 2013, 19). The media through which such communications can take place are numerous, and can include artefacts, finances, spaces and technologies. In this regard, mediated communication should "primarily be understood as opposed to direct, first-hand, or face-to-face communication" (Strömbäck and Esser 2009, 208). However, it is the usage of the term in the political communication literature that is most pertinent for our purposes, where mediation focuses on the use of communications media (particularly mass media). As Silverstone (2002, 762) puts it, mediation in this sense is defined as the "fundamentally, but unevenly dialectical process in which institutionalised media of communication (the press, broadcast radio and television, and increasingly the world wide web) are involved in the general circulation of symbols in social life". It is important to note that this is different from the process of mediatisation outlined in the previous chapter: mediatisation refers to the *historical process* by which the media's influence has reached into and changed in a fundamental way a number of societal spheres (including politics), whereas mediation is far more neutral and general, referring to the *transmission of messages, symbols and performances* (Krotz 2009, 26; Strömbäck and Esser 2009, 207–9).

Why is the concept of mediation generally absent from contemporary theories of populism? The view of populism as an 'unmediated' phenomenon whereby populist leaders are 'directly' in touch with their followers remains strong in the literature on populism. This is certainly the case in the literature on Latin American populism, where accounts of the phenomenon have tended to focus on how populist leaders have bypassed formal channels of representation to reach the 'the people' in an allegedly direct manner, with references to populists' "direct, unmediated, uninstitutionalized support" (Weyland 2001, 14) or their "unmediated relationships with atomized masses" (Roberts 1995, 113).[2] Other authors have focused less on the 'direct' organisational aspects of populism, and more on the apparent 'direct communication' that exists between populist leaders and followers: Urbinati (1998, 111) refers to populism's "direct language and politics", while March (2007, 66) refers to the populist leader's "unmediated communication with his people".

Yet there is a need to be careful when using such terms. While populists sometimes do indeed bypass traditional party structures or other usual mediating channels when appealing to 'the people', here we face a terminological dilemma: talk of 'unmediated' or 'direct' connections between the populist leader and 'the people' risks falling into the trap of unwillingly buying into leaders' claims that they do have 'direct' contact with 'the people'—and thus express insight into 'the people's' true desires and needs. This, however, is obviously incorrect; as the work of Ankersmit (1996, 2002) has demonstrated, when it comes to political representation, there is an ineradicable 'aesthetic gap' between those who are represented and those who claim to represent them that cannot ever be completely bridged. As such, we should not mistake attempts to cover up or deny this gap with the *actual closure* of the gap. So-called direct or unmediated populism always retains *some* element of nondirectness or mediation. As Knight (1998, 228–29) puts it: "At best, we might hypothesise that some populist movements—particularly in their infancy—are 'under-mediated'" rather than claiming that they are *unmediated*. Beyond this, when it comes to populist modes of communication and representation between the leader and 'the people', there have been a number of studies over the past fifteen years that have shown that these communications are not 'direct' but of course rely on numerous channels of mediation (Boas 2005; Jagers and Walgrave 2007; Kazin 1995; Mazzoleni, Stewart and Horsfield 2003; Pels 2003; Waisbord 2011; Walgrave and de Swert 2004).

The populist literature thus needs to let go of the myth of the populist leader who appeals 'directly' to 'the people' in an allegedly 'unmediated' fashion, and instead acknowledge that populist constructions of 'the people' are almost always mediated in some way or another. Contemporary populists do not 'go to the people' in the idealised style of the Russian *Narodnik* of the nineteenth century[3]—they 'go to the people' in the form of mediated messages, broadcasts, transmissions and performances. Today, mediation plays a vital role in the way that populist actors construct and transmit images, 'spectacles' or representations of 'the people'.

Yet the vital role of mediation remains relatively ignored in the literature on populism, even by those who have otherwise explored populist representations of 'the people' in depth. For example, those working broadly within the ideological approach (Canovan 2004, 2005; Mudde and Rovira Kaltwasser 2013b; Rovira Kaltwasser 2013) have made great conceptual progress by exploring 'the boundary problem' of populism (the question of how populists draw borders and boundaries around their definition of 'the people'), yet have ignored the role of media in setting these boundaries. Even Laclau, whose approach to populism as a political logic offers the most nuanced and cohesive account of the emergence of 'the people' so far attempted in the literature, ignores the vital role of mediation: as Simons (2011, 219–20) correctly notes, Laclau's work "would benefit from a media theory approach to the mediated character of the public . . . and a mediological approach to the transmission of political ideas".

This leaves us with a need for a media-centred conception of populism—an understanding of the phenomenon that can account for the complex dynamics involved in representing, rendering-present and speaking for 'the people'. The approach developed in this book—populism as a political style—allows us to do this. As such, the following section explains why representations of 'the people' require mediation, how representing 'the people' differs from representing other political subjects, and why populist modes of representation are well suited to the current media-political landscape.

Rendering-Present 'The People'

What makes 'the people' special? Unlike speaking for political subjects such as 'workers' or 'the middle class', which both have a relatively well defined social base—'workers' refers to those who are employed, while 'the middle class' refers to a particular socioeconomic stratum—'the people' has no particular social base automatically ascribed to it, and consequently, no inevitable constituency to fill the signifier (Laclau 2005b). In this regard, Canovan (2005, 140) is correct to claim that "'the people' is undoubtedly one of the least precise and most promiscuous of concepts. . . . 'The people' cannot be restricted to a group with definite characteristics, boundaries, structure or permanence, although it is quite capable of carrying these senses".

While this is not necessarily a problem—indeed, this ambiguity can actually be a strength as 'the people' can include a wide number of identities without ever really specifying their primary linking characteristics beyond a shared opposition to 'the elite' or an associated Other—it does raise an important question when it comes to political representation: how to represent 'the people' if the distinct attributes of 'the people' are not particularly clear? Who is it that populist representatives actually stand for? Arditi's (2007a) work on populist representation, or what he calls the "rendering-present" of 'the people',[4] is useful in thinking through this operation. As Arditi notes, populists simultaneously claim to speak for a group named 'the people' while remaining vague about who 'the people' are. So how to bridge this 'gap', whereby 'the people' are not identified or 'present' as a distinct constituency, yet are being spoken for?

According to Arditi (2007a, 65): "[T]he gap between the absent presence of the people and the action of representing them . . . is bridged by a 'presentation' that forgets the iterability at work in the 're-' of 're-presentation'". Here, populist leaders short-fuse the distance between representative and the represented by presenting themselves as having an extreme immediacy or intimacy with 'the people', or by going so far as to present themselves as actually *embodying* the expression of the popular will, as was presented in Chapter 4, in which case "the absent presence of the people turns out to be an absolute presence, and all that remains is the presence of the leader by fiat of tacit authorization" (Arditi 2007a, 65). If a populist leader's performance is convincing in this regard, 'the people's' spectrality and lack of ability to speak 'for itself' can thus link 'the people' and the leader together as one. Such performances are not uncommon within contemporary populism—Hugo Chávez's (AFP 2010) claim that "I am not an individual, I am the people" is a perfect example. It is also evident in organisational terms in Geert Wilders's Partij voor de Vrijheid, whereby Wilders is the only official member—members of the public can volunteer or donate money but cannot actually join the party (van der Pas, de Vries, and van der Brug 2013). In this case, Wilders claims to represent 'the people' without actually having to be accountable to any actual party members—just an imagined 'people' who may have voted for him in an election.

Arditi explicitly links such forms of populist representation of 'the people' with the contemporary mediatised political setting that was discussed in the previous chapter. While citizens may have once engaged 'directly' with their representatives or formal party structures through face-to-face meetings, rallies or events, most citizens today experience their representatives in a mediated form, through media channels such as television, Internet or newspapers.[5] Rather than 'real' immediacy with political representatives, we instead now have a "simulacrum of immediacy" or "virtual immediacy" aided by channels of mediation. According to Arditi (2007a, 68), this "virtual immediacy" that characterises contemporary representative politics "coincides with the imaginary identification characteristic of populist representation—the presumption of enjoying a direct relation with the people and the imaginary identification of the latter with the leader". This sense of directness or immediacy, however, does not mean that forms of mediation disappear from populism or other forms of representative politics. As Arditi (2007a, 68) argues, in this era of 'audience democracy', "mediations remain in place, denser than ever". As such, it is vital to bring mediation into discussions of how populist leaders construct idealised versions of 'the people' and simultaneously declare their closeness to them.

Mediating 'The People' through Image and Performance

If we agree that 'the people' is a mediated construction within contemporary populism, how can we think through the *processes* of mediated representation, and determine why some of these mediated constructions succeed while others fail? The work of two theorists proves useful here. The first is Situationist thinker Guy Debord, whose *Society of the Spectacle* (1994) presciently described "a media and consumer society organized around the production and consumption of images, commodities and staged events" (Kellner 2003, 2) wherein "all that once was directly lived has become mere representation" (Debord 1994, 12). The second is Michael Saward (2010), whose model of the 'representative claim' aims to put performance at the heart of understanding political representation by reconceptualising representation as a mediated 'event' or 'process' rather than following the traditional "presence approach" (2010, 43), which sees it as a relatively static institutional relationship. Their key concepts—'the spectacle' and the 'representative claim', respectively—provide the coordinates for understanding *how* mediated performances, images and representations of 'the people' are presented.

Debord: 'The People' as Image

As has been established, 'the people' is not a pre-existing social group, and as such, cannot directly present itself in an 'immanent' fashion (Laclau 2005b). Rather, 'the people' only come to be 'rendered-present' through mediated representation, which in populism is usually linked with the image of the leader. To speak for 'the people', then, is to present a "virtual image of the popular will", as the opening quotation of this chapter by Eco (2007, 130) indicates. Knowingly or not, we are firmly in the realm of Guy Debord here. Debord outlined a vision of society wherein social relations are reconstituted through images and mediated representations rather than being experienced 'directly'. As he noted: "The spectacle is not a collection of images; rather, it is a social relationship between people that is mediated by images" (1994, 12).

Indeed, there are hints of Debord's influence throughout the literature on populism. For example, writing on populism's relationship to the media, Mazzoleni (2008, 52) notes "the transformation of political language into spectacle" and refers to "the rise of an unprecedented 'spectacle-politics". Papadopoulos (2000, 7) has similarly claimed that "populists construct a 'political spectacle", while Lucardie (2008) has referred to the "spectacular politics" of populists. Elsewhere, Broxmeyer (2010), Sutherland (2012) and Žižek (2006a) have explicitly deployed the work of Debord in their analyses of populism.

How the relationship between populist leaders and their constituencies is mediated through idealised images of 'the people' within this context can be concretely illustrated by two quite disparate examples of populism—one from the side of the populist leader, the other from the side of the so-called people. The first is that of Silvio Berlusconi, and in particular the 2008 video for his party's official campaign anthem "Meno male che Silvio c'è", which roughly translates to 'Thank goodness for Silvio'. The video cuts between overhead shots of enormous crowds (presumably used to give a sense of the wide support for Berlusconi) and scenes of a range of 'ordinary Italians' of different professions—amongst them gelato servers, bakers, builders and taxi drivers—singing the praises of Berlusconi, with the repeated refrain of "President, we stand with you/Thank goodness for Silvio". Another version of the video, in typical Berlusconian fashion, features only females, many dressed in figure-hugging low-cut tops or swimsuits.[6] Beyond the general cheap aesthetics of the videos, three central things stand out in terms of understanding the image of 'the people' presented here. The first is that there are no visible minorities in either version of the video—Silvio's 'people' are 'native Italians', and employed or industrious native Italians at that. Second, the phrase "we are the people" is sung no less than five times across the two versions of the video, making clear that Berlusconi's idealised 'people' take the form of those identities presented in the video. Third, images of Berlusconi are absent from either video, with the focus purely on the image of 'the people' who find their unity in their leader, despite their disparate vocational backgrounds. This absence of Berlusconi gives the sense of grassroots support for the leader. Taken together, these three elements portray a sense of 'virtual immediacy' between Berlusconi and the idealised version of 'the people' that are portrayed in the video.

Berlusconi's keen understanding of the power of mediated images of 'the people' does not come as a surprise: the man is a media tycoon, and a number of scholars have made note of his impressive media skills (Campus 2010; Ginsborg 2004; Roncarolo 2005). Yet Berlusconi should not necessarily be viewed as an exceptional Italian case of "a demagogue who controls a corrupt demos properly tamed by his media" (Viroli 2012, xvii), but rather as a case par excellence of the populist ability to present appealing mediated representations and images of 'the people'. As Mancini (2008, 115) argues, Berlusconi actually offers various lessons for contemporary mediated representative politics—namely, that "politics is not a universe separated from daily life and its imaginary", and that images and spectacle are crucial in presenting an appealing and resonant claim to speak on behalf of 'the people'.

The second example of the importance of mediated images of 'the people' in the age of spectacle comes from the dramatic (and short-lived) 2002 Venezuelan coup in which Hugo Chávez was briefly ousted from office, and then returned as a result of to a mass outpouring of popular support. While it is beyond the limits of this chapter to describe the events in depth, the pertinent detail is that the battles over the legitimacy and 'meaning' of the coup were almost entirely inscribed in the language of mediated image: as Beasley-Murray (2002, 106) puts it, the coup "took place in the media, fomented by the media, and with the media themselves the apparent object of both sides' contention". He goes on to say that Venezuela "was brought down in the full, if confused, glare of media spectacle".[7] In a similar vein, Hernández (2004, 140) notes that "'media war', 'virtual coup' [and] 'media terrorism'" were some of the key terms used to describe the events. The primacy of the mediated image was made explicit when pro-Chávez groups took over state television stations in an attempt to broadcast their own messages of support for the ousted president, while other *Chavistas* demanded that the privately owned anti-Chávez networks present their side of the story. As Duno-Gottberg (2004, 130) reads the situation: "I think that this reveals the consciousness of these social groups of the importance of what Bourdieu has called 'media arbitration'. . . . It would appear that in this instance 'the mob' knew that mediation through television guaranteed social and political existence". In this case, in a time of significant uncertainty and unrest, it is telling that the struggles over the meaning of 'the people' took place primarily on the plane of televisual broadcast media.

These examples suggest that in the age of spectacle, mediated images are extremely important to the construction of 'the people'—from the perspective both of populist leaders and followers. These images have power in that they serve as "highly simplified and schematic mental representations" (Manin 1997, 227) of who makes up the legitimate 'people' within a given political community, condensing a great deal of information in an easily graspable aesthetic package. In this way, one could interpret these mediated spectacles as visual manifestations of the 'heartland' of populists, which Taggart explains as "a territory of the imagination" (2000, 95) that populists draw on as "an idealized conception of the community they serve" (2004, 274). These conceptions are always vague and blurry, and "owe their power to the heart, to evocation of sentiments that may not be necessarily either rationalized or rationalizable" (2000, 95). Mediated images of 'the people' evoke these complex notions of the heartland by combining potent symbolism (flags, signs, crowds, colours and so forth) with a visual sense of cohesion and homogeneity amongst 'the people'. Visual representations of 'the people' also give the heartland a certain sense of 'concreteness', strongly implying presence and corporeality—and thus existence—of 'the people'.

Importantly, these images also transmit information about who is *not* a resident of the heartland, and thus not part of 'the people'. This is usually done through the conspicuous absence of certain identities from the images of 'the people'—a handy method if a populist is keen to not be seen as outwardly discriminatory, as this exclusion takes the form of silent absence rather than open targeting of out-groups. The ability of images of 'the people' to combine these multiple levels of information in an appealing package aimed at evoking an affective reaction suggests that more attention needs to be paid to not just *what* is said of 'the people', but *how* they are portrayed and aestheticised through mediated spectacle.

Yet this is not simply a monodirectional operation, in which canny populist leaders (and their public relations teams) foist mediated images of 'the people' on an unsuspecting public who accept them in an uncritical manner. Images and representations of 'the people' are effective only insofar as they are *judged* to be convincing and resonant. But who makes such judgements? And on what grounds are these judgements made?

Saward: 'The People' as Performance

Saward's (2010) concept of the 'representative claim' offers us some clues in regards to these processes, and helps us understand the role of audiences and constituencies in judging claims made on behalf of 'the people'. Mapping neatly onto Debord's argument that images underlie all social and political relationships in the contemporary 'spectacular' milieu, Saward's work highlights the important role of aesthetics and performance at play in any form of political representation. According to Saward (2008, 273, emphasis in original):

> [P]olitical representation is a variable, dynamic and competitive process encompassing in principle a range of actors, and not a static and incontestable factual status that

some (the elected) possess utterly and others (everyone else) lacks utterly. It is also a phenomenon with strong aesthetic and cultural components—would-be representatives present themselves *as* such and such, to a constituency and perhaps a wider audience which itself is characterised (or portrayed) by the claimant in particular, selective ways.

Saward goes on to state that political representatives quite literally "need to 'make representations' (in the sense of artistic portrayals or depictions) of their constituents to try to get the latter to recognize themselves in the claims being made" (2010, 140).

There are two relevant points here for thinking about representations of 'the people' within contemporary populism. The first is that Saward stresses the contingency and constant negotiation at the heart of political representation. In this regard, political representation is seen as an ongoing *process,* rather than a particular *status* that is only conferred at elections that occur every few years. As such, we should understand that claims to represent 'the people' are never completely 'set', but rather are always in flux and open to contestation. The second is that it is *performance* that forms the basis of these ongoing negotiations around the meaning of 'the people': as Saward (2010, 67, emphasis in original) notes: "In order to *be* representative claims, these claims need to made, acted out, and packaged. . . . The successful performance of representative claims lies at the core of political success". Accordingly, the judgement of whether a claim to speak for 'the people' is successful or unsuccessful cannot be made on the basis of electoral success alone (although that is one partial indicator)—rather, this judgement relies on whether the representative performance 'resonates' and is accepted by certain audiences as convincing.

As such, there is more to successfully 'performing the people' than just speaking in their name—you could potentially walk around your local shopping centre claiming that you speak for 'the people', but it is doubtful that anyone would listen, care or accept your claim. Stressing the role of performance within representation captures the fact that for any claim to be resonant and effective, it relies on what Austin (1975, 16) called the "securing of uptake". This requires two things. First, there must be an audience to watch or hear your performance. Second, that audience needs to understand the performance, and choose to accept the claim: it must scan as both legible and convincing. There is a reflexive relationship at play here: audiences are not just voiceless masses waiting to be interpellated into popular subjects, but practice agency in regards to choosing to accept, reject or modify claims made about them. As Saward

(2010, 36–37) notes, audiences "may make counterclaims about themselves as subjects, or about the subjects proffered to them by others' claims".

However, how can 'the people', a group that does not empirically 'exist' prior to its constitution, answer a populist leader's mediated claim to speak on its behalf, or make counterclaims about themselves? Saward's distinction between constituencies and audiences is useful here in discerning who is in fact responsible for receiving and considering claims to speak for 'the people'. Constituencies are those whom the representative claims to speak *for*, while audiences are those whom the representative addresses the claim *to* (Saward 2010, 48–57).[8] So within populism, the constituency is made up of those identities who fit within the populist leader's characterisation of 'the people', while the audience is potentially (and usually) much larger—it may include journalists, other politicians, the citizens within the borders of the populist's electorate, state or country, or even international audiences. For example, Geert Wilder's conception of 'the people'—white, native Dutch citizens, as characterised by his oft-cited 'Henk and Ingrid' (van Zoonen 2012, 65)—is his constituency, yet his audience is far bigger, with his claims about representing those 'people' being broadcast and distributed across the globe through his media appearances, book, film and numerous international talks. In other words, Wilders is not interested solely in speaking directly to his 'people' (his constituency) but also as being *seen by others* (his audience) to be speaking in 'the people's' name through mediated performances.

Much of the success and efficacy of a performance of 'the people' thus lies in it gaining resonance with *both constituency and audience.* Let us take each of these separately: first, the constituency, or those who might identify as 'the people'. Obviously, there needs to be some uptake or acceptance of a populist's performance from whoever fills their notion of 'the people' for their claim to speak for 'the people' to resonate. Saward (2010, 151–53) refers to such uptake as "acceptance acts" or "acceptance events", and asks the important question: "How can we know if a given representative claim is or is not accepted by a citizen or citizens?" (Saward 2010, 152). There is not a clear-cut answer to this question, as such 'acceptance acts' can take a wide number of forms and can be expressed through a number of channels of mediation. As mentioned, the most obvious and easily measurable form of an 'acceptance event' is electoral success in the form of votes from those who you have characterised as 'the people'. If you do not secure these votes, then your claim to speak for 'the people' does not look particularly convincing: the rapid decline of a number of once prominent Tea Party candidates such as Christine O'Donnell and Herman Cain is evidence of this. Other visible and thus 'clear' signs of acceptance could include party memberships, donations, petitions in your favour or the formation of support groups; or outside the electoral arena, public displays of support whereby your 'people' visibly appear to support you, such as events like marches, rallies, speeches or television appearances in front of adoring crowds. Acceptance acts could even take the form of attracting Twitter followers or Facebook fans. At their most successful, such performances can invoke feelings of emotional commitment and affective investment in the populist leader. Saward also claims that silence can at times indicate acceptance, given that it can be read to imply tacit consent or approval of a claim (or at very least a lack of objection to the claim). On the other hand, 'deafening silence' could indicate the very opposite—not only that the claim does not resonate, but that it is seen as inconsequential enough that no one sees fit to challenge it (the farcical example raised earlier of walking around your local shopping centre claiming to speak for 'the people' might fit under this latter condition—silence in the face of such claims would likely indicate lack of interest rather than tacit acceptance).

However, perhaps just as important as being accepted by your constituency in the form of 'the people' is the reception and coverage you receive from other audiences—particularly in regards to being perceived as being in touch with or representing 'the people'. Saward acknowledges the complexity of this state of affairs when he evokes the situation in which "an invoked constituency may largely accept a given claim but a broader audience that is addressed by the claim may reject it, or express serious scepticism" (Saward 2010, 152). In populist terms, this would involve the invoked 'people' accepting the claim to speak on their behalf, but others outside the 'people' viewing the claim as false. We know that the wider audience matters because the kinds of events noted above—rallies, online displays of support, elections and so forth—are not just aimed at pleasing 'the people' but are often designed to be broadcast and disseminated (that is, mediated) to wider audiences. Such audiences play an important role: they can debate or deliberate the claims, participate in the dissemination of the claims, or confer a wider sense of legitimacy on the populist's claim by judging the claim to be resonant (Saward 2010, 150). So while the wider audience may not personally accept the populist's claim to speak for 'the people'—that is, they may not identify with the characterisation of 'the people' being offered, or may see the populist leader offering the claim as a charlatan— what they *do* need to 'buy' is the idea that the populist's claim to speak for 'the people' *resonates with those people*.

To give a concrete example: one might not agree with or fit into Sarah Palin's conception of 'the people' (that is, not be part of her constituency), but still be part of her audience by viewing footage on a news program of her speaking on behalf of 'the people' at a Tea Party rally. Having seen the feverish devotion of her followers at this rally, one might notionally accept that her message does resonate with her version of 'the people', and as such, judge her claim to speak on behalf of *a certain version of 'the people'* to be convincing (to those 'people'). Indeed, it is perfectly consistent to accept her claim to speak on behalf of 'the people', and at the same time utterly disagree with her political beliefs—what matters is that her claim *appears* to resonate. Judgements about the resonance of a mediated populist claim to speak for 'the people' are thus never made *just* by 'the people'.[9]

Mass Media as Proxy for 'The People'

The final question to ask about this process is: how do potential audiences and constituencies for these populist claims on behalf of 'the people' actually 'receive' the performances? While there are a number of channels of mediation that the performances can be transmitted through (electoral channels, clientelist networks and so forth), the obvious answer is that forms of media (particularly the mass media) play the central role in circulating, transmitting, printing, broadcasting and reproducing these performances in contemporary politics.[10] However, the mass media is not an impartial 'megaphone' for populists in this regard, and does not simply act as a neutral arbiter of these performances. Rather, the mass media is directly implicated in the back-and-forth negotiations of the meaning of 'the people' between populist leaders, constituencies and audiences in at least two central ways. The first way is unsurprising: journalists, editors and producers working within the mass media choose what images and characterisations of 'the people' to transmit, and how to frame them (Akkerman 2011; Bos, van der Brug and de Vreese 2010, 2011). The second way is less obvious and more interesting for our purposes—namely, the way that media sometimes positions itself as a proxy for 'the people'—not only receiving and transmitting mediated claims made on behalf of 'the people' but also actively *judging those claims on 'the people's' behalf*. This complexifies the processes involved in speaking for 'the people', and it is this situation—whereby media claims to speak for 'the people'—to which this final section of the chapter turns.

As has been established, the lack of an automatic social base of 'the people' means that it is open to a wide number of characterisations. However, this is not only the case in regards to making mediated claims on behalf of 'the people', but also in *answering* said claims on behalf of 'the people'. Pels (2003, 51, emphasis mine) gets at this process when describing the "continuous interplay between political professionals and citizens *(or rather: journalists who pose as the people's true spokespersons)*" within contemporary democracy, as does his portrayal of "media professionals increasingly play[ing] the part of the 'rational citizen' (always a mythical figure) as controllers of the political elite" (2003, 60). Similarly, Simons (2002, 171) argues that "today's public is necessarily a mediated public. Just as the bigger media networks compete for larger chunks of market share, those agencies seeking political rather than consumptive popular consent try to occupy a position from which they can speak in the name of 'the people'".

We can see this at play in both traditional and new media around the world. In regards to the former, we can think of the role played by newspapers like the UK's *The Sun*, Germany's *Bild*, the US's *New York Post* or Australia's *Daily Telegraph*, whereby these tabloids present themselves as self-appointed voices of 'the people' by adopting a register that allegedly resonates with 'the people', and by running certain campaigns that ostensibly represent 'the people's' concerns—such as demands to 'crack down' on illegal immigration, or 'get tough' on issues of law and order. We can also consider how such newspapers choose to present the claims of certain populist leaders versus other politicians—for example, when Pauline Hanson first emerged on the national political stage in Australia, the tabloid print media framed her as "a dinkum stirrer",[11] and "implied that Pauline Hanson's views were shared by many Australians, but that she had simply brought them into the public realm" (Scalmer 1999). Similarly, Art (2005) has outlined how Austrian tabloid the *Kronen Zeitung* continually lauded Jörg Haider and defended him against claims of Nazi apologism, while attacking rival politicians.

This is not just the case for newspapers. The prolonged support of the Tea Party by the Fox News Channel has been so intense that it has seen the characterisations of 'the people' offered by both the populist movement and the network become fused together. Writing on Tea Party protests, Skocpol and Williamson (2012, 131) claim that "Fox News directly linked the network's brand to these protests and allowed members of the 'Fox Nation' to see the Tea Parties as a natural outgrowth of their identity as Fox News viewers". Simons (2011, 216) has made similar arguments, arguing that Sarah Palin's populist conception of 'the real America' overlaps in a significant manner with the audience of Fox News. There is some limited evidence to suggest this might indeed be the case: a CBS News/New York Times poll (2010) found that Fox News was the primary source of news for Tea Party supporters, with 63 percent of supporters claiming that they get most of their political and current event news on television from the channel.[12] Congruence between 'the people' that these forms of media purport to represent and 'the people' that populists claim to speak for can also be seen in Venezuela, where members of the Bolivarian Circles tended to rely on the (pro-Chávez) state media as their primary source of news (Hawkins 2010). Elsewhere, Stewart, Mazzoleni and Horsfield (2003, 233) have concluded that the studies in their edited collection on media and neopopulism show "that the media outlets that reported positively on neo-populist movements also tended to be those whose main audiences were most likely to be supporters of the movements".

New media might be more indicative of 'the voice of the people' when it comes to answering the mediated claims of populists, given that blogs and social networking services like Twitter represent a far more multidirectional communicative dynamic than forms of old media. However, one must still have doubts about how representative of 'the people' certain forms of new media actually are—some voices within the blogosphere and social networks are louder than others, and certain levels of technical literacy are needed just to participate within such networks. This is particularly evident in the debates over just how participatory and representative the activities of Beppe Grillo's MoVimento 5 Stelle really are, with some reading the party's online activities as particularly inclusive (Navarria 2008; Turner 2012), while others are more cynical (Diamanti 2014). Similar concerns have been raised about the Tea Party's use of social networks (Rohlinger and Klein 2014), as well as about the role of social media in post-Thaksin Thailand, where Facebook groups have served as 'echo chambers' for opposing political camps (Grömping 2014).

Both traditional and new media thus play a multifaceted role within populism, broadcasting populist claims to 'the people' while at the same time judging the legitimacy of those claims by presenting themselves as representative of 'the people'. This effectively represents a situation where mediated representations of 'the people' have been short-fused: a populist actor makes a claim to represent 'the people', but rather than those who identify as 'the people' answering the claim, the mass media judges the claim for them, and speaks on their behalf. In such situations, the mass media acts both as the mediator of the image of 'the people' *and* as the voice of 'the people' simultaneously. A feedback loop is thus established between populist actors and media in regards to who represents 'the people', whereby those who might actually identify with 'the people' are merely left watching from the sidelines. To return to the terminology of Saward, the constituency is displaced here, with the audience (in the form of the mass media) appraising the populist's authenticity and legitimacy on 'the people's' behalf.

Yet those who may or may not identify with characterisations or mediated images of 'the people' are not just feckless spectators: they do have agency. If the claims made by the populist leader on behalf of 'the people' and the mass media's answer on behalf of 'the people' do not resonate with consumers of this media (who, after all, are the alleged 'people' everyone is talking on behalf of), it is likely that the claims will be rejected. As Pels (2003, 60) argues, people are not stupid, and generally know when a performance or claim is inauthentic: "Without formal expertise, ordinary citizens are quite capable of realistically judging what is performed on the media-political stage". This judgement of the mass media takes different forms, including protests, letters to the editor (Akkerman 2011; Rooduijn 2014a) or boycotts, as in the case of one faction of the Tea Party's boycott of Fox News for allegedly being too 'leftist', and thus not speaking for 'the people' in an accurate fashion (see Freedlander 2013). It can also take the form of the emergence of alternative voices of 'the people', or battles about who 'truly' represents 'the people' within new media (Lievrouw 2011). Or it could take the form of the worst fate of all for a media source that attempts to present itself as a proxy for 'the people'—a lack of interest, and consequently, dwindling relevance, circulation, viewers/readers, and most important, profit.

Conclusion

This chapter has explained the complex processes of mediation at play when speaking for 'the people' within contemporary populism. Questioning assumptions about populism's 'unmediated' or 'direct' nature, it has sought to make clear that mediation is a key part of contemporary populism, and that the representation of 'the people' is the outcome of a dynamic process between leaders, constituencies, audiences and media that takes place through channels of mediation—and that this process never finishes. As contemporary politics becomes more 'spectacular' and media-centred, it is likely that the focus on the aesthetic and performative elements of populism will becomes even more important to consider when seeking to understand the emergence of 'the people'.

There are three key lessons to be drawn from this chapter. The first is that when we think about populism, we must better acknowledge the dynamism at play in representations of 'the people' by engaging more robustly with the role of political representation and understanding the crucial role of mediation in any claim to speak on behalf of 'the people'. As Saward's work shows, populist representation is a *process,* not a status. A second lesson is that there is more to understanding populist 'success' than the votes received by populist actors. While studies of the electoral performance of populist leaders and parties are undoubtedly important, formulations of 'the people' go beyond this, with issues of 'uptake', resonance and the acceptance of performances of 'the people' being key to populist influence and success. In this regard, contemporary populism has much to teach us about the formulation of group identities in the contemporary mediatised political landscape, where rusted-on party supporters are ever-dwindling, and new audiences for political performances are being formulated and targeted all the time. Relatedly, a third lesson is that the resonance of populist performances of 'the people' is not just based on those who are characterised as 'the people' accepting them, but also on the reception of wider audiences. In other words, populist claims to speak for 'the people' are not just for 'the people' but for wider audiences as well. While these lessons may not provide solace for those seeking theoretical parsimony in the study of contemporary populism, they do acknowledge the richness and complexity at the heart of the seemingly very simple act of speaking for 'the people'.

7   The Stage II: Populism and Crisis

'Crisis' being a vague term, it is easily coined and devalued. Thus it is not difficult to associate 'populism' (or almost anything else) with 'crisis'. There is also a tautological tendency to impute populism (or anything else) to 'crisis', as if 'crisis' were a discernible cause, when, in fact, it is often a loose description of a bundle of phenomena. Disaggregation sometimes reveals that it was not 'crisis' which generated populism (or mobilisation, rebellion, etc.), but rather populism (or mobilisation, rebellion, etc.) which generated crisis.

—Knight (1998, 227)

As we find ourselves entering the adolescent years of the twenty-first century, it appears that we are well and truly living in the age of crisis—the Global Financial Crisis, the Eurozone crisis, environmental crisis, various humanitarian crises—the list goes on. More broadly, it is alleged that we are undergoing a crisis of faith in democracy (Crouch 2004; Zakaria 2013). In such a situation, it would seem that the stage has been set for populists to sweep in, appeal to 'the people' and enjoy great success by capitalising on a general loss of faith and disaffection with their representatives, 'the elite' and politics in general. Crisis breeds populism, doesn't it?

To some extent, this has occurred: Beppe Grillo's MoVimento 5 Stelle made a stunning political debut in Italy in 2013, capturing approximately a quarter of the overall votes in the national elections; populist parties in the Nordic countries have enjoyed a steady rise in popularity; while in Latin America, Rafael Correa is in his third term as president in Ecuador and Venezuelan president Nicolás Maduro continues to fly the Chavista flag. Yet elsewhere, populists are not doing so well in these times of crisis. Despite still commanding some influence within the Republican Party, the US Tea Party flailed following the humiliating defeat of a number of their star candidates; the much-vaunted Le Pen-Wilders alliance 'European Alliance for Freedom' failed to form an official group in the European Parliament following the 2014 EU elections; and in many countries allegedly undergoing crisis, populist challengers have simply not emerged or succeeded. This mixed evidence from across the world suggests a need to challenge the received wisdom regarding the causal relationship between populism and crisis, which tends to argue that crisis acts as either an external trigger or a necessary precondition of populism.

In this light, this chapter offers a new perspective on the relationship between populism and crisis, arguing that rather than just thinking about crisis as a trigger of populism, we should also think about how *populism attempts to act as a trigger for crisis*. This is due to the fact that crises are never 'neutral' phenomena, but must be mediated and 'performed' by certain actors, setting the stage for populist success. It argues that populist actors actively participate in this 'spectacularisation of failure' that underlies crisis, allowing them to pit 'the people' against 'the elite' or associated dangerous Others; radically simplify the terms and terrain of political debate; and advocate strong leadership and quick political action to stave off or solve the impending crisis. In making this argument, the chapter suggests that we should move from a conception of crisis as something that is purely external to populism, to one that acknowledges the performance of crisis as an *internal feature* of populism as conceptualised as a political style. In other words, if we do not have the performance of crisis, we do not have populism.

To put this position forward, this first section of this chapter examines accounts of the relationship between crisis and populism in the contemporary literature on populism, demonstrating that most dominant approaches continue to posit crisis as external to populism, and why this is a problem. The second section examines the concept of crisis, arguing that any definition of the phenomenon must take account of the necessary role of mediated performance and spectacularisation inherent in crisis. The third section then presents a six-step model of how populist actors go about 'performing' crisis, drawing on empirical examples of populists from across the world, and explaining how this differs from other forms of 'crisis politics'. Overall, it shows that while crisis may present an effective stage for populists, it is often the case that populists must play an important role in 'setting the stage' themselves.

Current Approaches to Populism and Crisis

Approaches to the role of crisis in the contemporary populist literature can be viewed on a spectrum. There are those authors who clearly draw a causal link between crisis and the emergence of populism; those who are unsure about the link; and a small few who argue that there is little to no link at all between the two phenomena. What connects each of these approaches is a persistent conception of crisis as *external* to populism. These positions are outlined below.

First, there are those who see crisis as a necessary precondition for populism. The strongest advocate for linking crisis to populism in this manner is Laclau. For Laclau, populism as a political logic simply cannot emerge without crisis: in his earlier writings he argued that "the emergence of populism is historically linked to a crisis of the dominant ideological discourse, which in turn is part of more general social crisis" (1977, 175), and more recently argued that "some degree of crisis . . . is a necessary precondition for populism" (2005b, 177). Indeed, he goes so far to claim that a number of historical figures would have remained sidelined without crisis paving their way:

> Without the slump of the 1930s, Hitler would have remained a vociferous fringe ringleader. Without the crisis of the Fourth Republic around the Algerian war, De Gaulle's appeal would have remained as unheard as it had been in 1946. And without the progressive erosion of the oligarchical system in the Argentina of the 1930s, the rise of Perón would have been unthinkable. (2005b, 177)

More widely, Laclau claims that "the crisis of representation . . . is at the root of any populist, anti-institutional outburst" (2005b, 139). Put bluntly, for Laclau, populism does not emerge or succeed without crisis spurring it into existence. Those analysts of populism influenced by the work of Laclau take a similar tack, tending to see crisis as offering a 'break' in hegemonic discourses, thus opening a space for counterdiscourses (like populism) to emerge. For example, Stavrakakis (2005, 247, emphasis in original) argues that "the emergence of new discourses and new identities is always related to the *dislocation* or crisis of previously hegemonic discursive orders. . . . This is also the case with populist discourses", and traces the emergence of a religious populist discourse in Greece in the early 2000s to a sense of crisis around Greece joining the European Economic Community. Elsewhere, Mouffe (2005a,b) links populism to a crisis of political representation and the emergence of 'post-politics', while Barros (2005, 269) links Menemism to a sense of terminal crisis.[1]

Strong causal links between crisis and populism are also evident in the contemporary literature among those who view populism as a strategy. For example, Roberts (1995, 113) argues that populism "surges most strongly in contexts of crisis or profound social transformation, when pre-existing patterns of authority or institutional referents lose their capacity to structure the political behaviour and identities of popular sectors", and has linked Chávez's rise to a "crisis of Venezuelan democracy" (2012, 138). Others have specifically focused on the role of crisis in neopopulism: Weyland (1999, 395) has argued that crises "trigger the emergence of neoliberal populism", and in reference to Carlos Menem, Fernando Collor de Mello and Alberto Fujimori, the prominent Latin American populist presidents of the 1990s, argues that "absent deep crises, these candidates would have had little chance to win government power". Elsewhere, Levitsky and Loxton (2012, 165) have claimed that "Fujimori's rise from obscurity to the presidency was rooted in a triple crisis"—crises of popular representation, the economy and security. This approach sees external crises as providing an opportunity for populist leaders to step in with their charismatic authority, flex their muscle and undertake extensive and dramatic reform in order to "sweep away the detritus of the past and usher in a new social order" (Roberts 1995, 113). It posits crisis as a necessary (or at least extremely conducive) precondition for the emergence of populism.

The second group are those who acknowledge there *may* be a link between populism and crisis but remain sceptical about it. Those working within the ideological approach tend to fall under this banner. The key advocate of this approach, Mudde (2007, 205) has acknowledged that "emphasis on the vital role of 'crisis' is a constant in studies of both historical and contemporary nativism and populism". However, he critiques this literature on the grounds that "most authors do not bother to articulate what constitutes a crisis" (2007, 205), meaning that the concept has remained vague and imprecise, and thus of limited analytic value. Nonetheless, Mudde does not believe that the concept should be rejected, as there does seem to be some significant correlation between variables we might associate with crisis—for example, economic instability, unemployment and political dissatisfaction—and the electoral success of European radical-right populists in the empirical literature. However, as Mudde (2007, 205) notes: "The key problem in this literature is the relationship between these variables and the overarching concept of crisis"—that is, these variables do not automatically equal crisis. More so, Mudde reminds us that nearly every modern political era has been alleged to be in crisis: for example, the 1950s and 1960s saw the 'end of ideology', the 1970s experienced a participation crisis, the 1980s witnessed the crisis of political parties, while the contemporary period has been marked by a crisis of political faith or trust, linked to cartelisation, clientism and corruption (Mudde 2007, 207). If crises are a permanent fixture of contemporary politics, it makes it difficult to claim that populism is an extraordinary phenomenon that arises only periodically during times of crisis.

Overall, Mudde remains relatively agnostic on the question of the relationship between crisis and populism.

Another key advocate of the ideological approach, Rovira Kaltwasser (2012, 186), has expressed similar reservations about how easily crisis can be linked to populism. He suggests that those who link populism's emergence to crisis fit snugly into what he calls the 'liberal approach' to populism. Here, populism is viewed as a democratic pathology—something that emerges only when democracy falters. Yet as Rovira Kaltwasser notes, the types of 'modernisation losers' hypotheses which argue that votes for populists come from those who suffer from the 'objective indicators' of crisis—political and economic disenfranchisement, unemployment and so forth—often do not stand up to empirical analysis: "[P]opulist radical right parties have shown a great success precisely in those regions of Europe where the structural prerequisites for their rise were hardly existent" (2012, 188). As such, a conception of crisis within populism cannot be simply structural, but also must refer to more subjective indicators, such as feelings of status loss (Lipset 1960) and moral collapse (Taggart 2000). Overall, while the adherents of the ideological approach do acknowledge the role of crisis in 'setting the scene' for populism, they do not see the relationship between the two as necessarily causal.

The third group of authors that can be identified are those who reject the link between crisis and populism outright. A number of these authors could be said to be sympathetic to a stylistic approach to populism. Knight (1998, 227) argues that (even more than populism) crisis is "a vague, promiscuously used, under-theorized concept which defies measurement and lacks explanatory power", and that the link between populism and crisis "may often be historically valid, but it does not afford a robust etiology. ... [T]his association is at best a rough tendency or correlation". Arditi (2007a, 63) is equally suspicious of the link between populism and crisis, arguing that the focus on crisis "narrows down the scope of the populist experience to moments when politics fails to address participatory, distributive or other demands. ... [T]he emphasis on the exception does not allow us to differentiate populist politics in opposition from populism in government". He is interested here in how populist actors, especially when in positions of power, are able to govern without an 'external' crisis to trigger their appeal within the electorate.

Despite their differences, all of these approaches—whether arguing for strong, weak or no causality at all in regards to the relationship between crisis and populism—perceive crisis as *external* to populism. That is, crisis is considered a phenomenon that does (or does not) cause, spur on, pave the way for or affect the development of populism. Indeed, this view of crisis as an externality is the mainstream view in political science, whereby we tend to look for causal relationships between discrete social or political phenomena.

However, there are two major problems with this view when it comes to crisis. The first is that the relationship between crisis and populism does not lend itself to simple causal explanations. This is due to (a) crisis being a contested phenomenon that lacks clear and discrete boundaries; (b) the fact that crisis itself is a product of complex causality (Byrne and Uprichard 2012); and (c) the aforementioned difference between crisis and the variables we associate with crisis (Mudde 2007). The second problem is that we cannot truly conceptualise a 'neutral' or 'objective' crisis that populism can be measured against. This is not to say that there is 'no such thing' as crisis, but rather to acknowledge that we hit something of an ontological brick wall when using the concept: we cannot separate 'crisis' from the words we use to describe the phenomenon.

Given these tensions, it is productive to move away from ostensibly 'objective' notions of external crisis, and instead towards a view of crisis as a phenomenon that can be experienced only through mediated performance, whereby a systemic failure is elevated to the level of perceived 'crisis'. In this light, the performance of crisis should be seen as *internal* to populism—not just as an external cause or catalyst for populism, but also as a *central feature of the phenomenon itself*.[2] In line with the political style approach put forward in this book, this means that populist actors actively 'perform' and perpetuate a sense of crisis, rather than simply reacting to external crisis. Moreover, this performance of crisis allows populists an effective way to divide 'the people' and 'the elite', and to legitimate strong leadership by presenting themselves as voices of the sovereign people.

There are traces of this argument—seeing populism as internal to populism—in the work of Taggart (2000, 2002, 2004), who has stressed that a *sense* of crisis is what the analyst of populism should be interested in, rather than an objective notion of crisis itself. The question of whether there 'really is' a crisis is not important—rather, the key focus should be on populist actors' ability to create a sense of crisis and how they "use that sense to inject an urgency and an importance to their message" (Taggart 2004, 275). De la Torre's (2007, 2010) work on Latin American populism also acts as an antecedent to this approach. Arguing against structuralist explanations that see populism as a transitory developmental stage caused by economic crises and upheaval, he contends that the appeal of populism "cannot be explained by the recurrence of a reified notion of crisis. . . . [E]conomic crises are experienced through common people's values, norms, and prejudices. The economy is always culturally mediated" (de la Torre 2010, 122). Both Taggart's and de la Torre's perceptive accounts of crisis and populism demonstrate that crisis is never merely a neutral phenomenon that is experienced 'objectively'. Rather, crisis is a phenomenon that is experienced culturally, socially and politically. It is a product of a *symbolically mediated performance.*

What We Talk about When We Talk about Crisis

Let us take a small step back, however, and make clear about what we are talking about when we use the term 'crisis'. The term has a long history within the social sciences, with some of its well-known theorists being Marx (1981), Schumpeter (1942), Habermas (1975) and Gramsci (1971, 276), who viewed crisis as the situation in which "the old is dying and the new cannot be born".

Koselleck (2006) provides the most complete intellectual history of the concept, tracing its etymological development from its early Greek origins through Christian theology, French medical grammar, the philosophy of history, German Idealism and Marxist theory among others. Put briefly, the term's initial Greek roots, *krinō*, referred to a decisive moment—"a crucial point that would tip the scales" (Koselleck 2006, 358)—as well as the subsequent action of reaching of a verdict. The key shift that Koselleck identifies in the term's development is the way that this initial concept of crisis became imbued with a sense of temporality in the late eighteenth century, meaning that crisis was not only that initial moment of decision, but also "an expression of a new sense of time which both indicated and intensified the end of an epoch" (Koselleck 2006, 358). As such, crisis became the name of the situation that necessitates a vital decision that is seen as so significant and all-encompassing as to both change and delineate the course of history.

Roitman (2011) captures the fusing of these two sense of crisis in her theorisation of the concept: "Crisis is mobilized in narrative constructions to mark out a 'moment of truth' or as a means to think 'history' itself. Such moments of truth might be defined as turning points in history, when decisions are taken or events are decided, thus establishing a particular teleology". However, these 'turning points' or 'moments of truth' are never clear-cut states of flux or change: as Roitman (2011) stresses: "Evoking crisis entails reference to a norm because it requires a comparative state for judgment: crisis compared to what?" As such, "there is not 'crisis' and 'non-crisis', which can be observed empirically". The attempt to objectively determine what 'is' or 'is not' a crisis is thus a relatively fruitless exercise, as the concept relies on notions of normalcy and stability that are themselves both culturally constructed and context-specific.

In contemporary usage, the way that crisis is most usually signified is through linking it to failure—whether that be of the financial system, political system, public policy, democracy, representation, masculinity and so on—and thus the impetus to act (or make the vital decision) comes from the need to correct the failure, and stem the crisis. Yet failure and crisis are not one and the same—as Hay (1995, 1999) has argued, there is a need to analytically distinguish between the two. While failure may provide "the structural preconditions for crisis" (1995, 64), crisis is "a condition in which failure is identified and widely perceived, a condition in which systemic failure has become politically and ideationally mediated" (1999, 324). In other words, a crisis only becomes a crisis when it is *perceived* as a crisis—when a failure gains wider salience through its mediation into the political or cultural spheres, and is commonly accepted as symptomatic of a wider problem.

If we take this distinction between failure and crisis seriously, we can see that those authors who claim that populism is spurred on by structural or institutional crises are often actually talking about failure—they see populism as a result of a market *failure* or system *failure*, rather than of market *crisis* or system *crisis*. In these cases, the term 'crisis' has been used uncritically, seen as an objective indicator of disorder, chaos or breakdown. However, the symptoms and the diagnoses have been confused here—the difference between failure and crisis hinges on mediation. A failure does not automatically necessitate a demand to act with immediacy and decisiveness. This demand to act only emerges with crisis—that is, when the failure becomes culturally or politically mediated, and gains an important temporal dimension. In other words, a crisis marks the *spectacularisation* of failure—the elevation of failure to crisis, in which the crisis becomes the foci for a historical decision and action. And as Taggart (2004, 282) notes: "The idea of living at a turning point in history is an important one for populist ideas". From this point of view, crisis is a phenomenon that is always mediated and performed, and thus can be thought of as *a key part of populism*, rather than just as something external to it.

Performing Crisis

So how do populist actors actually go about 'performing' crisis? How do they 'spectacularise' failure? There are six major steps that populist actors use to elevate a failure to the level of crisis, and in the process, seek to divide 'the people' from those who are responsible for the crisis, present simple solutions to the crisis, and legitimate their own strong leadership. In reality, these steps do not necessarily proceed in this exact order, nor are they necessarily discrete— however, they have been separated for analytical utility.

The model of populists' 'performance' of crisis is as follows:

1. Identify failure
2. Elevate the failure to the level of crisis by linking it into a wider framework and adding a temporal dimension
3. Frame 'the people' versus those responsible for the crisis
4. Use media to propagate performance
5. Present simple solutions and strong leadership
6. Continue to propagate crisis

Identify Failure

The first step is to identify or choose a particular failure and bring attention to it as a matter of urgency. The ability to elevate a failure to the level of crisis will likely be more successful if the chosen failure already has some political salience. For example, in times of economic instability, a populist actor may choose to focus on the failure of the political class to protect 'ordinary people' from bankers. At other times, sociocultural issues may prove more salient: for example, the central issue that both Pauline Hanson and Winston Peters initially chose to focus on was the 'failure' of Asian immigration and integration in Australia and New Zealand (Betz and Johnson 2004), while Geert Wilders has focused primarily on the 'failure' of Muslim immigration in the Netherlands (Vossen 2011). Another central failure that populist actors often focus on is the failure of political representatives or elites. This has been one of the core arguments of Beppe Grillo (Bordignon and Ceccarini 2013). None of this necessarily means that populists are 'single-issue' politicians, but rather that a particular failure is initially identified as a way of gaining attention and building up a sense of crisis.

Elevate the Failure to the Level of Crisis by Linking It into a Wider
Framework and Adding a Temporal Dimension

The next step is to link this chosen failure with other failures, thus locating it within a wider structural or moral framework. In doing this, populist actors attempt to make the failure appear as symptomatic of a wider problem, thus elevating the failure to the level of crisis. Laclau (2005b) has given us some indication of how this operation works in his discussion of what he calls "demands" in his theory of populist logic. As was outlined in Chapter 2, an initial demand that remains unanswered or unfulfilled by the actor, institution or system it is addressed towards (for example, a demand for reduced immigration levels addressed to the government) will begin to link with other unfulfilled demands in an "equivalential chain" (2005b, 74). The further that the equivalential chain between unfulfilled demands is extended, the weaker that the connection to the initial particular demand becomes. As such, the initial demand begins to function as a 'floating signifier' that represents the different demands entering the antisystemic equivalential chain—it stands as the "general equivalent representing the chain as a whole" (Laclau 2000, 302). It is this increasing 'emptiness' of the initial demand that is key to populism's political saliency: "the so-called 'poverty' of the populist symbols is the condition of their political efficacy" (Laclau 2005c, 40).

Laclau, however, does not explain *how* such demands become linked together. Demands, or in our case, perceived failures, do not simply link together in an automatic fashion, but have to be *actively* linked together—someone has to extend the 'equivalential chain'. This is where the performance of populist actors comes in—through mediated performances (whether speeches, rallies, interviews, written pieces, press releases or other media as discussed in the previous chapters), populist actors link failures in an attempt to homogenise a disparate set of phenomena as symptoms of a wider crisis, with these discrete 'failures' contextualised in the form of a temporally bounded and significant event.

Two key examples illustrate the linkage of the failures as crisis through performance. The first is Pauline Hanson's maiden speech to the Australian Parliament in 1996. Hanson managed to link an astounding number of perceived failures together in this one speech, including:

> the apparent existence of 'reverse racism', welfare payments to Aboriginal Australians, multiculturalism, bureaucracy, immigration, unemployment, foreign debt, living standards, family law, privatisation of government assets, foreign aid, the United Nations, government investment in large-scale development projects, national mil-

itary service, interest rates, and the (apparently threatening) status and size of Asian nations surrounding Australia. (Scalmer 2002, 149–50)

All of these failures were wrapped up in the central framework of multiculturalism, which she labelled "a national disgrace and crisis" (Hanson 1996, 3862). This spectacle drew "unprecedented Australian and international media attention" (Ward, Leach and Stokes 2000, 2), and successfully launched Hanson as a key player in Australian politics, with her chosen 'crisis of multiculturalism' garnering a huge amount of attention and debate.

Another example of linking issues through spectacle and performance is the US Tea Party's Taxpayer March on Washington, which was held on September 12, 2009. While the initial issue that arguably spurred the creation of the Tea Party was the Obama administration's mortgage bailouts, as expressed by CNBC host Rick Santelli's rant at the Chicago Mercantile Exchange (CNBC 2009; Lo 2012), the speeches at this march extended to such disparate issues as taxation, healthcare reform, abortion, free-market capitalism and big government, while signs held by the protestors compared Obama to Hitler and Stalin, and questioned his 'true' nationality. The overall concern here was not just about bailouts—the initial 'failure'—but rather the looming crisis that was to be brought about by Obama's alleged 'socialist' plan for the United States, taking in a number of heterogeneous issues.

An important temporal dimension underlies these performances of crisis. Populists present their appeal as having to be enacted within short timelines—and if they are not, terrible things will occur. This sense of impending doom presents society at a precipice, which if stepped over, cannot be reversed. For example, in her maiden speech to parliament, Hanson (1996, 3862) claimed that "time is running out. We may only have 10 to 15 years to turn things around" before Australia was doomed by multiculturalism. Using a similar metaphor, Sarah Palin (in Newton-Small 2011) has argued that America is "at a crossroads". Even more dramatically, Hugo Chávez (in Hawkins 2010, 55) claimed during the 1998 Venezuelan presidential election that "we are in the times of the Apocalypse. You can no longer be on the side of the evil and the side of God". The urgency of these claims elevates the situation to one in which the crisis must be dealt with immediately, and decisions made in order to stave off the crisis, rather than considering the many different options on the table. The 'slow politics' (Saward 2011) of consensus, deliberation and negotiation are presented as ineffectual, while strong and decisive political action, unencumbered by the procedural checks and balances, are seen as desirable.

The metaphors that are commonly used by populist actors in such performances also reflect this urgency. Metaphors of contagion or pathology, such as Jobbik's Gábor Vona's (2013) argument that Hungarians are "sick passengers on a sinking European ship. ... [W]e must get off the ship, then cure our diseases" are used alongside metaphors of natural disaster, such as Pauline Hanson's (1996, 3861) claim that Australia was "in danger of being swamped by Asians" or Geert Wilder's (2013b) claim that Western nations "must stand together, otherwise we will be swept away by Islam". As Brassett and Clarke (2012) have argued, such metaphorical framing devices invoke a sense of shared trauma and concern, with a common threat bringing together 'victims' through a shared sense of vulnerability.

Frame 'The People' versus Those Responsible for the Crisis

Once the initial failure has been linked and elevated into a wider framework of crisis, the populist actor is able to identify those who are responsible for the crisis, and set them against 'the people', who are presented as being most negatively affected by the crisis. This is useful, given that 'the people' often remains a vague signifier, reliant on identification of the enemy in order to give meaning to 'the people's' identity. As Taggart (2000, 94) argues: "[P]opulists are often more sure of who they are not than of who they are. The demonization of social groups, and particularly the antipathy towards 'the elite', provides populists with an enemy, but it is also a crucial component of the attempt to construct an identity".

The performance of crisis facilitates this group identification in two major ways. First, it allows populist actors a way of linking 'the elite' with the aforementioned demonised social groups, who *together* are portrayed in concert as being opposed to 'the people' in presenting, causing or perpetuating the crisis. For example, Western European populist radical right actors have tended to focus their exclusionary efforts on non-native groups, such as the Roma, Muslims or Turks, *as well as* 'the elite', including bureaucrats, journalists and academics. Similarly, the Reform Party of Canada used a 'crisis' of Canadian democracy (Laycock 1994; Wegierski 1998) to target 'the elite' (in the form of old parties and bureaucrats) *as well as* 'welfare mothers', juvenile delinquents and 'special interest groups' amongst others who allegedly drain the country's coffers (Laycock 2012). In each of these cases, 'the elite' is construed as designing, promoting and advocating the policies that benefit the minority groups, who in turn have taken advantage of the situation, leading to a crisis that has ultimately hurt 'the people'.

Secondly, the performance of crisis offers populist actors a seemingly 'objective' rationale for targeting their enemies, beyond outright discrimination. As noted, Hanson was able to demonise Asian immigrants by linking them to the crisis of multiculturalism. Here she did not explicitly attack the personal character of Asian immigrants, but rather framed the need to stop immigration in order to ensure "that our dole queues are not added to by, in many cases, unskilled migrants not fluent in the English language" (Hanson 1996, 3862). Geert Wilders (in Traynor 2008) has framed his opposition to Islam in similar terms. He claims that "I don't hate Muslims—I hate Islam", and has argued for the need for the Dutch people to stand against the impending crisis of the Islamisation of Europe by invoking a threat to the cornerstones of liberal democracy: "If we do not oppose Islamization, we will lose everything: our freedom, our identity, our democracy, our rule of law, and all our liberties. It is our duty to defend the legacy of Rome, Athens, and Jerusalem" (Wilders 2012, 216).

Use Media to Propagate Performance

Much of the success or failure of performing crisis relies on the circulation of the populist's performance through media. Media plays a central role in the 'breaking' of a crisis, disseminating information about crisis, and perpetuating a continuing sense of crisis. However, media attention does not always come easily in a media-saturated age. As Bos et al. (2010, 142–43) have shown in their study of European radical right populist actors, to combat this situation and "get media attention, these politicians will have to be somewhat unusual in their behaviour, style, or in terms of their messages. . . . By exploiting their novelty and outsider position, their news value can in fact become very high, thereby assuring prominence". Indeed, speaking as a harbinger of imminent doom or perpetuating a critical threat can help to gain this vital media attention.

One of the most obvious ways that populist actors promote and perform a sense of crisis is through the types of media events outlined in the previous two chapters, designed as spectacles to attract wide attention, garner salience for the particular threat, and identify the enemies of 'the people'. While Ociepka (2005b, 210) argues that "populists often inspire media events by introducing issues into the public discourse in order to launch the process of opinion building", it is equally correct to claim that they actively *promote* or *stage* these events as a central element of performing crisis. The political communication literature on populism provides us with some evidence of the forms that these events take. These include press conferences, radio or television appearances, speeches that privilege "hot button issues" (Jenkins 2003, 158) such as immigration or crime, and the making of inflammatory or controversial statements in public arenas. For example, Mazzoleni (2008, 60) writes of "Haider's remarks about the Nazis and the Jews, Fortuyn's outspoken statements on Islam . . . [as] 'newsworthy' realities that the mass media will automatically cover in their pursuit of corporate goals", given that the spectacle of creating crisis helps gain viewers, listeners or readers due to its controversial or spectacular nature.

Indeed, these spectacles and performances fit firmly within the mass media's pecuniary interests, helping to sell newspapers, attract viewers and gain page views. A dramatised, salacious crisis makes for more entertaining reading or viewing than a sober and even-handed account of an event. Mazzoleni (2008, 55) makes this mutually beneficial relationship between populist leaders and the media clear:

> This convergence of goals sees the media pursuing their own corporate ends by striking emotional chords on issues such as security, unemployment, inflation, immigration and the like. At the same time, populist leaders and their movements gain status, visibility and popular approval by generating controversy, scuffling with incumbent political leaders and resorting to inflammatory rhetoric.[3]

As noted in Chapter 5, with many contemporary populist parties, movements and leaders now having professional public relations managers and media liaisons, these links become even more professionalised, and thus performances of crisis become more sophisticated and spectacular.

Other media events used by populists to perform crisis include gatherings, marches or performative rituals (Biorcio 2003) that may initially appear 'unmediated'—that is, as 'grassroots' events—but of course then often gain a large degree of media attention as a result of the spectacular nature of the event. Examples include the aforementioned Tea Party's '9/12 Taxpayer March on Washington' and the 2011 antigovernment 'Convoy of No Confidence' in Canberra, Australia (Wear 2014). These seemingly 'unmediated' events operate to give feelings of threat and crisis a semblance of legitimacy by presenting 'the people' as the central drivers of these concerns, rather than populist leaders.

Present Simple Solutions and Strong Leadership

Once a failure has been spectacularised, and a sense of crisis has been created and propagated, the next important step is to present oneself as having the solution to the crisis. Populist actors are able to do this using a number of performative methods including portraying other political actors as incompetent and feckless, offering simple answers for the crisis, and advocating the simplification of political institutions and processes.

The portrayal of other political actors as incompetent and ignorant of the true urgency of the crisis allows populist actors to position themselves as 'straight-shooters' who cut through the 'bullshit' (Frankfurt 2005) of mainstream politics, with ideological differences and the actual practicalities of multiparty democracy being portrayed as superfluous for the practice of governing in times of threat and breakdown. Populists thus present themselves as being 'beyond' ideology or the minutiae of party politics, and rather focused on the urgent crisis at hand, ready for action and armed with solutions. In an example of this positioning, Silvio Berlusconi has made clear that he is not interested in the "'abstract principles' or 'complicated ideology' of party politics" (in McCarthy 1996, 134), and claimed that "whenever I hear that *Forza Italia* is a party, I get shivers down my spine" (Berlusconi 2000, 140). Similarly, in the run-up to the 2012 Republican primaries in the United States, Herman Cain (in Jones 2011) claimed: "I am not a politician, I'm a problem solver". Such manoeuvres allow populists to paint other politicians as self-interested and disengaged from the 'real world'—caught up with the internal workings of party politics, like true technocrats, rather than seeking to put a definitive end to crisis.

The second performative method is the offering of simplistic solutions to the crisis. These often take the form of what Rosanvallon (2011) has called "a procedural and institutional simplification" inherent to populism. Procedural simplification is evident in the often crude and immediate policy solutions offered by populist actors in the effort to stop crises. An example of this can be found in Geert Wilders's (in de Bruijn 2011, 35) ideas for solving the impending crime and immigration 'crisis' in the Netherlands:

> Problem: Moroccans throw stones at the Dutch Police.
> Solution: Arrest them, prosecute them and deport them . . .
> Problem: This government is breaking record after record in the area of mass immigration.
> Solution: Don't allow in any more Eastern Europeans and shut the borders to immigrants from Muslim countries. Now! . . .
> Problem: Rotterdam, the second largest city in the Netherlands, will have an immigrant majority by 2012.
> Solution: Repatriation, repatriation, repatriation. What comes in can also come out.

The logic behind these kinds of solutions are simple: remove or eradicate the enemy of 'the people', and the crisis will be either staved off or solved. Rather than acknowledging that many complex and intertwined factors cause systemic failures, the aim of the populist performance of crisis is to point the finger squarely at the enemy of 'the people'.

Institutional simplification, meanwhile, is evident in the way populist actors use crisis to attack and attempt to simplify the existing political system, as it is perceived as being perverted or corrupted. Here, intermediary or unelected bodies that stand between 'the people' and their elected representatives are seen as illegitimate, while anything that stands in the way of 'solving' the crisis—such as the political opposition or checks and balances—is to be bulldozed over. This has been most obvious in those situations where populist leaders have been able to win high office. In Thailand, Thaksin Shinawatra leveraged the Asian financial crisis to great effect in this regard. Tejapira (2006, 28–29) details Thaksin's 'institutional simplification' as such:

> Making full use of his financial resources, enhanced executive power and overwhelming parliamentary majority, Thaksin lost no time in packing or bending the constitutionally created bodies set up as checks and balances, to undermine or neutralize their power. The government has intervened in the selection of candidates for some of these organs, refused to co-operate with them, obstructed their work or even offered them bribes.

In Italy, Silvio Berlusconi similarly spent much of his time in office attempting to discredit the judiciary, calling it "a dictatorship of leftist judges" (in Reuters 2011), and painting it as unnecessary and dangerous interference to the voice of the sovereign people (Tarchi 2008). In Ecuador, under the guise of a 'citizen's revolution', President Rafael Correa has illegally closed the Congress and concentrated power in the executive (de la Torre 2013b). Perhaps most dramatically, Yoweri Museveni was able to use the Ugandan Bush War to push through a 'no-party' democracy in which political parties were banned for nineteen years (Carbone 2005).

Continue to Propagate Crisis

It is difficult to continually propagate and perform crisis: after all, the efficacy of the invocation of crisis often stems from its episodic and 'out of the ordinary' character, whereby crises are constructed as temporally limited events. This presents a set of challenges for perpetuating a sense of crisis—it can be difficult to continue to attract attention and prolong panic and concern about one's chosen crisis, especially if it becomes clear that one's notion of crisis is not particularly convincing, or if the issues that one's notion of crisis revolve around become less salient to voters or the attention of the mass media. In an illustrative example of this dilemma, Rydgren (2006, 71) has shown that the failure of the Swedish Ny Demokrati was due in a large part to the 1990s economic crisis, which made socioeconomic issues far more salient (particularly issues around Sweden's political economy and the welfare state) than the sociocultural issues that Ny Demokrati campaigned on (an immigration 'crisis'), and thus saw them suffer a humiliating defeat in the 1994 general elections.

One way that populists sometimes attempt to stem this loss of interest or salience is by switching the notion of crisis that they employ: for example, in the 2012 Dutch elections, Geert Wilders temporarily attempted to switch the focus of his party's campaign from the crisis of the Islamisation of Europe to the European financial crisis, advocating the Netherland's exit from the European Union (Partij Voor de Vrijheid 2012). Similarly, Pauline Hanson has cycled through numerous impending crises from which Australia is allegedly suffering—from an 'Asian invasion', to a health crisis brought on by 'diseased' African immigrants, to a privatisation crisis resulting from the selling off of public services (Australian Associated Press 2006; Clennell, Keene and Budd 2011). These attempts to 'switch' crises have been met with some degree of failure, with Wilder's Partij voor de Vrijheid losing nine seats and 5 percent of its 2010 vote share in the 2012 election, and Hanson failing to gain office past 2001.[4]

Another tactic is to extend the purview and size of the crisis or breakdown. Hugo Chávez was successful in doing this, beginning with a breakdown of trust in regards to old party elites, moving onto attacks on the domestic opposition, and then to a far-reaching imperialist conspiracy spearheaded by the United States (Hawkins 2010, 61). This was met with increasing electoral success, perhaps because Chávez was able to build up his notion of crisis in a gradual and linear manner, rather than switching his focus suddenly. De la Torre (2013b) has argued that Rafael Correa has extended his vision of his enemies and the crisis that Ecuador allegedly faces in a similar manner.

Of course, none of these tactics are guaranteed to work. Different environments and audiences will prove more receptive to certain types of performance of crises than others—as noted in the previous chapter, the gaining of 'uptake' of populist claims and performances is a highly complex and contingent operation. While some populist actors' successes in performing crisis are short-lived and of their time (such as Hanson), others (like Chávez and Correa) have been able to perpetuate a sense of panic over an extended period. This latter condition, when successfully presented, can be rather effective, moving crisis from being an extraordinary phenomenon to an ordinary one, thus allowing these populist actors to strengthen their authority as 'crisis managers' and as the sovereign voices of 'the people'.

Populist Performances of Crisis versus 'Crisis Politics'

Taken together, this model of how populist actors go about performing crisis raises an important question: how do such performances differ from 'crisis politics' in general? In other words, what makes these performances unique to populism? This is a particularly timely question at the present moment, given that 'crisis politics' seems to be common across the board in the so-called 'age of austerity' (Streeck and Schäfer 2013). 'Crisis politics' here can be understood as the type of politics and responses outlined by Boin et al. (2005, 2008) that seek to deal with large-scale crises—examples include the governance of cities after natural disasters (such as Hurricane Katrina), political reactions to terrorist attacks (such as the September 11 attacks), the politics of large-scale disasters (such as the Fukushima Daiichi nuclear disaster), or the politics of responding and adapting to financial crisis (such as the Greek government-debt crisis).

There are two central differences that can be identified between the performances of crisis that are a feature of populism, and 'crisis politics' more generally: the centrality of 'the people' and the necessary perpetuation of crisis. In regards to the first, the primary aim of populist performances of crisis is to divide 'the people' from those allegedly responsible for the crisis—whether that is 'the elite', some dangerous Other or a combination of the both. If it does not succeed in this regard, the populist performance of crisis fails. This is not the case for more general forms of 'crisis politics'. They *can* invoke 'the people', but this is not *necessarily* the key political subject that all forms of 'crisis politics' attempt to mobilise or 'render-present'. For example, those involved in performing more general forms of 'crisis politics' can invoke subjects as different as distinct classes (such as in times of economic crisis), ethnicities (such as in times of ethnic conflict), religions (in times of religious conflict) or genders (such as the 'crisis of masculinity') amongst others. None of these political subjects need be couched in the language of 'the people' for 'crisis politics' to operate efficiently. Relatedly, the enemy of these political subjects does not have to be 'the elite'—this is culturally and politically contingent.[5] So while populist performances of crisis *always* divide 'the people' from 'the elite' and connected Others, other 'crisis politics' more generally do not *need* to invoke 'the people'—indeed, they quite often invoke different political subjects.

Second, if populism is "a powerful reaction to a sense of extreme crisis", as Taggart (2000, 2) puts it, then its existence and continued success is reliant on the continued propagation and perpetuation of crisis. As has been argued, this means that we should see the performance of populism as a *core feature* of populism, because its perpetuation is necessary for populist actors' political survival. This is simply not the case for all other forms of 'crisis politics'. Many forms of 'crisis politics' blatantly seek to *end* the specified crisis at hand, rather than continuing to perpetuate it for political gain (t' Hart and Tindall 2009a).[6] For example, prolonging a sense of crisis is probably not in the interests of leading political actors in some of the European countries that have been hit the hardest by the Eurozone sovereign debt crisis, given that they are facing disenchanted, desperate and disgruntled citizens who are likely to be keen to punish them at the ballot box—here, an *end* to the crisis stands as the key goal. As such, while narratives within more general forms of 'crisis politics' tend to have a broadly teleological structure—they have a defined beginning, middle and, most important, end—the performances of crisis by populist actors are ongoing, in that they either extend the scope of the crisis, or alternatively switch their notion of crisis so that the sense of crisis continues. Unlike 'crisis politics' in general, populist performances of crisis never really end.

Conclusion

This chapter has argued that the performance of crisis is a vital part of contemporary populism. While dominant conceptions of populism tend to view crisis as only *external* to populism, it has argued that crisis should also be seen as an *internal* feature of populism, given that crises are never 'neutral' events, but are actively performed by populist actors who attempt to 'spectacularise' failure so as to propagate a sense of crisis. In other words, while crisis is an important 'stage' on which populist performances play out, populist actors play a crucial role in 'setting the stage' of crisis. Having outlined the mechanisms of this performance, it has shown that this performance allows populists a method for dividing 'the people' against 'the elite', for presenting themselves as the sovereign voice of 'the people', and for radically simplifying procedures and institutions. It must be stressed that the performance of crisis should not be viewed as just a particular political strategy amongst others that populists can choose to deploy if they feel it would politically advantageous—rather, the performance of crisis should be seen as an essential core feature of populism itself, as outlined in the concept of populism as a political style developed in Chapter 3.

This argument has five key ramifications for thinking about populism. First, it makes clear the importance of performance in contemporary populism, demonstrating that crisis can *become* a crisis only through performance or mediation. Second, it provides a more nuanced notion of crisis for those who study populism, showing that crisis can be thought of as an external trigger *as well as* an internal feature of populism. Third, it demonstrates that the performance of crisis helps to define 'the people', in that it can identify and link together 'the people's' enemy in the form of 'the elite' and other minority groups, and can offer populists a seemingly 'objective' rationale for targeting 'the people's' enemies. Fourth, it presents a model of the steps that populist actors take in performing crisis, which could be tested against and applied to different empirical cases of populism across the world. Fifth, it shows that there are differences between the ways that populists perform crisis and 'crisis politics' more generally.

In a world that is allegedly beset by a number of crises, this shift in perspective allows us to question arguments about the simple causality between populism and crisis, and to interrogate the very notion of crisis as a discrete and objective phenomenon. By addressing the performative repertoires, practices of mediation and role of spectacle inherent in populist use of crisis, it is clear that crisis offers an important 'stage' for populism to play out upon—but one that requires careful and deliberate construction.

8   Populism and Democracy

> *The populist 'dimension', however, is neither democratic nor anti-democratic: it is an aspect of a variety of political cultures and structures.*
>
> —Worsley (1969, 247)

> *The debate over the meaning of populism turns out to be a debate over the interpretation of democracy.*
>
> —Urbinati (1998, 116)

Is populism good or bad for democracy? For all the words spilt in newspapers, editorials, academic journals and books on populism over the past two decades, this is perhaps *the* key question to which authors on the topic keep returning. While some portray populism as the enemy of democracy—a particularly prominent view in contemporary European debates, evident in the constant hand-wringing over populist candidates in national and European elections— others see it as a panacea for the democratic deficit that characterises many contemporary political systems, viewing it as a way to enfranchise 'the people' and return them to their rightful place as the sovereign voice of democracy. However, the answer is more complicated than the one that either of these positions might present.

Using the conception of populism as a political style developed over the preceding chapters, this chapter presents a new perspective, arguing that populism tells us very little about the democratic 'content' of any political project. Questioning attempts to draw causal conclusions regarding populism's effect on democracy, it rejects the strict binary between populism and democracy and instead examines both the democratic and antidemocratic tendencies *within* populism as conceptualised as a political style. In doing so, it shows that lining up such tendencies side-by-side cannot determine 'once and for all' if populism is or is not democratic, as these tendencies manifest differently in diverse contexts and environments—and sometimes are present at the same time.

The chapter extends this case over three sections. The first section outlines the three central arguments regarding populism's relationship with democracy in the contemporary literature: those who believe populism is a negative force for democracy, those who see it as a positive force, and those who remain equivocal on the matter. The second section questions attempts to draw causal conclusions regarding populism's 'effect' on democracy, showing that these conclusions are very much dependent on the actors and institutions that are privileged as indicators of democracy. To avoid following this same route, the third section then examines both the democratic and antidemocratic tendencies within populism as conceptualised as a political style. It draws together elements of contemporary populism that have been discussed over the preceding chapters, including 'bad manners', the performance of 'the people', the targeting of 'the elite' and associated Others, populism's tendency towards simplification and the extreme personalisation of the leader, and assesses these elements on the grounds of whether they can be considered as democratic or antidemocratic. Overall, this chapter demonstrates that the relationship between populism and democracy is far from straightforward, and that the category of political style can help us think it through in a more nuanced manner.

Before proceeding, there is a need to acknowledge that discussing democracy is always a fraught exercise, given the long history and complexity of the concept (Dunn 2005; Keane 2009b; Osbourne 2011). While it is not within the scope of this chapter to cover these debates and definitions of democracy, there is a need for a working definition to guide the analysis. As such, within this chapter, democracy is not only understood as a minimal set of institutions and procedures (including free and fair elections), but as a political form and 'way of life' (Dewey 1987) in which relationships of power are submitted to public restraint, and where there is a commitment to and recognition of contingency, pluralism and equality (Keane 2009b). This is of course an ideal-type, and it stands in tension with democracy's expression in terms of its multiple historical forms. It does not, however, necessarily commit to a particular normative model or form of democracy—liberal, radical or otherwise, as shall discussed below—and as such, it stands as a useful compass from which to guide the following discussion.

Diagnosing Democracy and Populism: The Good, the Bad and the Equivocal

There are three main approaches to populism's relationship with democracy within the contemporary literature on populism: those who see it as a negative force, those who see it as positive, and those who remain on the fence.[1] These approaches tend to be tied to specific regional literatures and theoretical approaches to populism, and are outlined in detail below.

Populism as a Negative Force for Democracy

The argument that populism is a negative force for democracy is undoubtedly the most prominent view in the academic literature and wider political debates today. This view tends to see populism as a 'pathology' of democracy—that is, an anomaly or abnormality that occurs only as a result of particular social decay or disease (Rosanvallon 2008; Taggart 2002). As such, it tends to locate populism as a dangerous 'outside' of democracy or as a kind of 'return of the repressed' (Arditi 2007a) of older, more archaic forms of politics. Underlying some of these arguments is a version of the social psychology of the late nineteenth century, in which 'the people', associated with uncontrollable crowds, masses or mobs are considered an unruly remainder of 'politics as such', and as a result, populism is seen as a phenomenon that should be viewed with fear and concern (see Laclau 2005b, 21–64).

This view has been particularly popular in Europe, where work on populism has been tied to the radical right in recent years, resulting in a rather partial assessment of the wider phenomenon of populism and its democratic credentials. The influence of the terms introduced by Betz (1993, 1994) and Mudde (2007)—'radical right-wing populism' and the 'populist radical right', respectively—is difficult to overstate here, with a number of authors associated with the ideological approach to populism following their lead in focusing only on this specific variant of populism (Abts and Rummens 2007; Akkerman 2003; Mény and Surel 2002).[2] This view of populism as a dangerous form of politics is not limited just to academia—in recent years, a number of European think-tanks have launched projects on how to combat or neutralise populism's increasing influence, demonstrating that it is seen as a potent threat to European democracy in civil society as well (Bartlett, Birdwell and Littler 2011; Fieschi, Morris and Caballero 2012; Painter 2013). Yet as has been demonstrated throughout this book, populism is not a phenomenon exclusively associated with the radical right, meaning that this view of populists as antidemocratic extremists is rather blinkered. Critiquing this exclusive association between the radical right and populism, Stavrakakis and Katsambekis (2014, 136) argue that

> many of the existing analyses suffer from a certain euro-centrism that reduces the conceptual spectrum covered by the category 'populism' in its global use to a very particular European experience— extreme right-wing xenophobic movements and

parties—and then essentializes the resulting association, overextending the application of this contingent European meaning and elevating it into a universal and trans-historical criterion.

The pathological view is not limited only to Europe, however. It is also evident in the work of a number of authors who examine Latin American populism (Corrales and Penfold 2011; Krauze 2011; McCoy and Myers 2004), particularly those influenced by the strategic approach to populism (di Piramo 2009; Levitsky and Loxton 2013). Here, despite the achievements of figures like Chávez, Morales and Correa in bringing levels of material and social equity to various sectors of their respective countries, their abuses of the procedures and rules of democratic process, as well as their Manichean discourse and slide towards *caudillismo*, are seen as threatening to democracy.

It is clear that many of those who fall into this camp favour liberal democracy. These authors' antipathy towards populism can be seen to stem from the tensions that characterise contemporary liberal democracy: a split between its democratic pillar, which emphasises participation, majoritarianism and the sovereignty of 'the people', and its liberal/constitutional pillar, which emphasises the rights of the individual, and locates the ultimate authority of the state in the law. In democratic theory, this tension has alternatively been labelled as 'the democratic paradox' (Mouffe 2000) or the 'two-strand model' of democracy (Abts and Rummens 2007; Canovan 2004). In practice, it is argued that these two reflexive strands or pillars keep each other in check, as the universal constitutionalism of the liberal pillar safeguards individual human rights and protects citizens from the whims of other citizens or the state, while the democratic pillar locates sovereign rule within 'the people' and allows for the possibility of reforming constitutional matters. The issue for those who see populism as a threat to democracy is that populism tips the scales too heavily towards the democratic pillar, and consequently, liberal safeguards such as the protection of minorities or checks and balances are threatened. Populists do this by presenting the liberal elements of contemporary liberal-democratic systems as diluting the 'true' democratic ideal—'the people's' sovereignty. This is evident in the way that "all populist movements speak and behave as if democracy meant the power of the people and only the power of the people" (Mény and Surel 2002, 9). Given that the populist appeal to unbridled majoritarianism can result in the targeting of minorities, the general response is that populism must be reined in or defeated in order to return the democratic landscape to its 'proper' state, thus realigning the liberal-democratic balancing act.

While such a position explains the very real and valid concerns that people have about the deleterious effects that certain forms of populism can have on the social fabric of their societies, the conceptual framework of viewing populism as a pathology can sometimes be misguided—as Mény and Surel (2002, 3) point out: "A pathology is meaningful only by comparison with a situation defined as normal, a definition which in this case is, to say the least, problematic". More so, while the explanation of populism's emergence as a reaction against liberalism may make sense in the European or North American contexts, the same does not hold for understanding populism in a number of countries in Latin America, Africa and the Asia-Pacific that are not liberal-democratic.

Populism as a Positive Force for Democracy

On the other side of the divide are those who see populism as a positive force for democracy. Here, populism is viewed as a core element of democracy, in that it emphasises the sovereignty of 'the people', appeals to majoritarianism, and offers a powerful critique of those who distort or disfigure democracy. Figures like the Morales and Chávez are held up as heroes who have helped the poor of their countries, while figures like Grillo are seen as returning power to 'the people' through bottom-up initiatives.

In the academic literature, this argument is put forward most prominently by Laclau and those who subscribe to his view of populism as a political logic. Laclau long advocated the adoption of a normative model of democracy that he called 'radical democracy' (Laclau and Mouffe 1985), and as he stated affirmatively of populism: "[R]adical democracy is always populist" (2005a, 259). This is because, for Laclau, "the construction of a 'people' is the *sine qua non* of democratic functioning" (2005b, 169)—without populism we have no 'people', and without 'the people', we do not have democracy. Unlike political struggles based around particular categories like class, gender or race, Laclau saw populism's appeal to 'the people' as opening up the democratic horizon to an ever-expanding number of identities. Obviously, then, this approach does not view populism as a pathology of democracy, nor a return to archaic politics, but rather sees populism as a necessary feature of democracy. Laclau's support for populism was also reflected in his visits to Bolivia, Ecuador and Venezuela on the invitations of Morales, Correa and Chávez, respectively (Precious 2009).

Others who fit into this camp are more cautious in their admiration of populism. Kazin argues that populism has the potential to help "to improve the common welfare" (1995, 7) in the United States, but also worries about its right-wing manifestations. In Latin America, Cannon (2009) has praised elements of

137

Chávez's populist project, framing it as an effective and understandable corrective to Venezuela's broken political system, but has also expressed wariness about the populist tendency towards clientism and corruption. Elsewhere, in the mid-to-late 1990s, the critical theory journal *Telos,* led by Paul Piccone, took up populism as both a way to critique liberalism and a possible method by which to deliver local autonomy to citizens, but remained wary of its tendency to prey on minorities (Raventos 2002).

Indeed, if we return to the two-strand approach discussed above, these positive conceptualisations of populism are often formulated as part of a critique of liberalism. For these advocates of populism, the liberal pillar of liberal democracy has been taken too far, with the rule of law and individual rights overpowering the democratic pillar. Here, unelected officials and supranational bodies like the European Union and the United Nations are seen as constraining, undermining or ignoring the sovereign people, who are the true source of democratic legitimacy. These critiques see liberalism as a method for constraining democratic involvement, or as a way for elites to ensure continued control of the political sphere. Populism offers a way to remedy this situation.

However, there are a number of problems with this approach. One is that it puts too much faith in the populist leader—while populist leaders can certainly act as a voice for a group of heterogeneous demands, the flipside is that they can use their role as the voice of 'the people' to present themselves as infallible and unchallengeable. As Arditi (2010) warns, such situations can sometimes morph into an authoritarian cult of personality or demagogy. Such views can also overlook the power struggles, coercion and exclusion that see certain demands emerge as worthy of representation as opposed to those that get suppressed or omitted. In this sense, some of those working within this approach are too rosy in their view of populism as an emancipatory and radically democratic force, willing to 'look the other way' when it comes to abuses of individual rights and corruption, as these are seen as 'necessary evils' in order to make gains in the name of 'the people'.

The Equivocal Approach

In between these two positions, we find equivocation about populism's effect on democracy. This equivocal approach does not make a general argument about whether populism is positive or negative for democracy, but rather examines specific case studies or compares regional examples of populism to determine its effect in certain contexts. A wide range of authors and conceptual approaches fit under this heading, whether purposefully or the result of the simple fact that they choose not to make their normative position on their ideal notion of democracy clear.

Mudde and Rovira Kaltwasser, the leading authors in the ideological approach to populism, have worked most strenuously to defend this approach. As has been mentioned, they label their approach the 'minimal approach' to populism, and claim that "the scepticism about establishing a clear relationship (either positive or negative) between populism and democracy is the defining condition of scholars that adhere to the minimal approach" (Rovira Kaltwasser 2012, 194). As such, they claim that populism is 'ambivalent' when it comes to democracy, acting as both a threat *and* corrective for democratic politics (Mudde and Rovira Kaltwasser 2012c). Further, Mudde (2010) pushes against the liberal approach that views populism as what he calls a "normal pathology" by arguing that we rather need to see populism as a "pathological normalcy"— that is, a radicalisation of mainstream views, not something that comes from outside 'normal' politics. To put it another way, Rovira Kaltwasser (2012, 195) has argued that "populism is a sort of democratic extremism".

There is much to admire in Mudde and Rovira Kaltwasser's argument in this regard. Their consideration of populism's positive and negative effects on democracy is balanced and convincing in many regards, and they are careful to note that populism has a different effect on different *kinds* of democracy: as they claim: "[P]opulism can play a positive role in the promotion of an electoral or minimal democracy, but it tends to play a negative role when it comes to fostering the development of a full-fledged liberal democracy" (Mudde and Rovira Kaltwasser 2013b, 507). Avoiding knee-jerk reactions that paint populism as a democratic bogeyman or as democracy's saviour, they have also been able to assemble an impressive array of authors to commit to and test their approach across populist cases in Europe and the Americas (Mudde and Rovira Kaltwasser 2012b). Even if the position put forward in this book disagrees with their wider ideological approach, it finds much commonality in their conviction that populism is neither clearly democratic nor antidemocratic.

However, there are reasons to be cautious regarding Mudde and Rovira Kaltwasser's (2012a, 16) attempt to "come to a non-normative position on the relationship between populism and democracy". Although their goal of putting empirics first is admirable, the question of whether a 'non-normative position' is even possible when it comes to discussing something as fraught as democracy lingers over their project. Ochoa Espejo (2015, 60) has been especially critical of such an equivocal approach, claiming that scholars often use such framing to disguise the normative assumptions that underlie their argument:

> [S]cholars tend to avoid issues of political morality in their work on populism. This is particularly true of those scholars who study the phenomenon empirically and claim to eschew normative judgments yet unwittingly introduce such judgments by virtue of accepting the distinction between democracy and populism. Given that most contemporary scholars agree that liberal democracy is the best form of political organization, describing a movement as "populist" rather than "liberal-democratic" is a way of sneaking a normative judgment in through the back door.

As the ideological 'minimal' approach becomes more hegemonic within the literature, it would be better that the authors working within the approach make their commitment to liberal democracy and pluralism (which is implicit in much of their work) clearer rather than obfuscating it in the name of a 'non-normative' approach to populism. Finally, if those authors working within this approach are committed to conceptualising populism as an ideology, then there is a need to acknowledge that ideologies—even if they are 'thin' or 'minimal'—can have nondemocratic totalising tendencies. Hawkins (2010, 33) gets at this sense of populism when he discusses it as a totalising worldview, and acknowledges how populism is "moralizing, dualistic, and teleological", and claims that it "ultimately has a kind of directionality, carrying democracy down an authoritarian, or to be more precise, totalitarian path as it imposes a uniform moral ideal on citizens" (2010, 37). These tendencies are obviously not 'ambivalent' when it comes to democracy, and demand further exploration.

Populism, 'The Political' and Democratic Politics

As can be seen, no single approach to the relationship between populism and democracy is unproblematic or value-free—even if they attempt to be. Attempting to discern the relationship between two contested concepts is a difficult task, and as Ochoa Espejo's critique shows, the very *framing* of the discussion in the literature—that is, populism and democracy as two discrete phenomena—has a tendency to automatically exteriorise populism as a phenomenon that is *not* part of democracy. While this may be sound (and perhaps necessary) from a methodological perspective when it comes to measuring certain *indicators* of democracy, the metaphors used to characterise the relationship between populism and democracy in the theoretical literature—populism as a 'mirror' (Panizza 2005a), 'shadow' (Canovan 1999) or 'spectre' (Albertazzi and McDonnell 2008; Arditi 2007a) of democracy—suggest a more complex picture where populism and democracy are intertwined with each other. Indeed, in an attempt to show that populism lingers *within* democratic practice, Arditi (2007a) goes so far as to suggest that populism is an 'internal periphery' of democracy.

In exteriorising populism and fixing the meaning of democracy to a particular normative framework, authors tend to privilege certain institutions, actors and subjects as indicators of democracy (whether this is acknowledged or not). This can cause very different outcomes in terms of the assessment as to whether populism is good or bad for democracy. For example, if one looks at Chavismo's democratic credentials from the view of the independence of institutions and the protection of minority rights, one might conclude that Chávez was antidemocratic. However, if one looks at the indicators of democracy as economic equity, empowerment of previously excluded sectors and the strengthening of civil society, one might conclude that Chávez's rule was very positive for Venezuelan democracy. To add to this confusion, the 2013 Latinobarómetro poll report claimed that when 87 percent of Venezuelan respondents offered their support for democracy, they were "not talking about institutional and normative quality but, rather, about the way in which the population feels included in the country's political and social life or, in other words, intangible goods with great power in the region that determine many people's vision of their democracies" (Corporación Latinobarómetro 2013, 8–9). So whom are we to listen to—academics who see populism in Venezuela as democratic, those who see it as antidemocratic, or the Venezuelan people themselves, who seem to be utilising their own measure of democracy?

In this regard, Motta (2011, 28) has convincingly argued that when assessing populism's relationship with democracy, many "'Western' political scientists" make

> a variety of assumptions regarding the main actors that shape politics and the desirable institutional form of democracy. Accordingly, politics is conflated with policy making by political elites and bureaucrats, and the procedures of democratic institutions premised upon representative democracy, in which the role of the people is to delegate power, via elections, to elected elites. . . . Thus alternative ways of organizing power and institutionalizing government are excluded from analysis, as are nonliberal articulations of democracy.

Motta reminds us that there is more at play in democratic politics than the safeguarding of certain institutions. Democratic politics can take liberal and nonliberal forms, as well as representative and post-representative forms (Tormey

2015). While what we call 'politics' obviously does take the shape of what most mainstream political scientists focus on—parties, elections, policies and so forth—it also includes many nonelectoral and noninstitutional practices. Consequently, questions about populism's relationship with democracy should not always be taken at face value—rather, they often conceal larger questions about what constitutes so-called correct or legitimate forms of political practice.

From this perspective, tracing causal correlations between populism and the quality of democracy purely based on institutional outcomes may be a flawed enterprise. Instead of continuing to ask how populism affects democracy—that is, assuming that populism is a completely separate external entity to democracy—it is possible to shift our viewpoint slightly and consider the democratic and antidemocratic tendencies *within* populism. This perspective acknowledges the complex interplay between populism and democracy, and concedes that populism's democratic and antidemocratic tendencies can be present at the same time—often with tension between the two. Utilising the notion of populism as a political style developed throughout the preceding chapters of this book, the following sections identify and explore these tendencies, showing that populism is not 'ambivalent' but rather torn between two competing directions.

The Democratic Tendencies of Populism

Populism has a number of democratic tendencies. These include its drive to make politics more accessible and 'popular'; its potential to include previously excluded or disenfranchised identities within its conception of 'the people; and its ability to reveal the sometimes less-than-democratic tendencies of contemporary forms of democratic politics.

First, as was argued in Chapter 5, populism can be considered democratic in that it renders politics far more comprehensible and understandable for everyday citizens. The populist embrace of the political 'low', 'bad manners' and tendency towards simplification can provide an appealing and comprehensible contrast to the increasingly rarefied and technocratic styles of politics that characterise the contemporary political landscape. Rather than speaking in the convoluted language of technocrats or relying on abstraction, populists' blunt style can enable "citizens to regain their grip on a complex political reality by restoring mundane political experience to the centre of democratic practice" (Pels 2003, 50). This goes beyond ideology or policies—for example, there is little doubt that the rise of the Tea Party in the United States was not just a matter of its ideological opposition to Obama's presidency and his taxation policies, but due to the fact that figures like Sarah Palin and Glenn Beck were able to offer a 'resonant' and attractive political performance, and render a very complicated political reality into a more easily graspable political perspective. This is done by appealing to emotion as much as rationality, and utilising embodied, symbolically mediated performance as much as policy platforms to shape the political narrative. Populism thus acknowledges that modern politics is not just a matter of putting forward policies for voters to deliberate rationally upon as some kind of *homo politicus*, but rather appealing to people with a full 'package' that is both attractive and relevant.

Second, populism can be considered democratic in that populist actors have the ability to include previously excluded identities within their performances of 'the people', thus symbolically transforming these identities and associated sites of contestation into 'legitimate' political actors and sites. Let us take the cases of 'the people' represented by Evo Morales, Hugo Chávez and Thaksin Shinawatra as examples of this operation. Morales has been able to put forward an inclusive conception of 'the people' that has not only comprised the traditional populist 'base' of disaffected urban *mestizos*, but the usually ignored indigenous population of Bolivia as well.[3] In Venezuela, one of Chávez's chief successes was providing the tools for the "formation of the popular democratic subjects who are basic to new forms of popular democracy" (Motta 2011, 43), including those who live "at the margins of civil society" (Hellinger 2001, 19) in his conception of 'the people'. In Thailand, Thaksin was ostensibly the first politician to harness the developing political involvement of the informal masses, with his 'people' including the rural poor, the urban middle class, and northern small-business and land owners (Phongpaichit and Baker 2009a). Yet it is not just that these leaders spoke for these previously excluded groups: it is that they adopted their clothing, speech and dress, thus proving their authenticity and 'closeness' to 'the people'. Morales never wears a regular suit, instead donning his traditional Bolivian *chompa* or sweater, even at meetings of world leaders; Chávez wore tracksuits, sang and danced to traditional Venezuelan songs, and took calls from 'the people' on his television show; while Thaksin swapped his suit-and-tie attire and technocratic style for unbuttoned shirts, sleeping in tents on his reality television show, and talking about his sex life on radio to prove his everyday credentials with 'the people'.[4] These symbolically inclusive gestures sought to legitimise previously excluded identities within the political and cultural sphere.

Third, populism can effectively reveal the dysfunctions of contemporary democratic systems. The most obvious way it does this is by revealing corruption or elite collusion, and by calling for the increased sovereignty of 'the people' in the name of democracy. In the Latin American experience, populism has often been an understandable reaction to hollowed-out, corrupt and exclusionary 'democratic' systems, while in Europe, many populist actors' opposition to the European Union has effectively revealed the 'democratic deficit' at the heart of elite projects (Ivarsflaten 2008; Taggart 2004). In such environments, the populist demand of increased accountability of representatives to their constituents is entirely plausible. More broadly, populists have been at the forefront of engaging with the much-discussed 'crisis of representative politics', whereby "citizens perceive their representatives as incapable of acting according to the messages they have sent through their votes, protests, or other forms of mobilization" (Mény 2003, 256–57). This is a situation exacerbated by corruption, political scandals and lack of transparency in politics, and is evident in the declining numbers of people who are voting, joining political parties, or becoming involved with party politics in general (Crouch 2004; Hay 2007; Tormey 2015).

Populists not only can hold a finger to the pulse of representative democratic politics, but also can offer effective critiques of the structural shortcomings and inefficiencies of democratic systems. For example, figures like Ross Perot and Pauline Hanson have made significant attempts to expose the deficiency of political vision in two-party systems such as the United States and Australia, making clear the lack of choice offered to voters in these countries. Similarly, one of the key drivers of Beppe Grillo's MoVimento 5 Stelle has been the disaffection of voters with the entire Italian political system. Populists can thus shine a light on the fact that democratic systems often do not live up to their full potential. If we return to Arditi's 'drunken dinner guest' metaphor for populism raised in Chapter 4, we find that "populism calls the bluff on claims that gentrified politics is democratic politics 'as such'. It also shows that the 'table manners' of democratic politics are often little more than props to bestow an aura of public virtue on elected officials that have none" (Arditi 2007a, 80). In its refusal to 'play nice' and instead flaunt its 'bad manners', populism can deliver contemporary democratic systems some awkward truths that they may not wish to hear.

It is clear that populism offers a wider view of what is considered as 'legitimate politics' than the constrained democratic horizon that it sometimes seems that we are stuck within. It reveals that if the official stock-and-trade of what passes for democratic politics today is the chance for citizens to spend ten minutes every few years voting for representatives from a seriously constrained field of choice, then this is not good enough. Populism can show that there is more to legitimate political action in democracies—riots, protests, gatherings, online campaigns, self-organised civil society groups and so forth—than just voting. As such, populism, in its evocation and performance of 'the people', can instead work to correct notions of democratic politics that see 'the people' as a purely constituted democratic subject that exists to delegate power to representatives to rule on their behalf. Rather, in its ability to make politics more accessible and relatable, as well as stressing the power of 'the people', populism acknowledges the constituent power of 'the people'—that is, the notion that 'the people' is an active entity that is responsible for the shaping of its own political destiny (Kalyvas 2005). In drawing together 'bad manners', a focus on the sovereignty of 'the people', offering an accessible view of the political, and calling out democratic dysfunction, populism displays a number of important democratic tendencies.

The Antidemocratic Tendencies of Populism

While populism may have strong democratic tendencies, these stand in tension with a number of antidemocratic tendencies that can manifest concurrently. These include populism's targeting of Others associated with 'the elite'; its denial of complexity and heterogeneity; and its tendency towards extreme personalisation.

As has been stressed throughout this book, the populist invocation of 'the people' makes little sense without an Other to which it is opposed. This is due to the fact that within populism, 'the people' does not refer to all people within a certain political community, but rather operates synedochically, elevating one part of the community to the position of embodying or representing the whole community (Laclau 2005b). In doing so, populism excludes certain identities from 'the people', deeming them as illegitimate and not part of the community. So while populist invocations of 'the people' can sometimes open spaces for new democratic subjects, this inclusivity always comes at the price of the exclusion—sometimes virulent and violent exclusion—of the Other.

This becomes clear if we return to the 'inclusive' examples of Chávez, Morales and Thaksin mentioned earlier. In the process of extending their conception of 'the people', each of these figures has, to some extent, excluded significant sectors of their societies in the process. Morales has isolated major business sectors of Bolivian society (Eaton 2011) and has been accused of stifling critique by labelling journalists who disagree with his government as "instrument[s] of neoliberalism" (Dangl 2007). Chávez allegedly withheld social insurance from those who offered political support to opposition parties (Weyland 2009) and accused his enemies of being aligned with the devil. Thaksin deployed a wide range of attacks on 'the people's' enemy (an alliance of liberal reformers and conservative forces drawn from the monarchy, military and public service) including the intimidation of the opposition, bullying of nongovernmental organisations, shutting down media outlets and even extrajudicial killings (Tejapira 2006). So even though these populists have brought about a large degree of democratic renewal in their countries, it has always been at the price of exclusion and a significant threat to pluralism.

Elsewhere, the targeting of 'the people's' Other has been at least as bad—or even more explicit—than these examples. Muslims have taken the brunt of the venom of contemporary Western European populists (Betz 2007); 'Gypsies', 'Turks' and the Roma have been the central targets of Central and Eastern European populists' attacks (Stewart 2013); Asian, Arab and African immigrants have been attacked by populists in Australia and New Zealand (Betz and Johnson 2004; Poynting 2002); while in Africa, populists have targeted ethnic minorities, 'deviant' women and homosexuals (Vincent 2009). Each of these groups has been subjected to violence, intimidation and discrimination, treated less as legitimate political opponents than enemies to be excluded or destroyed.

It is this explicit targeting of the Other that has attracted Žižek's (2006a, 2006b) concern in his debates with Laclau (2006) about the normative implications of advocating populism as the basis for an emancipatory democratic project. The issue for Žižek (2006a, 555) is that populism "displaces the antagonism and constructs the enemy ... [T]he enemy is externalized and reified into a positive ontological entity (even if the entity is spectral) whose annihilation would restore balance and justice". In this operation, populism ignores the 'true' enemy—the causes of 'the people's' problems are never complex issues like the ruthless speed of modern capitalism, globalisation, structural imbalances, sexism, racism, poverty and so on. Rather, it is 'the elite', who are at the helm of all that is threatening, evil and harmful, or the Other whom 'the elite' have 'let in' or been too lax towards, as they are taking away jobs/spending welfare money/introducing diseases/causing crises and so forth. This scapegoating and conspiracy-theorising ultimately represents a refusal to deal with the complexity of contemporary political and social reality, instead introducing an overarching schema that explains everything, with the Other/elite as "the singular agent behind all threats to the people" (Žižek 2006a, 556). In this way, populism is always a reactive and negative politics—it throws its hands up in exasperation, and then points the blame at the enemy figure. The key message is that *somebody* must be responsible for this mess.

This denial of complexity is also reflected in its myth of the homogenised and unified 'people'. Populism tends to deny difference or division within 'the people', and in this sense, Mudde and Rovira Kaltwasser (2013b) are correct to argue that populism can be considered as a challenge to pluralism. This presents contemporary populism with a real problem in the contemporary political landscape, criss-crossed as it is by difference and heterogeneity. The flows of global capital, migration, cross-border and transnational bodies and identities have seen political communities become ever more diverse, and identities more complex. To deny diversity in the common age is to deny the lived experience of late modernity. As mentioned in Chapter 6, this disavowal of complexity often manifests itself in the invocation of what Taggart (2000) has identified as the populist 'heartland', the territory of the imagination that glances towards the past to remind 'the people' of simpler times. It is here that populists cast "their imaginative glances backwards in an attempt to construct what has been lost by the present" (Taggart 2000, 95). This nostalgic view of the unified community of the past is evident in various examples of contemporary populism, whereby immigrants or 'the elite' are seen as 'diluting' or threatening the lifestyle and existence of the 'people', who were allegedly unified in the past.

The populist tendency towards extreme personalisation can also be viewed as antidemocratic. As has been shown throughout this book, populism tends to rely on a singular leader to 'render-present', represent and embody the hopes, desires and voice of 'the people'. 'The people' in this regard do not emerge ex nihilo, awaiting representation, but are constituted through the performance of populist actors. As such, 'the people' and the leader become symbolically tied together: the populist leader is not a mere representative of 'the people' but rather becomes the figure who truly knows what 'the people' want, or as shown in Chapter 4, becomes the figure who purports to actually *embody* the sovereign will of 'the people'.

Such personalisation can lead to two problematic outcomes: the strict dichotomisation of political space and the dangerous monopolisation of power in the hands of the leader. In the first case, the political community is split in a Schmittian friends/enemies manner between those who support the leader ('the people') and those who do not. As de la Torre (2007, 388) puts it, under populism "the political field is reduced to a camp where citizens can choose either to acclaim the leader or to be condemned to ostracism as enemies of the leader and hence of the people and of the nation". We can see this split around the world today: Ostiguy (2009a, 2009b) has argued that the central political cleavage in Argentina is still between Peronism and anti-Peronism, while in Venezuela, the central cleavage remains between Chavismo and anti-Chavismo, even after Chávez's death. Baldini (2011) has argued that a similar cleavage exists between those who support and those who are against Berlusconi in Italy, and the case is the same regarding Thaksin in Thailand. Populism basically comes down to this: if you are not with us, you are against us.

The second issue—the monopolisation of power in the hands of the leader—stems from the leader's ostensible infallibility: if the leader represents or embodies 'the people's' will, and 'the people' are always right, then the leader is also always right. As a consequence, the granting of more power to the populist leader is not seen as a problem, as this is ultimately giving more power to 'the people'. This tendency worries many analysts of populism, given that a number of prominent populist actors have gone on to abuse their powers by utilising this logic, and shifted towards authoritarianism. To touch on a few central examples: in Latin America, Hawkins (2010, 15) characterised Chávez's time in office as "a semidemocratic regime headed in an increasingly authoritarian direction"; de la Torre (2013b) has written of Correa's 'authoritarian project'; while Levitsky and Loxton (2012, 2013) have grouped these leaders together with Fujimori and Morales as examples of 'competitive authoritarianism'. Elsewhere, Museveni has demonstrated an increasing authoritarianism in Uganda (Carbone 2005); while in Thailand, Thaksin has admitted himself that he slipped into 'soft authoritarianism' (in Plate 2011, 23).[5] As Arditi (2007a, 83) notes, when leaders starts seeing themselves as the preordained voice of 'the people', "the danger of an authoritarian streak enters the scene".

This 'authoritarian streak', especially when populists are in high office, can manifest itself in the attempt to extend state control to previously open sites of contestation and opposition, particularly within civil society. As was noted in Chapter 5, a number of Latin American populists have attempted to bring about 'media statism' in their countries, which is "a model that places the state at the center of media systems and approaches market and civil society as either opposed or subjected to the designs of government" (Waisbord 2012, 3). In

Europe, Berlusconi's attacks on the judiciary using his own media have been well documented (Quigley 2011; Viroli 2012). Meanwhile, in Thailand, Thaksin attacked intellectuals, nongovernment organisations and civil society groups as 'enemies of the nation' and claimed that he wanted "kanmueang ning, quiet or calm politics" (Baker and Phongpaichit 2009, 367–68), expressing open admiration for the Singaporean political system—not a particularly shining model of democracy. Taken together, populism's targeting of Others, monopolisation of power, its political polarisation and denial of complexity offer a rather worrying approach to democracy.

Populism as Democratic and Antidemocratic

Having outlined the democratic and antidemocratic tendencies of populism, can we make an ultimate judgement on whether populism 'is' or 'is not' democratic? Unfortunately, it is not that simple: lining up these tendencies side by side and counting which list has more attributes will not give us a conclusive answer regarding populism's democratic credentials. As can be seen throughout this chapter, this is because these tendencies manifest differently in different settings. Populism can appear as a democratic force in some contexts, and antidemocratic in others. Additionally, these tendencies are often at play and in tension with one another simultaneously: as we have seen, populists flaunt their democratic tendencies at the same time as undoing democratic guarantees. Populism can thus go either way when it comes to democracy: as Arditi (2005, 98) notes: "Populism can remain within the bounds of democracy but also reach the point where both enter into conflict, and perhaps even go their separate ways". This is ultimately because populism does not offer any positive 'content' regarding how democratic a political project should be, but rather only offers certain tendencies: populism is indeed 'empty-hearted' (Taggart 2004) in this regard.

This argument lines up with the equivocal approach identified earlier in this chapter, which contends that there is no ultimate clear relationship between populism and democracy, and that each case or regional subtype must be considered in its own right to determine its democratic credentials. However, this chapter shows that there are more nuanced ways of doing this than the usual analyses that seek to determine populism's 'effect' on democracy. By focusing instead on populism's democratic and antidemocratic *tendencies,* and how these manifest in different settings, it easier to account for populism's complex and sometimes contradictory relationship with democracy, instead of being beholden to a particular normative model of democracy and the associated privileging of certain actors and institutions as indicators of democracy.

More so, the exploration of populism's democratic and antidemocratic tendencies throws into question the equivocal approach's characterisation of populism as 'ambivalent'. Ambivalence implies uncertainty, indecisiveness or the inability to choose a course of action or how one feels about something. As can be seen, populists do not display ambivalence towards democracy as much as *opportunism*: they are usually quite clear and passionate about the kind of democracy they favour—the kind that will allow them to get in power, or if they are already in power, allow them stay in power. The democratic and anti-democratic tendencies within the populist playbook are thus there for selective picking and choosing, to be invoked and used when strategically useful—and ignored when they are not. This democratic opportunism thus underlines the notion that populism is ultimately a political style that has no set ideological or democratic/antidemocratic credentials—it is used by a wide range of actors in different contexts across the globe.

Conclusion

This chapter has sought to unravel the question of how to understand populism's relationship with democracy. It first outlined the central approaches to populism and democracy within the literature: those who see populism as negative for democracy, those who see it as positive, and those who are equivocal when it comes to the relationship between the two. Rather than following the example of these other approaches, whereby they seek to discern a *causal* relationship between populism and the quality of democracy, this chapter instead laid out the democratic and antidemocratic tendencies *within* populism as conceptualised as a political style. This was done in order to move away from analyses that unwittingly privilege certain actors and institutions as indicators of democracy (and thus as 'good' political practice), and to instead shift our focus to the performative elements of populism.

This shift has particular pertinence at this present historical juncture, where democracy itself has been stylised. As Brown (2010) argues: "Democracy has historically unparalleled global popularity today yet has never been more conceptually footloose or substantively hollow", becoming a global 'brand' that is used and abused by many different political actors to give themselves a sheen of legitimacy. In other words, when all call themselves democrats, democracy's image, as invoked by various actors, states and institutions across the globe, has been increasingly severed from its 'content'. In this context, style becomes even more important to analyse, as various political actors seek to lay claim to the key stylistic feature of populism that resonates with democracy: appeal to 'the people'.

Indeed, if we really "are all democrats now" (Brown 2010)—if only in name—then populism is likely to be a reoccurring and possibly more common phenomenon across the global political landscape, given that democracy and populism share this central political subject and audience. As such, future assessments of the relationship between populism and democracy may have to rethink the strict binary separation of the two phenomena, and move beyond traditional institutional analyses of democracy. Instead, there will be a need to pay close attention to the way that populism, as a style, manifests across different political contexts and how it adapts and reconfigures democracy's performative tropes and repertoires in its own image. While it might be nice to state clearly that populism 'is' or 'is not' democratic, it is only by acknowledging the complexity of the relationship between the two phenomena, and noting populism's both democratic and antidemocratic tendencies, that we do it justice.

9   Conclusion:
The Future of Populism

Populism is here to stay.
—Panizza (2005a, 19)

As the contemporary political landscape changes, so does populism. In an era in which we face a rapidly shifting media environment, a prolonged sense of crisis and the development of new forms of political identification and representation, this book has argued that we need to rethink contemporary populism in order to make sense of its changing shape in this context. It has done this by developing a new understanding of populism as a political style, and providing the coordinates for how to understand populism in the mediatised and 'stylised' political environment of the early twenty-first century. In undertaking this task, it has sought to make sense of populism's ability to cut across a number of different political, ideological and organisational contexts by focusing on its *performative* dimension, arguing that populism is not a particular entity or 'thing' but a political style that is *done*. Laying out a new and original way of seeing the phenomenon, it has examined the central actors, audiences, stages and mise-en-scènes at play within contemporary populism, and in the process, investigated populism's relationship to media, crisis and democracy.

While this is far from the 'mainstream' view of populism, it represents an important way of making sense of contemporary populism's ability to appear across the world, performed as it is by leaders as disparate as Yoweri Museveni, Jörg Haider, Joseph 'Erap' Estrada and Preston Manning. Taking a wide view, the book has drawn on different area literatures in order to locate populism as a global phenomenon that transcends regional boundaries. The book has also crossed boundaries in terms of the disciplines it has drawn upon to make sense of contemporary populism, combining insights from the political science, political theory, political communications and political sociology literatures to create a more interdisciplinary and comprehensive view of the phenomenon.

This shift in perspective provides a number of lessons for understanding contemporary populism, as well as opening up a number of future research paths. As such, this concluding chapter highlights the central arguments made throughout this book—that populism is a political style, that populism's relationship with the media must be accounted for, that populism is a global phenomenon and that populism has both democratic and antidemocratic tendencies—and how they contribute to our understanding of populism. It also sketches out the potential directions for further research on the phenomenon across the globe. Finally, the book closes with a reflection on what the future might hold for populism—and why debates over it will continue to matter.

Understanding Contemporary Populism as a Political Style

First, this book has aimed to put forward a developed and systematic notion of populism as a political style that can be used by others to analyse the phenomenon. While a number of other authors have used the term 'political style' to label populism (Canovan 1999; Jagers and Walgrave 2007; Kazin 1995; Knight 1998; Taguieff 1995), the term has remained vague and undertheorised. More often than not, the question of what the term 'political style' actually means has been left unanswered, and the phrase has been used to name various attributes that do not quite fit within the other four dominant approaches to populism as laid out in Chapter 2—ideology, strategy, discourse or political logic. This vagueness and inconsistency has made it particularly difficult for the political style approach to stand as a viable alternative to these approaches. This book has aimed to change that. It has built on these previous authors' works, and has systematically set out, explained and defended the political style approach to populism, demonstrating that political style is a compelling, important and nuanced category for understanding populism at the present time, worthy of use in both theoretical and empirical analyses of populism.

Drawing on the work of Ankersmit (1996, 2002), Hariman (1995) and Pels (2003) from the fields of rhetoric, political philosophy and political sociology, political style was conceptualised as *the repertoires of embodied, symbolically mediated performance made to audiences that are used to create and navigate the fields of power that comprise the political, stretching from the domain of government through to everyday life.* This concept was then used to discern the key features of populism as a political style by examining twenty-eight cases of leaders identified as populist in the literature from across the globe. These features were: appeal to 'the people' versus 'the elite'; 'bad manners'; and crisis, breakdown or threat, each of which was examined in detail throughout the following chapters of the book.

Thinking of populism in this way has four major repercussions. The first is that it gives us a way to understand populism not only across regional contexts but across ideological and organisational contexts as well. No matter whether populism is left or right, grassroots or 'top-down', the concept presented in this book allows us to compare populism as a *general phenomenon*. The second is that it moves populism from being a black-and-white concept—in that a political actor 'is' or 'is not' a populist—towards a more nuanced concept that accounts for the 'gray area' in between the black and white. The third repercussion is that we can make sense of populism's alleged lack of 'substance' or its 'emptiness', not by seeing at as somehow deficient or 'thin' but instead by taking its *stylistic characteristics* seriously. What is 'on the surface' when it comes to populism matters. Fourth, the political style approach offers up a new conceptual vocabulary to studying populism, focusing on performers, audiences, stages and the mise-en-scènes of the phenomenon. This vocabulary captures the inherent theatricality of contemporary populism, while also bringing the mechanisms of populist representation into focus.

This new approach opens up a number of directions for future research. The first area involves continuing to develop and apply the political style approach to populism. One promising direction would be to explore the concept in depth by applying it to individual or more focused regional case studies, as this book has only offered an introduction and broad overview of what can be done with the approach. This development would allow us to compare the performative repertories at play in different cases of populism across the world: it would certainly be interesting to see how notions of 'the people' versus 'the elite', 'bad manners' and crisis manifest in different contexts. Subtypes of populism could potentially be developed on this basis.

On a related track, another potential area of research could see more work being done to compare populism to the political styles that have been identified by Hariman (1995) or by identifying other contemporary political styles for comparison. The obvious one that has been identified in this book is the technocratic style, characterised by an appeal to expertise, 'good manners', and a focus on stability. In this regard, it would certainly be interesting to track how some ostensibly populist leaders have oscillated between populist and technocratic styles: de la Torre (2013b) has recently suggested that Correa's political project in Ecuador is one of "technocratic populism", combining populist style with a faith in expertise and top-down policies, and this represents a case that would certainly be worthy of further analysis under this rubric. It may also be the case that there are other political styles that can be identified and compared to populism: one possibility here would be a 'post-representative' (Tormey 2015) political style of the type presented by the Occupy and 15-M movements. A comparison of the populist style (represented by the Tea Party) and post-representative style (represented by the Occupy movement) would be very useful in terms of clearing the still present conceptual confusion about the status of Occupy and its splinter movements, and outlining the similarities and differences between the two movements.

Another important avenue of enquiry opened up by the concept of political style involves its gradational nature. As has been noted throughout this book, populist actors can be more or less populist at certain times, depending on how intensely and consistently they utilise the populist style. Yet this does not mean the gradational technocracy—populism spectrum can only apply to populists. We should ostensibly be able to track 'mainstream' politicians along this spectrum, and it can be expected that most of these actors will fall somewhere in the middle of the spectrum, balancing the two styles (or perhaps even leaning towards the technocratic side). Yet as been hinted at throughout this book, there are a number of examples of where populism has been increasingly adopted by a number of 'mainstream' political actors, who may use it in a less consistent or 'softer' manner than those who are usually cited as populists in the literature. In order to make sense of this phenomenon, future research could utilise the spectrum presented in this book and operationalise it further. The most promising work in terms of making sense of these mainstream appropriations of populism has come from Hawkins (2010, 2012), whose research on populist discourse (in the form of speeches of a number of different political leaders) has shown that some figures who are not often thought of as populists within the literature—such as George W. Bush—have a similar, if not higher 'populism score' than some of the mainstays of the literature, such as Carlos Menem or Evo Morales. As populism continues to become 'mainstreamed', it is important to build on this avenue of enquiry, as it remains one of the foggiest questions in the populist literature—how do we account for these 'borderline' cases? In this regard, a number of promising collaborative possibilities exist between those who utilise the discursive and political style approaches, and it may be the case that the political style approach can supplement the discursive approach's lack of engagement with the aesthetic and performative dimensions of populism to make more sense of this matter.

Populism and the Media

The book's second central argument has been that the media landscape needs to be considered in much more detail when thinking about populism. It has demonstrated this by showing that we need to move beyond just examining media coverage of populists or how populists interact with different types of media—what the limited literature on populism and media has tended to focus on—but also towards focusing on the process of *mediatisation* and the key role of *mediation*. As Chapter 5 argued, processes of mediatisation have buttressed the rise of contemporary populism, with populism standing at the intersection of media and political logics. Chapter 6, meanwhile, demonstrated that the concept of mediation is vital to understanding populist representations of 'the people' today, and that talk of populism being an unmediated or direct phenomenon must be abandoned. In doing so, the book has brought together work on populism from the political communications and political science literatures, aiming for cross-pollination that might help provide the directions for future research.

There is obviously still much work to be done in this area. While the broader populist literature has tended only to pay lip service to the role of the media (and by extension, mediatisation and mediation), there are some tentative signs that this might be changing—an encouraging number of empirical case studies have recently been published that examine populism's links with media (Bale, van Kessel and Taggart 2011; Bos, van der Brug and de Vreese 2010, 2011; Burack and Snyder-Hall 2012; Rooduijn 2014a; van der Pas, de Vries and van der Brug 2013; Waisbord 2012), while Krämer (2014) and Mazzoleni (2014) have made efforts to draw together insights on 'media populism' and 'political populism'. However, the majority of the empirical work has tended to focus on older forms of mass media. As such, future studies should consider populist use of new media, as has been set out by Demos's project on online populism in Europe (Bartlett, Birdwell and Littler 2011). We are potentially only on the cusp of being able to see the impact of new media on populism, and it is likely that this arena will prove to be vital in understanding populism as we look towards the future, particularly given that new media offers populists an ever-available stage on which to perform and reach 'the people'. Another important area in this regard would be empirical research on the professionalised communication and public relations expertise behind populist actors, as discussed in Chapter 5. As was mentioned, this area is particularly under-researched, given that populists are notoriously cagey about what goes on 'behind the scenes', lest it suggest any in-authenticity on their part. Nonetheless, it would be useful to know more about these operations, and compare them with more 'mainstream' political actors. Do populists and mainstream leaders and parties treat the media differently? Do they utilise different media strategies? How do they overlap, and where do they differ? These questions are important if we wish to understand populism more fully, and especially if those who aim to combat populism want to be effective in their struggles.

Beyond this, more work is needed to discern and untangle the complex links between mediatisation, channels of mediation and populism. This is partic-ularly relevant to considering the mechanisms of populist representations of 'the people'—that is, the very question of *how* populists go about representing 'the people'. The model presented in Chapter 6, which outlined the relationship between populist leaders, audiences, constituencies and media, offers a way of mapping these processes, and can be applied (and refined) through being ap-plied to empirical cases. More consideration needs to be given to what makes speaking for 'the people' different from speaking for other political subjects, and many empirical studies on the assorted ways that populists claim to speak for and 'render-present' 'the people'—via mass media, reality television, radio broadcasts, social media and so forth—remain to be written. Fortunately, rep-resentation has emerged as a key theme of a number of leading authors' recent work (Arditi 2007a, 2010; Roberts 2015; Rovira Kaltwasser 2013; Taggart 2004): hopefully this signals a broader engagement with the concept within the pop-ulist literature.

Populism beyond Europe and the Americas

The book's third central argument has been that we need to consider popu-lism on a more global scale. This argument is twofold. First, it involves putting an end to extrapolating the features of a certain case study or regional variant of populism to account for populism in toto. Despite Ionescu and Gellner's (1969b) classic edited collection showing over four decades ago that populism is not a purely regional phenomenon, but rather a feature of countries all across the world, this lesson has sometimes been forgotten within the populist lit-erature. This regional siloing thankfully seems to be breaking down, but old habits die hard, as demonstrated in the 'common wisdom' so usually proffered in European circles that populism is a dangerous right-wing form of politics. Second, it means looking beyond the sometimes myopic focus on Europe and the Americas, and taking into account populist cases from Africa and the Asia-Pacific. These areas are not just 'outliers' but deserve in-depth analysis and consideration. There are understandable reasons for the 'Atlantic bias' (Moffitt 2015a) of the literature on populism—a term used here to reflect the fact that the majority of the work on populism both focuses on and is produced in those regions bordered by the Atlantic Ocean—including the geographic concentration of researchers in this region, numerous rich cases of study in these regions, and the fact that 'populism' is only a very recent term in some languages, meaning that is has not been applied in detail in some contexts (Phongpaichit and Baker 2009b, 69). Yet these reasons are not an excuse to continue to ignore these understudied regions.

In order to move towards overcoming these tendencies, this book has sought to develop the lineaments of a more global view of populism. Its inductive concept of populism as a political style is a result of comparing leaders commonly identified in the literature as populists from each of the five regions noted above. More so, it has further used illustrative examples from all of these regions to back up its argument throughout the book. While it has leant more heavily on the European and Latin American examples at times, this is a result of there simply being more literature available on those areas than others. More work on the African and Asia-Pacific regions in the future will help to change this situation, and allow us to develop and refine more globally applicable theories of populism.

Populism, Crisis and Democracy

Finally, this book has contributed to recent debates around populism's vexed relationship with democracy, especially in the wake of the crises of the first decade of the twentieth century. In regards to crisis, it showed that while there is a strong tendency within the literature to argue that crisis is a trigger for populism, we should also think about how *populism attempts to act as a trigger for crisis*. This is because crisis is not a neutral phenomenon but something that must be mediated and 'performed' in order *to be perceived as crisis*. Chapter 6 demonstrated that populists actively participate in this process, and developed a six-step model to show how populists 'perform' crisis. One of the central implications for democracy shown in this model is populism's worrying tendency to use crisis to set 'the people' against 'the elite' and Others, sometimes in such a virulent fashion that the removal or eradication of 'the people's' enemy is seen as the only way to 'solve' the crisis.

Yet this does not automatically mean that populism is an antidemocratic force. As Chapter 8 showed, populism tells us very little about the democratic 'content' of any political project. In exploring the democratic and antidemocratic tendencies *within* populism by focusing on its performative features, the book has added credence to the equivocal approach to populism and democracy set out by Mudde and Rovira Kaltwasser (Mudde and Rovira Kaltwasser 2012b; Rovira Kaltwasser 2012, 2013)—albeit with some reservations about their overall project—and contributed to a more nuanced and complex understanding of the relationship between populism and democracy. By slightly shifting the perspective on the question of the democratic credentials of populism, the book opens a path for future research in this area. While this book has set out a general understanding of populism's democratic and antidemocratic tendencies, it would be interesting to look in depth at how these tendencies manifest in different cases and contexts. Do certain democratic or antidemocratic tendencies within populism become more pronounced in different regions? Are they sublimated into 'mainstream' democratic politics in particular cases? And are certain types of democratic regimes more susceptible to populism than others? These questions are ripe for analysis, and the political style approach developed in this book could help answer them as it moves beyond purely institutional understandings of the relationship between populism and democracy.

The Future of Populism?

This leaves us with the million-dollar question: what does the future hold for populism? Will populist actors continue to enjoy political success across the globe? Can we expect populism to continue to be 'mainstreamed' in a number of different contexts? To put it bluntly, if conditions continue as they currently stand, the chances for populism's sustained ascent are high. These are good times for populism. The talk of a "populist Zeitgeist" (Mudde 2004, 542) or "populist revival" (Roberts 2007, 3) noted in the introductory chapter of this book is convincing. There are populist presidents across Latin America; powerful populist actors in governments across Europe as well as in the European Parliament; a number of prominent Republicans in the United States are affiliated with the Tea Party; and numerous populist actors are making inroads in Africa and the Asia-Pacific. All of these figures are benefitting from populaces that are disenchanted with party politics, cynical about the intentions of 'the elite' and tired of an exhausted political paradigm. A prolonged global financial downturn, rising unemployment in a number of areas and a loss of faith in perceived elite projects like the European Union are helping fuel the flames. Wherever there are dissatisfied citizens who feel as if their voice is not being heard, there is space for populists to appeal to 'the people'.

Yet dissatisfaction is not the only thing fuelling populism's ascent. As this book has shown, populism is particularly attuned to the contours of the contemporary mediatised landscape, whereby 'communicative abundance' reigns supreme and media touches upon on almost all aspects of modern life. As the march of mediatisation continues onwards, we can expect populist actors to benefit as they continue to straddle the line between politics and media in the clever ways that they perform for 'the people'. In such a context, we might also expect populism to continue to become subsumed within so-called mainstream politics across the political landscape. Here, we will see populist figures become increasingly brought into the 'mainstream' fold, while ostensibly 'mainstream' politicians will likely crib from the populist playbook given its increased efficacy and timeliness.

In other words, populism is here to stay. It is not a 'pathology' or democratic disease that has only appeared because of some mysterious imbalance to the workings of democracy across the globe. Nor is it simply a derogatory term to be used glibly to tar those we do not like, trust or understand. Instead, populism is a permanent feature of contemporary democratic life that deserves to be taken far more seriously. Consequently, the ongoing debates about the meaning of populism will continue to be vital, not only in deciding how we conceptualise the phenomenon but in deciding how we deal with it as well. These debates are not just the splitting of hairs amongst ivory tower academics, and the ongoing quest to understand and define the phenomenon should not be snidely swept aside as a petty nuisance. These debates matter. In a much-needed defence of the literature on populism, Fieschi (2013) recently described the way that:

> [T]he field is dismissed as at best ineffectual, and at worst the product of neo-liberal delusion. But this work is neither undecipherable, useless nor pernicious. It is meaningful and its very abundance could just as easily be testimony to the interest and urgency of the task. . . . Populism is a complex concept—and so the discussion around it reflects that complexity.

This defence of the concept is entirely correct. Populism *is* a complex concept, and as a result, conceptual debates will continue to rage around it. But *populism itself* will also continue to change, and we will need to adjust our conceptual understandings of it accordingly. This means remaining vigilant about what is going on directly in front of our eyes, and being open to new perspectives on populism rather than tying ourselves in strict conceptual straitjackets for the sake of parsimony and elegance. We are no longer living in the times of the populists on the prairies of the Midwest United States or the rural villages of Russia. We are not living in the time of Juan Perón or Huey Long. Contemporary populism has changed. As such, it is time for the populist literature to fully engage with the relationship between populism and media; to recognise the global nature of populism; and to take account of the key performative repertoires underlying contemporary populism across a number of contexts. Until that is done, we will have only a blinkered view of contemporary populism. While there is no 'holy grail' when it comes to definitions of populism, the notion of populism as a political style offers a new understanding of the phenomenon that is sensitive to the mediatised and 'stylised' context of contemporary populism. The aim of this book has been to develop the concept and show that it is viable for making sense of contemporary populism across the globe. As populism continues to spread and become more familiar, the notion of populism as a political style will only prove more vital. Let us hope it is up to the task.

Appendix

Table of Leaders Used to Discern Features of Populism as a Political Style

Leader	Country	Authors who classify the leader as populist
Carlos Menem	Argentina	(Barros 2005, Conniff 1999, Knight 1998, Roberts 1995, Szusterman 2000, Weyland 1999, 2001)
Pauline Hanson	Australia	(Curran 2004, Mason 2010, Melleuish 2000, Snow and Moffitt 2012, Stokes 2000, Taggart 2000)
Jörg Haider	Austria	(Betz 2001, Fallend 2012, Mouffe 2005a, Mudde 2004, Mudde and Rovira Kaltwasser 2013a, Plasser and Ulram 2003)
Evo Morales	Bolivia	(de la Torre 2015a, Hawkins 2010, Madrid 2008, Panizza and Miorelli 2009, Rousseau 2010, Seligson 2007)
Fernando Collor	Brazil	(Cammack 2000, Conniff 2010, de la Torre 1998, Panizza 2000, Roberts 1995, Weyland 2001, 2003)
Preston Manning	Canada	(Flanagan 2009, Harrison 1995, Johnson, Patten, and Betz 2005, Laycock 2005, 2012, Patten 1996, Taggart 2000)
Rafael Correa	Ecuador	(Carrión 2009, Conaghan and de la Torre 2008, de la Torre 2013b, Levitsky and Loxton 2013, Montúfar 2013, Sosa 2012)
Abdalá Bucaram	Ecuador	(de la Torre 1999, 2010, de la Torre and Arnson 2013, Di Tella 1997, Levitsky and Loxton 2013, Sosa-Bucholz 2010, Weyland 2001)
Marine Le Pen	France	(Bar-On 2013, Betz and Meret 2013, Mayer 2013, Mondon 2012, 2013, Shields 2013, M. H. Williams 2010)
Gábor Vona	Hungary	(Bíró-Nagy, Boros, and Vasali 2013, Feischmidt and Szombati 2012, Kovács 2013, Minkenberg and Pytlas 2013, Pirro 2014, van Kessel 2015)
Silvio Berlusconi	Italy	(Edwards 2005, Ginsborg 2004, Jones 2009, Mudde 2004, Tarchi 2008, Zaslove 2008)
Beppe Grillo	Italy	(Bartlett et al. 2013, Bordignon and Ceccarini 2013, Fella and Ruzza 2013, Hartleb 2013, Lanzone 2014, McDonnell 2012)
Raila Odinga	Kenya	(Cheeseman and Larmer 2015, Chege 2008, Gibson and Long 2009, Kagwanja 2009, MacArthur 2008, Resnick 2010)
Andrés Manuel López Obrador	Mexico	(Basurto 2012, Béjar 2006, Bruhn 2012, Edwards 2010, Knight 2010, Ochoa Espejo 2015)

Appendix

Geert Wilders	Netherlands	(Akkerman 2011, Bos, van der Brug, and de Vreese 2011, de Bruijn 2011, de Lange and Art 2011, Mudde 2011, Vossen 2010, 2011)
Pim Fortuyn	Netherlands	(de Lange and Art 2011, Koopmans and Muis 2009, Lucardie 2008, Mudde 2004, Pels 2003, Vossen 2010)
Winston Peters	New Zealand	(Bale and Blomgren 2008, Beilharz and Cox 2006, Betz 2005, Betz and Johnson 2004, Denemark and Bowler 2002, Miller 1998)
Alberto Fujimori	Peru	(Barr 2003, Ellner 2003, Levitsky and Loxton 2012, McClintock 2013, Roberts 1995, Rousseau 2010)
Joseph Estrada	Philippines	(De Castro 2007, Hedman 2001, Karaos 2006, Raquiza 2013, Rocamora 2009, M. R. Thompson 2010a, 2010b, 2013)
Jacob Zuma	South Africa	(Hart 2013, Mathekga 2008, Piper 2009, Resnick 2012, Southall 2009, Vincent 2009, 2011)
Bert Karlsson	Sweden	(Bale and Blomgren 2008, Eatwell 2005, Kamali 2009, Rydgren 2006, 2008, Taggart 1995, 1996, Widfeldt 2000)
Thaksin Shinawatra	Thailand	(Funston 2009, Hewison 2010, Khoo 2009, Laothamatas 2006, Phongpaichit and Baker 2009b, Tamada 2009)
Yoweri Museveni	Uganda	(Carbone 2005, Izama and Wilkerson 2011, Kassimir 1999, Mudde and Rovira Kaltwasser 2014, Mwakikagile 2012, Alex Thompson 2010)
Herman Cain	USA	(Langman and Lundskow 2012, Lepore 2011, Michael 2015, Pieper 2013, Rosenfeld 2011, Sarver Coombs 2014)
Sarah Palin	USA	(Broxmeyer 2010, Kahl and Edwards 2009, Larson and Porpora 2011, Mason 2010, Mead 2011, Wasburn and Wasburn 2011)
Ross Perot	USA	(Canovan 2004, Kazin 1995, Laurence 2003, Rooduijn 2014b, Taggart 2000, Westlind 1996)
Hugo Chávez	Venezuela	(Corrales and Penfold 2011, de la Torre 2007, Ellner 2003, Hawkins 2009, 2010, Panizza and Miorelli 2009, Roberts 2012)
Michael Sata	Zambia	(Cheeseman and Hinfelaar 2010, Cheeseman and Larmer 2015, Hess and Aidoo 2010, 2014, Larmer and Fraser 2007, Ochieng' Opalo 2012, Resnick 2010, 2012)

Notes

Chapter 1

1. Important exceptions to the rule include Mudde and Rovira Kaltwasser (2012b, 2013a) and de la Torre (2015b).

2. A phenomenon like populism lends itself to interpretivist research rather than purely positivist work on the grounds that the term itself is a site of contention, with debates about democracy, 'the people', legitimacy and sovereignty hinging on its meaning. Following the linguistic turn in the social sciences (Carver 2002; Patton 2008), it is important to acknowledge that the debates about the meaning of populism are part and parcel of the phenomenon itself.

3. The benefit of working in this manner is that the theory developed is "sufficiently abstract to deal with differing spheres of social behavior and social structure, so that they transcend sheer description or empirical generalization" (Merton 1968, 68), yet at the same time "it offers a way of engaging the complexity of empirical reality that is simply avoided with universal claims" (Ziblatt 2006, 8). In developing theory around more abstract concepts of representation, leadership and media communications in regards to populism, the book thus "falls somewhere between grand theories and empirical findings" in attempting "to understand and explain a limited area of social [and political] life" (Bryman 2012, 22).

Chapter 2

1. While most authors would agree that the term itself emerged only in the mid-to-late nineteenth century, Houwen (2011) traces populism's roots to early Greek thought as well as democratic revolutions in the United States and France in the eighteenth century, while Canovan (1981) sees populism in the US Jacksonian movement.

2. Not all authors fall neatly into the approaches identified in this chapter—for example, Taggart (2000) and Mény and Surel (2002) arguably combine ideological and strategic elements in their definitions of populism, while Zaslove (2008) combines discursive and strategic elements in his 'ideal type' of populism.

3. It should be noted that at least one noted adherent of this approach, Roberts, has recently shifted his position to one more sympathetic to discursive or ideological approaches that hinge on 'the people' (Roberts 2015).

4. For example, Hawkins (2010, 33) uses five elements to measure populist discourse: Manichean outlook; identification of Good with 'the people'; identification of Evil with 'the elite'; emphasis on systemic change; and an 'anything-goes' approach to minority rights and democratic procedure.

5. Laclau's approach to discourse is far removed from the typical discursive approach to populism outlined earlier in this chapter, moving beyond speech and text, and rather referring to meaning-forming processes of any kind. The approach, developed with Mouffe (Laclau and Mouffe 1985), has even inspired its own 'school' of thought—the 'Essex School' of discourse analysis (see Howarth, Norval and Stavrakakis 2000; Townshend 2003).

6. See Chesters and Welsh (2006), Robinson and Tormey (2009), Tormey (2015) and Arditi (2012) for examples of how these movements attempt to escape the populist logic.

Chapter 3

1. Despite indicating that populism is a political style in the noted article, Canovan elsewhere refers to populism as an ideology (Canovan 2002), specifically drawing on a Freeden-influenced view of ideology (the same definition of ideology utilised by Mudde and his followers), thus making it unclear about her ultimate view of what *kind of phenomenon* populism might be.

2. Referring to the frustration of theorising style, Ewen (1988, 2–3) notes that "I was about to tackle a subject that was, at best, amorphous, a subject that had no clear shape to it, and lacked the kind of concreteness that has shaped the catalogs of knowledge that scholars and students depend upon for intellectual guidance". More recently, Vivian (2011, xii) has spoken of "the paradoxical promise and problem of style: one deploys the category in order to describe matters of rich cultural, political, or aesthetic significance but the matter of style itself remains unresolved".

3. On multiple understandings of 'the political', see Lasswell (1935), Arendt (1958) and Foucault (1991, 2007, 2010).

4. Laclau (2005b) criticised inductive approaches to defining populism's features, and instead used deductive principles to build his model of the phenomenon. However, his critique of inductive approaches drew on a very dated literature, with Laclau primarily targeting the conceptual approaches in the Ionescu and Gellner edited collection (1969b) and Canovan's *Populism* (1981), in the process overlooking almost a quarter-century of theoretical and empirical development. Laclau thus failed to acknowledge that there has been a fair consensus on populist *cases* in re-

cent years in the literature, which means that an inductive approach is far more useful today than it might have been earlier.

5. Rooduijn (2014b) has made a similar argument in his development of a definition of populism that seeks to find the phenomenon's 'nucleus'.

6. This is not to say that parties and movements cannot have their own engrained political styles. However, these styles will always be the result of individuals' performances within these structures. It thus makes sense to look to the populist leader as the central figure of analysis when examining populism when conceptualised as a political style.

7. While much work has been done in the populist literature on formulations of 'the people', significant conceptualisations of 'the elite' in terms of populism are rare. This is a problem, as signifiers like 'the elite', 'the establishment' or 'the system' are just as 'empty' as that of 'the people'. As such, these groups can be construed in different ways: for example, in the United States, the 'cultural establishment' and 'economic establishment' are very different groups—possibly even opposed to each other—but can serve the same antagonistic purposes for populists.

8. Saurette and Gunster (2011, 199) have labelled this as 'epistemological populism'. Its rhetorical techniques include: "[T]he assertion that individual opinions based upon first-hand experience are much more reliable as a form of knowledge than those generated by theories and academic studies; the valorisation of specific types of experience as particularly reliable sources of legitimate knowledge and the extension of this knowledge authority to unrelated issues; the privileging of emotional intensity as an indicator of the reliability of opinions; the use of populist-inflected discourse to dismiss other types of knowledge as elitist and therefore illegitimate; and finally, the appeal to 'common sense' as a discussion-ending trump card".

9. The understanding of the technocratic political style offered here combines elements of Hariman's (1995) 'bureaucratic' style and Ostiguy's (2009b) conception of the political 'high' with the characterisation of technocracy offered by Centeno (1993) and the technocratic 'mode of reasoning' outlined by Ribbhagen (2013).

10. While populists may sometimes promise stability, this stability will always be balanced or at the cost of constructing a crisis or emphasizing an imminent threat: for example, while Correa has sought stability in some regards in Ecuador, this has been framed in terms of a 'citizens' revolution' that "paints politics as a clash of opposing historical projects" (de la Torre 2013b: 37) and seeks to identify and destroy Correa's many enemies.

11. This is an issue that has been wrestled with by a number of authors, with Mazzoleni (2008, 58) attempting to conceptualise this divide by putting forward a difference between 'hard' and 'soft' populism, Snow and Moffitt (2012, 274) put-

ting forth the notion of 'mainstream populism', and Bos et al. (2012, 3) testing how mainstream parties can "adopt the presentation style of populists", and how this is received by different audiences.

12.   'Astroturf' is a play on the term 'grassroots', and refers to "the artificial formation of apparently spontaneous grassroots movements by sectional interests, such as business groups, issue or pressure groups, or political parties" (Wear 2014, 55).

Chapter 4

1.   According to McDonnell (2013, 222), 'personal parties' have four central characteristics: their lifespan is seen as dependent on the political lifespan of their founder-leader; their organisation at the local level is neither manifest nor permanent; there is strong concentration of power in the leader; and the party's image and campaign strategies focus on the leader. Examples include Silvio Berlusconi's Forza Italia and Popolo Della Libertà, Geert Wilder's Partij voor de Vrijheid, Ross Perot's Reform Party and Pauline Hanson's One Nation (McDonnell and Moffitt 2013).

2.   See Mudde and Rovira Kaltwasser (2014) on 'leaderless populism', although their claim that Occupy Wall Street and the Arab Spring are examples of populism is contentious, especially given Rovira Kaltwasser's claim elsewhere that Occupy is a "borderline case" (Rovira Kaltwasser 2013, 16) and their insistence that populism is opposed to pluralism—a ideology that Occupy strongly articulates.

3.   While in most cases this manifests in strong *singular* figures, there are a few cases of populism where there have been a number of concurrent strong populist leaders attached to a populist party or movement. For example, the US Tea Party has had a number of "expressive leaders" (Michael 2015, 274), including Sarah Palin, Michele Bachmann, Glenn Beck, Herman Cain, Ron Paul and Rand Paul amongst others. The Belgian Vlaams Blok had a leadership 'triumvirate' of Frank Vanhecke, Filip Dewinter and Gerolf Annemans, while the Swedish Ny Demokrati had two concurrent key leaders in Bert Karlsson and Ian Wachtmeister (these two examples were pointed out by Sarah L. de Lange and Duncan McDonnell). However, these examples of multiple concurrent leaders remain exceptions to the rule.

4.   It is for this reason that populism should not been confused with recent forms of 'post-representative' politics exemplified by Occupy Wall Street or Movimiento 15-M, which clearly revoke such forms of leadership. For more on 'post-representative' politics, see Tormey (2015).

5.   Poguntke and Webb (2005, 5) trace such changes to the internationalisation of politics, the growth of the state, the mediatisation of contemporary politics and the erosion of traditional social cleavages.

6.   Ostiguy develops his high-low axis to explain Latin American politics, but it is useful and applicable for comparative politics more widely.

7. Hugo Chávez's body was also to have been embalmed and displayed permanently in Caracas following his death, but it was not prepared soon enough for the embalming to be done in a hygienic and effective manner.

Chapter 5

1. Much of the literature on populism still refers to 'the media' as a singular entity, despite the fact that drastic shifts in the field of technology and media communications mean that we now have plural types of media, rather than the singular noun. These include (but are not limited to) the following overlapping categories: mass media, news media, old media, new media, social media, broadcast media, print media, electronic media, mobile media, online media and digital media. In this regard, Couldry (2009, 447) prefers to use the term 'the media field' rather than 'the media' but concedes that "the construction 'the media' will continue to frame not only the activities of media institutions, large and small, but also the actions of individuals that operate across the producer-consumer divide".

2. The key exceptions to this rule are Mazzoleni, Stewart and Horsfield's edited collection, *The Media and Neo-Populism* (2003), which examines the relationship between neopopulist parties/leaders and media coverage across the globe, and to a lesser extent, Ociepka's edited collection, *Populism and Media Democracy* (2005a). Ellinas's *The Media and the Far Right in Western Europe: Playing the Nationalist Card* (2010) is also an excellent comparative study, but obviously focuses on the Western European far right, rather than populism in general.

3. Mass media can be understood as "organizations that use technological channels to distribute messages for the purpose of attracting an increasingly large audience and conditioning those audiences for repeated exposures so as to increase one's resources such that the enterprise is at least self-supporting" (Potter 2011, 905), which differs from non–mass media in that the latter is not necessarily concerned with maximising their audience. For more on definitions of mass media, see Noll (2006), Potter (2009), J. B. Thompson (1995) and Traudt (2005).

4. A number of authors have criticised Laclau for ignoring the media dimension, with Simons (2011, 202) arguing that "key among the practices, processes and institutions that are missing from Laclau's theory of the construction of 'the people', as well as his historical examples, are those of the mass media and popular culture".

5. Some scholars prefer the term 'mediation' to 'mediatisation' to describe this process. However, the latter term is more useful given that it avoids any confusion with discussion of 'mediated' and 'unmediated' forms of politics, particularly within the populist literature. The role of mediation in 'rendering-present' 'the people' is examined in detail in the next chapter. For more on the differences between mediation and mediatisation, see Krotz (2009, 26) and Strömbäck and Esser (2009, 207–9).

6. While Hjarvard (2008, 2013) and a number of other central authors (Jansson 2002; Strömbäck 2008) refer to mediatisation as a process, Krotz (2007) refers to mediatisation as a "meta-process", as it is not linear, does not have a stable beginning or end, nor is confined to a particular culture or region. According to Krotz, other meta-processes include industrialisation, globalisation, individualisation and commercialisation. However, for purposes of conceptual clarity and consensus within the literature, the term 'process' is used here to describe mediatisation.

7. For a complete picture of Thaksin's abuses of the media, see Phongpaichit and Baker (2009a) and Lewis (2006).

8. See Bos et al. (2011) for a refutation of this claim when it comes to right-wing populist leaders in Europe.

9. For example, Palin's daughter Bristol has appeared on two series of *Dancing with the Stars,* has her own reality television series, *Bristol Palin: Life's a Tripp* and has written a memoir (Palin and French 2011)*;* Bristol's former partner, Levi Johnson, has posed for *Playgirl;* and Todd Palin, Sarah's husband, has appeared as a contestant on military-themed reality television show *Stars Earn Stripes* and presented a television special on dogsled racing.

Chapter 6

1. It must be acknowledged that the question of how 'the people' are formulated is not just limited to the populist literature but is also central to debates within contemporary democratic theory. However, rather than wade into these wider debates, this chapter remains focused specifically on the role of 'the people' in contemporary populism. Authors who have offered nuanced analyses of the role of 'the people' in this wider vein include Canovan (2005), Kalyvas (2005), Näsström (2007), Ochoa Espejo (2011) and Smith (2003).

2. It should be noted that Roberts (2006, 127) has since acknowledged that a lack of mediation is not a core feature of Latin American populism: as he notes: "Whereas some populist leaders opt for direct, noninstitutionalized, and unmediated relationships with unorganized followers, others have constructed formidable party organizations to encapsulate and discipline adherents".

3. The term 'idealised' is used, as even though the *Narodnik* went directly 'to the people' by leaving Russian cities for rural villages, they still relied on mediation in the forms of pamphlets and written propaganda to make their point (Taggart 2000).

4. Arditi borrows the term from Jacques Derrida (1982).

5. According to Manin (1997), whom Arditi draws upon to make his argument, "audience democracy" has replaced "party democracy" in this regard. As the 'audience' metaphor indicates, this a primarily supply-side form of democracy, whereby political actors 'perform' for potential voters and supporters, rather than the so-

called 'good old days' of party democracy, with its higher levels of party membership, loyalty and participation. In this situation, "a new elite of experts in communication has replaced the political activist and party bureaucrat" (Manin 1997, 220).
Consonant arguments have been more recently been made by Jeffrey Edward Green
(2010) with his theory of 'ocular democracy'.

6. Both versions of the video referred to here can be found on YouTube (Choppolona 2009; harrypotter86 2008).

7. It is important to note that Beasley-Murray (2002, 105–6), while outlining
the media spectacle inherent to the 2002 coup, also reads the coup as exposing "the
limit of a televisual regime of visibility" in that "Chávez and the opposition sought
legitimacy through television; and both failed".

8. Saward further notes that audiences and constituencies can be either 'intended' or 'actual', depending on whether a claim is accepted or not. The question
of whether the audience or constituency moves from being 'intended' into 'actual'
thus hinges on the decisions of the recipients of the claim.

9. Although it is beyond the limits of this chapter, Saward has developed a
number of conditions from which to judge the democratic legitimacy of representative claims in his recent work (Saward 2014).

10. While it lurks in the background of his exploration of 'the representative
claim', Saward (2010) does not really addresses the role of 'the media', nor the fact
that most representative claims are in fact mediated.

11. In Australian slang, 'dinkum' means true or genuine, while 'stirrer' is an af-
fectionate term for some who 'stirs up' trouble.

12. Williamson, Skocpol and Coggin (2011, 30) have gone so far as to argue
that Fox News acts not just as a journalistic or even as a propagandist source of
information, but rather, to use Minkoff's (2001) term, a 'national social movement
organization' that provides an infrastructure and venue for collective action, and
helps to build collective identities and solidarity.

Chapter 7

1. The relationship between crisis and populism in the other forms of discursive approaches is less clear. On one hand, Hawkins (2010, 94) links Chavismo's rise
to "a crisis of legitimacy rooted in the breakdown of the rule of law and the perceived corruption of the political system", while Bruhn (2012) links Mexican presidential candidate Andrés Manuel López Obrador's leftist populism to economic
crisis, with both authors backing up their claims with ample empirical evidence.
However, other authors within this approach have avoided looking at crisis, perhaps for pragmatic reasons: it may be difficult to code for crisis in discursive analysis, especially the computer-based content analysis method outlined by Rooduijn
and Pauwels (2010), given that crisis and the variables we associate with crisis are

different things (Mudde 2007, 205). Hawkins has made the closest attempt at capturing crisis in his coding rubric for populist speeches: he looks for the ascription of "cosmic proportions" to moral dimensions of the speech, as well as the claim that "system change is/was required, often expressed in terms such as 'revolution' or 'liberation' of the people" (2010, 252–53).

2.   Adding credence to this position is Rooduijn's (2014b) review of the populist literature to find a 'lowest common denominator' definition of the phenomenon, in which he argues that that the proclamation of crisis is one of four central features of populism.

3.   An example of the disproportionate amount of media coverage given to a populist actors is that of Tea Party figure Herman Cain, who in 2011 was the most covered Republican candidate in the US media, and indeed, the third most covered figure overall, after Barack Obama and Muammar Gaddafi (Pew Research Center's Project for Excellence in Journalism 2011).

4.   However, this does not necessarily mean changing tack in terms of crisis is always a negative experience. From early 2014 until the time of writing (mid-2015), Wilder's Partij voor de Vrijheid has tended to be either the most popular or second-most popular party in the Netherlands according to opinion polls (Louwerse 2015).

5.   In some situations, 'the elite' can even be portrayed as the victims of crisis: for example, the US Justice Department has depicted a number of banks (including divisions of Citigroup and Bank of America) as victims of Standard & Poor's credit ratings during the financial crisis (Wall Street Journal 2013, A14)—a new twist on the usual narratives that have emerged from the Global Financial Crisis.

6.   There are however, some forms of nonpopulist politics that seek to perpetuate crisis and 'normalise' it to create a permanent 'state of exception'. See Agamben (2005) for examples and discussion of this phenomenon.

Chapter 8

1.   Rovira Kaltwasser (2012) has labelled these the 'liberal approach', the 'radical approach', and finally, the one that he advocates, the 'minimal approach'. Although these divisions are sound, they have been relabelled here as the negative, positive and equivocal views of populism's effect on democracy, as there are a number of authors (Arditi 2007a; de la Torre 2010; Kazin 1995; Panizza 2005a; Panizza and Miorelli 2009) who take nuanced positions that do not quite fit into the liberal or radical approaches, but also do not subscribe to Mudde and Rovira Kaltwasser's (2013b) 'minimal' position, instead utilising a different definition of populism. The term 'equivocal' is borrowed from Ochoa Espejo's (2015) insightful discussion of the normative dimensions of discussing populism.

2.   It should be noted that Mudde is not part of the 'liberal' camp that sees pop-

ulism as a negative force: rather, he and Rovira Kaltwasser have been the leading advocates of the 'minimal' (or what is referred to here as 'equivocal') approach to populism. However, he is mentioned here because of his influence on those who have focused exclusively on European radical right populism as a threat to democracy. Similarly, Betz has also pointed out that populism can have positive effects on democracy, in that it can "point out the gaps and contradictions between the abstract principles and claims informing representative democracy and their application in the real world" (Betz and Johnson 2004, 323–24).

3.   Madrid (2008) has gone so far as to conceptualise this form of populism as 'ethnopopulism', noting that some key watchers of Latin American populism would not have predicted such a development given that 'the people' is most often conceptualised as a homogenous and undifferentiated body.

4.   For more on how these symbolically inclusive gestures link with social and political inclusion, see Moffitt (2015a) on Thaksin, and Mudde and Rovira Kaltwasser (2013a) on Chávez and Morales.

5.   In this interview, Thaksin blamed his authoritarianism on his training as a policeman. As he noted: "[M]y personal weak point is my culture of being trained as a police officer. Sometimes I rely on the techniques and instruments of law and order too much. . . . [W]e were taught to use the 'iron fist in a velvet glove', but in this modern world, in the open world, in this more transparent world, you have to use more of the velvet glove and less of the iron fist . . . much less. If not extremely necessary, do not use these techniques if you want to nurture true democracy" (in Plate 2011, 211–12).

Bibliography

Abts, Koen, and Stefan Rummens. 2007. "Populism versus Democracy". *Political Studies* 55(2): 405–24.

Ackerman, James S. 1962. "A Theory of Style". *Journal of Aesthetics and Art Criticism* 20(3): 227–37.

AFP. 2010. "'I Am the People,' Chávez Tells Followers Ahead of Polls". *Sydney Morning Herald*, January 24. Accessed August 19, 2013. http://news.smh.com.au/breaking-news-world/i-am-the-people-chavez-tells-followers-ahead-of-polls-20100124-mryf.html.

Agamben, Giorgio. 2005. *State of Exception*. Translated by Kevin Attell. Chicago: University of Chicago Press.

Akkerman, Tjitske. 2003. "Populism and Democracy: Challenge or Pathology?" *Acta Politica* 38(2): 147–59.

Akkerman, Tjitske. 2011. "Friend or Foe? Right-wing Populism and the Popular Press in Britain and the Netherlands". *Journalism* 12(8): 931–45.

Akkerman, Tjitske. 2012. "Populism". In *Encyclopedia of Global Studies*, edited by Helmut K. Anheier and Mark Juergensmeyer, 1358–60. Thousand Oaks, CA: SAGE.

Albertazzi, Daniele, and Duncan McDonnell. 2008. "Introduction: The Sceptre and the Spectre". In *Twenty-First Century Populism: The Spectre of Western European Democracy*, edited by Daniele Albertazzi and Duncan McDonnell, 15–29. Basingstoke: Palgrave Macmillan.

Alexander, Jeffrey C. 2011. *Performance and Power*. Cambridge, MA: Polity Press.

Alexander, Jeffrey C., Berhard Giesen, and Jason L. Mast, eds. 2006. *Social Performance: Symbolic Action, Cultural Pragmatics and Ritual*. Cambridge: Cambridge University Press.

Alexander, Jeffrey C., and Jason L. Mast. 2006. "Introduction: Symbolic Action in Theory and Practice: The Cultural Pragmatics of Symbolic Action". In *Social Performance: Symbolic Action, Cultural Pragmatics and Ritual*, edited by Jeffrey C. Alexander, Berhard Giesen and Jason L. Mast, 29–90. Cambridge: Cambridge University Press.

Allcock, John B. 1971. "'Populism': A Brief Biography". *Sociology* 5(3): 371–87.

Ankersmit, Frank. 1996. *Aesthetic Politics: Political Philosophy beyond Fact and Value*. Stanford: Stanford University Press.

Ankersmit, Frank. 2002. *Political Representation*. Stanford: Stanford University Press.

Arditi, Benjamin. 2005. "Populism as an Internal Periphery of Democratic Politics". In *Populism and the Mirror of Democracy*, edited by Francisco Panizza, 72–98. London: Verso.

Arditi, Benjamin. 2007a. *Politics on the Edges of Liberalism: Difference, Populism, Revolution, Agitation*. Edinburgh: Edinburgh University Press.

Arditi, Benjamin. 2007b. "Post-hegemony: Politics Outside the Usual Post-Marxist Paradigm". *Contemporary Politics* 13(3): 205–26.

Arditi, Benjamin. 2010. "Review Essay: Populism Is Hegemony Is Politics? On Ernesto Laclau's *On Populist Reason*". *Constellations* 17(3): 488–97.

Arditi, Benjamin. 2012. "Insurgencies Don't Have a Plan—They *Are* the Plan: Political Performatives and Vanishing Mediators in 2011". *JOMEC Journal: Journalism, Media and Cultural Studies* 1(1). Accessed February 26, 2013. http://www.cardiff.ac.uk/jomec/jomecjournal/1-june2012/arditi_insurgencies.pdf.

Arendt, Hannah. 1958. *The Human Condition*. Chicago: University of Chicago Press.

Arendt, Hannah. 2004 [1951]. *The Origins of Totalitarianism*. New York: Schocken Books.

Armey, Dick, and Matt Kibbe. 2010. *Give Us Liberty: A Tea Party Manifesto*. New York: William Morrow.

Armony, Ariel C., and Victor Armony. 2005. "Indictments, Myths, and Citizen Mobilization in Argentina: A Discourse Analysis". *Latin American Politics and Society* 47(4): 27–54.

Art, David. 2005. *The Politics of the Nazi Past in Germany and Austria*. New York: Cambridge University Press.

Austin, J. L. 1975. *How to Do Things with Words*. Cambridge: Harvard University Press.

Australian Associated Press. 2006. "Hanson Turns on 'Diseased' Africans". *Sydney Morning Herald*, December 6. Accessed November 25, 2014. http://www.smh.com.au/news/national/hanson-turns-on-diseased-africans/2006/12/06/1165081010724.html.

Azzarello, Stefania. 2011. "Populist Masculinities: Power and Sexuality in the Italian Populist Imaginary". M.A. diss., Women's Studies Department, University of Utrecht.

Baker, Chris, and Pasuk Phongpaichit. 2009. *A History of Thailand*. Melbourne: Cambridge University Press.

Baldini, Gianfranco. 2011. "Italy: Politics in the Age of Berlusconi". In *Europe Today:*

A Twenty-first Century Introduction, edited by Ronald Tiersky and Erik Jones, 133–60. Plymouth: Rowman and Littlefield.

Bale, Tim, and Magnus Blomgren. 2008. "Close but No Cigar? Newly Governing and Nearly Governing Parties in Sweden and New Zealand". In *New Parties in Government: In Power for the First Time*, edited by Kris Deschouwer, 85–103. Abingdon: Routledge.

Bale, Tim, Stijn van Kessel and Paul Taggart. 2011. "Thrown around with Abandon? Popular Understandings of Populism as Conveyed by the Print Media: A UK Case Study". *Acta Politica* 46(2): 111–31.

Bangkok Post. 2013. "Thaksin Tweets He's Definitely Not Dead". *Bangkok Post*, April 2. Accessed April 8, 2013. http://www.bangkokpost.com/news/politics/343453/thaksin-tweets-he-definitely-not-dead.

Bar-On, T. 2013. *Rethinking the French New Right: Alternatives to Modernity*. Abingdon: Routledge.

Barlai, Melani. 2012. "Jobbik on the Web: Right-Wing Extremism in Hungary". In *CeDEM12: Proceedings of the International Conference for E-Democracy and Open Government*, edited by P. Parycek, N. Edelmann and M. Sachs, 229–40. Krems: Edition Donau-Universität Krems.

Barr, Robert R. 2003. "The Persistence of Neopopulism in Peru? From Fujimori to Toledo". *Third World Quarterly* 24(6): 1161–78.

Barr, Robert R. 2009. "Populists, Outsiders and Anti-Establishment Politics". *Party Politics* 15(1): 29–48.

Barros, S. 2005. "The Discursive Continuities of the Menemist Rupture". In *Populism and the Mirror of Democracy*, edited by Francisco Panizza, 250–74. London: Verso.

Bartlett, Jamie, Jonathan Birdwell, Mona Bani and Jack Benfield. 2012. *Populism in Europe: Denmark*. London: Demos.

Bartlett, Jamie, Jonathan Birdwell and Sarah L. de Lange. 2012. *Populism in Europe: Netherlands*. London: Demos.

Bartlett, Jamie, Jonathan Birdwell and Caterina Froio. 2012. *Populism in Europe: CasaPound*. London: Demos.

Bartlett, Jamie, Jonathan Birdwell, Péter Krekó, Jack Benfield and Gabor Gyori. 2012. *Populism in Europe: Hungary*. London: Demos.

Bartlett, Jamie, Jonathan Birdwell and Mark Littler. 2011. *The New Face of Digital Populism*. London: Demos.

Bartlett, Jamie, Jonathan Birdwell and Duncan McDonnell. 2012. *Populism in Europe: Lega Nord*. London: Demos.

Bartlett, Jamie, Caterina Froio, Mark Littler and Duncan McDonnell. 2013. *New Political Actors in Europe: Beppe Grillo and the M5S*. London: Demos.

Basurto, Jorge. 2012. "Populism in Mexico. From Cárdenas to López Obrador". In

Populism in Latin America, edited by Michael L. Conniff, 86–109. Tuscaloosa: University of Alabama Press.

Baudrillard, Jean. 1994. *Simulacra and Simulation*. Ann Arbor: University of Michigan Press.

BBC News. 2006. "In Quotes: Berlusconi in His Own Words". *BBC News*, May 2. Accessed April 8, 2014. http://news.bbc.co.uk/2/hi/3041288.stm.

BBC News. 2012. "Dutch Gripped by 'Shop a Migrant' Website". April 7. Accessed June 12, 2012. http://www.bbc.co.uk/news/world-europe-17078239.

Beasley-Murray, Jon. 2002. "Media and Multitude: Chronicle of a Coup Unforetold". *Journal of Iberian and Latin American Research* 8(1): 105–16.

Beasley-Murray, Jon. 2010. *Posthegemony*. Minneapolis: University of Minnesota Press.

Beck, Ulrich. 2006. *The Cosmopolitan Vision*. Cambridge: Cambridge University Press.

Beilharz, Peter, and Lloyd Cox. 2006. "Nations and Nationalism in Australia and New Zealand". In *The SAGE Handbook of Nations and Nationalism*, edited by Gerard Delanty and Krishan Kumar, 555–64. London: SAGE.

Béjar, Alejandro Álvarez. 2006. "Mexico's 2006 Elections: The Rise of Populism and the End of Neoliberalism?" *Latin American Perspectives* 33(2): 17–32.

Bennett, W. Lance, and Alexandra Segerberg. 2013. *The Logic of Connective Action: Digital Media and the Personalization of Contentious Politics*. New York: Cambridge University Press.

Berlusconi, Silvio. 2000. *L'Italia che ho in mente*. Milano: Mondadori.

Betz, Hans-Georg. 1993. "The New Politics of Resentment: Radical Right-Wing Populist Parties in Western Europe". *Comparative Politics* 25(4): 413–27.

Betz, Hans-Georg. 1994. *Radical Right-Wing Populism in Western Europe*. London: Palgrave Macmillan.

Betz, Hans-Georg. 2001. "Exclusionary Populism in Austria, Italy, and Switzerland". *International Journal* 56(3): 393–420.

Betz, Hans-Georg. 2005. "Against the System: Radical Right-Wing Populism's Challenge to Liberal Democracy". In *Movements of Exclusion: Radical Right-Wing Populism in the Western World*, edited by Jens Rydgren, 25–40. Hauppage, NY: Nova Science.

Betz, Hans-Georg. 2007. "Against the 'Green Totalitarianism': Anti-Islamic Nativism in Contemporary Radical Right-Wing Populism in Western Europe". In *Europe for the Europeans: The Foreign and Security Policy of the Populist Radical Right*, edited by Christina Schori Liang, 33–54. Aldershot: Ashgate.

Betz, Hans-Georg, and Carol Johnson. 2004. "Against the Current—Stemming the Tide: The Nostalgic Ideology of the Contemporary Radical Populist Right". *Journal of Political Ideologies* 9(3): 311–27.

Betz, Hans-Georg, and Susi Meret. 2013. "Right-wing Populist Parties and the Working-class Vote: What Have You Done for Us Lately?" In *Class Politics and the Radical Right*, edited by Jens Rydgren, 107–21. Abingdon: Routledge.

Biorcio, Roberto. 2003. "The *Lega Nord* and the Italian Media System". In *The Media and Neo-Populism: A Contemporary Comparative Analysis*, edited by Gianpietro Mazzoleni, Julianne Stewart and Bruce Horsfield, 71–94. Westport, CT: Praeger.

Birenbaum, Guy, and Maria Villa. 2003. "The Media and Neo-Populism in France". In *The Media and Neo-Populism: A Contemporary Comparative Analysis*, edited by Gianpietro Mazzoleni, Julianne Stewart and Bruce Horsfield, 45–70. Westport, CT: Praeger.

Bíró-Nagy, András, Tamás Boros and Z. Vasali. 2013. "More Radical than the Radicals: The *Jobbik* Party in International Comparison". In *Right-Wing Extremism in Europe*, edited by Ralf Melzer and Sebastian Serafin, 229–54. Berlin: Friedrich-Ebert-Stiftung.

Blumler, Jay G. 2003. "Foreword: Broadening and Deepening Comparative Research". In *The Media and Neo-Populism: A Contemporary Comparative Analysis*, edited by Gianpietro Mazzoleni, Julianne Stewart and Bruce Horsfield, xv–xx. Westport, CT: Praeger.

Boas, Taylor. 2005. "Television and Neopopulism in Latin America: Media Effects in Brazil and Peru". *Latin American Research Review* 40(2): 27–49.

Boin, Arjen, Allan McConnell and Paul t' Hart, eds. 2008. *Governing after Crisis: The Politics of Investigation, Accountability and Learning*. New York: Cambridge University Press.

Boin, Arjen, Paul t' Hart, Eric Stern and Bengt Sundelius. 2005. *The Politics of Crisis Management: Public Leadership under Pressure*. New York: Cambridge University Press.

Bordignon, Fabio, and Luigi Ceccarini. 2013. "Five Stars and a Cricket: Beppe Grillo Shakes Italian Politics". *South European Society and Politics* 18(4): 427–49.

Bos, Linda, Wouter van der Brug and Claes de Vreese. 2010. "Media Coverage of Right-Wing Populist Leaders". *Communications* 35(2): 141–63.

Bos, Linda, Wouter van der Brug and Claes de Vreese. 2011. "How the Media Shape Perceptions of Right-Wing Populist Leaders". *Political Communication* 28(2): 182–206.

Bos, Linda, Wouter van der Brug and Claes de Vreese. 2012. "An Experimental Test of the Impact of Style and Rhetoric on the Perception of Right-Wing Populist and Mainstream Party Leaders". *Acta Politica* 48(2): 192–208.

Brading, Ryan. 2013. *Populism in Venezuela*. New York: Routledge.

Brassett, James, and Chris Clarke. 2012. "Performing the Sub-Prime Crisis: Trauma and the Financial Event". *International Political Sociology* 6(1): 4–20.

Brown, Wendy. 2010. "We Are All Democrats Now". *Theory and Event* 13(2). Accessed June 14, 2014. http://muse.jhu.edu/journals/theory_and_event/summary/vo13/13.2.brown.html.

Broxmeyer, Jeffrey D. 2010. "Of Politicians, Populism, and Plates: Marketing the Body Politic". *WSQ: Women's Studies Quarterly* 38(3): 138–52.

Bruhn, Kathleen. 2012. "To Hell with Your Corrupt Institutions!: AMLO and Populism in Mexico". In *Populism in Europe and the Americas: Threat or Corrective for Democracy?*, edited by Cas Mudde and Cristóbal Rovira Kaltwasser, 88–112. New York: Cambridge University Press.

Bryman, Alan. 2012. *Social Research Methods*. 4th ed. Oxford: Oxford University Press.

Bucy, Erik P., and Maria Elizabeth Grabe. 2007. "Taking Television Seriously: A Sound and Image Bite Analysis of Presidential Campaign Coverage, 1992–2004". *Journal of Communication* 57(4): 652–75.

Burack, Cynthia, and R. Claire Snyder-Hall. 2012. "Introduction: Right-Wing Populism and the Media". *New Political Science* 34(4): 439–54.

Burant, Stephen R. 1987. "The Influence of Russian Tradition on the Political Style of the Soviet Elite". *Political Science Quarterly* 102(2): 273–93.

Burke, Kenneth. 1957 [1941]. *The Philosophy of Literary Form: Studies in Symbolic Action*. New York: Vintage.

Burke, Kenneth. 1965. *Dramatism and Development*. Barre, MA: Clark University Press.

Butler, Judith. 1990. *Gender Trouble*. New York: Routledge.

Byrne, David, and Emma Uprichard. 2012. "Useful Complex Causality". In *The Oxford Handbook of Philosophy of Social Science*, edited by Harold Kincaid, 109–29. New York: Oxford University Press.

Cain, Herman. 2012a. "Rabbit". *YouTube [online video clip]*, March 26. Accessed June 25, 2012. http://www.youtube.com/watch?v=EdpN5C1_flQ&list=PLFC6170BD3784F524.

Cain, Herman. 2012b. "This Is the Economy on Stimulus". *YouTube [online video clip]*, March 1. Accessed June 25, 2012. http://www.youtube.com/watch?v=YYN-Awrq3og&list=PLFC6170BD3784F524.

Cain, Herman. 2012c. "Chicken". *YouTube [online video clip]*, April 11. Accessed June 25, 2013. http://www.youtube.com/watch?v=V1rjf7zdD-M.

Cammack, Paul. 2000. "The Resurgence of Populism in Latin America". *Bulletin of Latin American Research* 19(2): 149–61.

Campus, Donatella. 2010. "Mediatization and Personalization of Politics in Italy and France: The Cases of Berlusconi and Sarkozy". *International Journal of Press/Politics* 15(2): 219–35.

Cannon, Barry. 2009. *Hugo Chávez and the Bolivarian Revolution*. Manchester: Manchester University Press.

Canovan, Margaret. 1981. *Populism*. London: Junction Books.

Canovan, Margaret. 1982. "Two Strategies for the Study of Populism". *Political Studies* 30(4): 544–52.

Canovan, Margaret. 1984. "People, Politicians and Populism". *Government and Opposition* 19(3): 312–27.

Canovan, Margaret. 1999. "Trust the People! Populism and the Two Faces of Democracy". *Political Studies* 47(1): 2–16.

Canovan, Margaret. 2002. "Taking Politics to the People: Populism as the Ideology of Democracy". In *Democracies and the Populist Challenge*, edited by Yves Mény and Yves Surel, 25–44. Basingstoke: Palgrave Macmillan.

Canovan, Margaret. 2004. "Populism for Political Theorists?" *Journal of Political Ideologies* 9(3): 241–52.

Canovan, Margaret. 2005. *The People*. Cambridge: Polity Press.

Carbone, Giovanni M. 2005. "'Populism' Visits Africa: The Case of Yoweri Museveni and No-Party Democracy in Uganda". *Crisis States Research Centre Working Papers Series* 73. London: Crisis States Research Centre, London School of Economics and Political Science.

Carrión, J. 2009. "The Persistent Attraction of Populism in the Andes". In *Latin American Democracy: Emerging Reality or Endangered Species?*, edited by Richard L. Milett, Jennifer S. Holmes and Orland J. Perez, 233–51. New York: Routledge.

Carroll, Dean. 2013. "Beppe Grillo Has 'Votes but No Policies' Says Herman Van Rompuy". *Public Service Europe*, February 28. Accessed March 1, 2013. http://www.publicserviceeurope.com/article/3153/beppe-grillo-has-votes-but-no-policies-says-herman-van-rompuy.

Carver, Terrell. 2002. "Discourse Analysis and the 'Linguistic Turn'". *European Political Science* 2(1): 50–53.

Castañeda, Jorge G. 2006. "Latin America's Left Turn". *Foreign Affairs* 85(3): 28–43.

Castells, Manuel. 2010. *The Rise of Network Society*. 2nd ed. Oxford: Wiley Blackwell.

CBS News/New York Times. 2010. "The Tea Party Movement: Who They Are". April 3. Accessed June 14, 2013. http://www.cbsnews.com/htdocs/pdf/poll_tea_party_who_they_are_041410.pdf.

Centeno, Miguel Angel. 1993. "The New Leviathan: The Dynamics and Limits of Technocracy". *Theory and Society* 22(3): 307–35.

Chávez Frias, Hugo. 2005. "Transcript: Hugo Chávez Interview". *Nightline*, September 16. Accessed February 17, 2012. http://abcnews.go.com/Nightline/International/story?id=1134098&page=1#.Tz2—FwSo1I.

Cheeseman, Nic, and Marja Hinfelaar. 2010. "Parties, Platforms, and Political Mobilization: The Zambian Presidential Election of 2008". *African Affairs* 109(434): 51–76.

Cheeseman, Nic, and Miles Larmer. 2015. "Ethnopopulism in Africa: Opposition Mobilization in Diverse and Unequal Societies". *Democratization* 22(1): 22–50.

Chege, M. 2008. "Kenya: Back from the Brink?" *Journal of Democracy* 19(4): 125–39.

Chesters, Graeme, and Ian Welsh. 2006. *Complexity and Social Movements: Protest at the Edge of Chaos*. Abingdon: Routledge.

Chongkittavorn, Kavi. 2001. "Media Reform in Thailand: New Prospects and New Problems". 'Thailand: The Next Stage' conference, SAIS, Johns Hopkins University, Washington, DC, November 30.

Choppolona. 2009. "Meno male che silvio c'è?" *YouTube [online video clip]*, October 11, 2009. Accessed May 25, 2014. https://www.youtube.com/watch?v=TX-giqPAVR7Y.

Clennell, Andrew, Neil Keene and Henry Budd. 2011. "Pauline Hanson Reborn over Asset Sale Fight". *Daily Telegraph*, March 10. Accessed November 25, 2012. http://www.dailytelegraph.com.au/news/nsw/pauline-hanson-reborn-over-asset-sale-fight/story-fn7q4q9f-1226018699281.

CNBC. 2009. "Santelli's Tea Party". *CNBC Video [online video clip]*, February 19. Accessed November 21, 2012. http://video.cnbc.com/gallery/?video=1039849853.

Committee to Protect Journalists. 2009. "Bill Punishing 'Media Crimes' in Venezuela a Serious Setback". July 30. Accessed March 29, 2012. http://cpj.org/2009/07/bill-punishing-media-crimes-in-venezuela-a-serious.php.

Comroff, Jean. 2011. "Populism and Late Liberalism: A Special Affinity?" *Annals of the American Academy of Political and Social Science* 637(1): 99–111.

Conaghan, Catherine, and Carlos de la Torre. 2008. "The Permanent Campaign of Rafael Correa: Making Ecuador's Plebiscitary Presidency". *International Journal of Press/Politics* 13(3): 267–84.

Conniff, Michael L. 1999. "Introduction". In *Populism in Latin America*, edited by Michael L. Conniff, 1–21. Tuscaloosa: University of Alabama Press.

Conniff, Michael L. 2010. "Women and Populism in Brazil". In *Gender and Populism in Latin America: Passionate Politics*, edited by Karen Kampwirth, 110–21. University Park: Pennsylvania State University Press.

Corbetta, Piergiorgio, and Rinaldo Vignati. 2013. "Left or Right? The Complex Nature and Uncertain Future of the 5 Star Movement". *Italian Politics and Society* 72/73 (Spring–Fall): 53–62.

Corner, John. 2003. "Mediated Persona and Political Culture". In *Media and the Re-styling of Politics*, edited by John Corner and Dick Pels, 67–84. London: SAGE.

Corner, John, and Dick Pels. 2003a. "Introduction: The Re-styling of Politics". In *Media and the Restyling of Politics*, edited by John Corner and Dick Pels, 1–18. London: SAGE.

Corner, John, and Dick Pels, eds. 2003b. *Media and the Restyling of Politics*. London: SAGE.

Corporación Latinobarómetro. 2013. *Latinobarómetro 2013 Report*. Santiago: Corporación Latinobarómetro.

Corrales, Javier, and Michael Penfold. 2011. *Dragon in the Tropics: Hugo Chávez and the Political Economy of Revolution in Venezuela*. Washington, DC: Brookings Institution Press.

Couldry, Nick. 2009. "Does 'the Media' Have a Future?" *European Journal of Communication* 24(4): 437–49.

Couldry, Nick, and Tim Markham. 2007. "Celebrity Culture and Public Connection: Bridge or Chasm?" *International Journal of Cultural Studies* 10(4): 403–21.

Critchley, Simon. 1993. "Re-tracing the Political: Politics and Community in the Work of Philippe Lacoue-Labarthe and Jean-Luc Nancy". In *The Political Subject of Violence*, edited by David Campbell and Micheal Dillion, 73–93. Manchester: Manchester University Press.

Crouch, Colin. 2004. *Post-Democracy*. Cambridge: Polity Press.

Curran, Giorel. 2004. "Mainstreaming Populist Discourse: The Race-Conscious Legacy of Neo-Populist Parties in Australia and Italy". *Patterns of Prejudice* 38(1): 37–55.

Dangl, Benjamin. 2007. "New Politics in Old Bolivia: Public Opinion and Evo Morales". *Upside Down World,* November 28. Accessed February 13, 2014. http://upsidedownworld.org/main/bolivia-archives-31/1021-new-politics-in-old-bolivia-public-opinion-and-evo-morales.

de Baecque, Antoine. 1997. *The Body Politic: Corporeal Metaphor in Revolutionary France, 1770–1800*. Translated by Charlotte Mandell. Stanford: Stanford University Press.

de Bruijn, Hans. 2011. *Geert Wilders Speaks Out: The Rhetorical Frames of a European Populist*. The Hague: Eleven International.

De Castro, Renato Cruz. 2007. "The 1997 Asian Financial Crisis and the Revival of Populism/Neo-Populism in 21st Century Philippine Politics". *Asian Survey* 47(6): 930–51.

de la Torre, Carlos. 1997. "Populism and Democracy: Political Discourses and Cultures in Contemporary Ecuador". *Latin American Perspectives* 24(3): 12–24.

de la Torre, Carlos. 1998. "Populist Redemption and the Unfinished Democratization of Latin America". *Constellations* 5(1): 85–95.

de la Torre, Carlos. 1999. "Neopopulism in Contemporary Ecuador: The Case of Bucaram's Use of the Mass Media". *International Journal of Politics, Culture, and Society* 12(4): 555–71.

de la Torre, Carlos. 2007. "The Resurgence of Radical Populism in Latin America". *Constellations* 14(3): 384–97.

de la Torre, Carlos. 2010. *Populist Seduction in Latin America*. 2nd ed. Athens: Ohio University Press.

de la Torre, Carlos. 2012. "The People, Democracy, and Authoritarianism in Rafael Correa's Ecuador". XXX Congress of the Latin American Studies Association, San Francisco, May 23–26.

de la Torre, Carlos. 2013a. "The People, Populism, and The Leader's Semi-Embodied Power". *Rubrica Contemporanea* 2(3): 5–20.

de la Torre, Carlos. 2013b. "Technocratic Populism in Ecuador". *Journal of Democracy* 24(3): 33–46.

de la Torre, Carlos. 2015a. "The Contested Meanings of Insurrections, the Sovereign People, and Democracy in Ecuador, Venezuela, and Bolivia". In *The Promise and Perils of Populism: Global Perspectives*, edited by Carlos de la Torre, 349–71. Lexington: University Press of Kentucky.

de la Torre, Carlos, ed. 2015b. *The Promise and Perils of Populism: Global Perspectives*. Lexington: University Press of Kentucky.

de la Torre, Carlos, and Cynthia Arnson. 2013. "Introduction: The Evolution of Latin American Populism and Debates over Its Meaning". In *Latin American Populism in the Twenty-First Century*, edited by Carlos de la Torre and Cynthia Arnson, 1–36. Washington, DC: Woodrow Wilson Center Press with Johns Hopkins University Press.

de Lange, Sarah L., and David Art. 2011. "Fortuyn versus Wilders: An Agency-Based Approach to Radical Right Party Building". *West European Politics* 34(6): 1229–49.

de Wilde, Pieter. 2013. "Representative Claims Analysis: Theory Meets Method". *Journal of European Public Policy* 20(2): 278–94.

Debord, Guy. 1994. *The Society of the Spectacle*. Translated by Donald Nicholson-Smith. Cambridge: MIT Press.

Denemark, David, and Shaun Bowler. 2002. "Minor Parties and Protest Votes in Australia and New Zealand: Locating Populist Politics". *Electoral Studies* 21(1): 47–67.

Derrida, Jacques. 1982. "Sending: On Representation". *Social Research* 49(2): 294–326.

Dewey, John. 1987. "Democracy and Educational Administration". In *The Later Works*, edited by Jo Ann Boydston, 229–39. Carbondale: Southern Illinois University Press.

di Piramo, Daniela. 2009. "'Speak for Me!': How Populist Leaders Defy Democracy in Latin America". *Global Change, Peace and Security* 21(2): 179–99.

Di Tella, Torcuato S. 1965. "Populism and Reform in Latin American". In *Obstacles to Change in Latin America*, edited by Claudio Véliz, 47–73. Oxford: Oxford University Press.

Di Tella, Torcuato S. 1997. "Populism into the Twenty-first Century". *Government and Opposition* 32(2): 187–200.

Diamanti, Ilvo. 2014. "The 5 Star Movement: A Political Laboratory". *Contemporary Italian Politics* 6(1): 4–15.

Disch, Lisa. 2011. "Toward a Mobilization Conception of Democratic Representation". *American Political Science Review* 105(1): 100–114.

Disch, Lisa. 2012. "Democratic Representation and the Constituency Paradox". *Perspectives on Politics* 10(3): 599–61.

Dunn, John. 2005. *Democracy: A History*. New York: Atlantic Monthly Press.

Duno-Gottberg, Luis. 2004. "Mob Outrages: Reflections on the Media Construction of the Masses in Venezuela (April 2000–January 2003)". *Journal of Latin American Cultural Studies* 13(1): 115–35.

Eaton, Kent. 2011. "Conservative Autonomy Movements: Territorial Dimensions of Ideological Conflict in Bolivia and Ecuador". *Comparative Politics* 43(3): 291–310.

Eatwell, Roger. 2005. "Charisma and the Revival of the European Extreme Right". In *Movements of Exclusion: Radical Right-Wing Populism in the Western World*, edited by Jens Rydgren, 101–20. Hauppauge, NY: Nova Science.

Eco, Umberto. 2007. *Turning Back the Clock: Hot Wars and Media Populism*. Translated by Alastair McEwen. Orlando, FL: Harcourt Books.

Edwards, Phil. 2005. "The Berlusconi Anomaly: Populism and Patrimony in Italy's Long Transition". *South European Society and Politics* 10(2): 225–43.

Edwards, Sebastian. 2010. *Left Behind: Latin America and the False Promise of Populism*. Chicago: University of Chicago Press.

Ellinas, Antonis A. 2010. *The Media and the Far Right in Western Europe: Playing the Nationalist Card*. New York: Cambridge University Press.

Ellner, Steve. 2003. "The Contrasting Variants of the Populism of Hugo Chávez and Alberto Fujimori". *Journal of Latin American Studies* 35(1): 139–62.

Engels, Jeremy. 2008. "Some Preliminary Thoughts on Democratic Style". *Rhetoric and Public Affairs* 11(3): 439–40.

Ewen, Stuart. 1988. *All Consuming Images: The Politics of Style in Contemporary Culture*. New York: Basic Books.

Faine, Jon. 2005. "Talk Radio and Democracy". In *Do Not Disturb: Is the Media Failing Australia?*, edited by Robert Manne, 169–90. Melbourne: Black Inc.

Fallend, Franz. 2012. "Populism in Government: The Case of Austria (2000–2007)". In *Populism in Europe and the Americas: Threat or Corrective for Democracy?*, edited by Cas Mudde and Cristóbal Rovira Kaltwasser, 113–35. New York: Cambridge University Press.

Feischmidt, Margit, and Kristof Szombati. 2012. *Gyöngyöspata 2011: The Laboratory of the Hungarian Far-Right*. Budapest: Ecopolis Foundation.

Fella, Stefano, and Carlo Ruzza. 2013. "Populism and the Fall of the Centre-Right in Italy: The End of the Berlusconi Model or a New Beginning?" *Journal of Contemporary European Studies* 21(1): 38–52.

Fieschi, Catherine. 2004a. *Fascism, Populism and the French Fifth Republic: In the Shadow of Democracy*. Manchester: Manchester University Press.

Fieschi, Catherine. 2004b. "Introduction". *Journal of Political Ideologies* 9(3): 235–40.

Fieschi, Catherine. 2013. "Who's Afraid of the Populist Wolf?" *OpenDemocracy,* June 25. Accessed June 26, 2013. http://www.opendemocracy.net/catherine-fieschi/who%E2%80%99s-afraid-of-populist-wolf.

Fieschi, Catherine, Marley Morris, and Lilla Caballero. 2012. *Recapturing the Reluctant Radical: How to Win Back Europe's Populist Vote.* London: Counterpoint.

Filc, Dani. 2011. "Post-Populism: Explaining Neo-Liberal Populism through the Habitus". *Journal of Political Ideologies* 16(2): 221–38.

Flanagan, Tom. 2009. *Waiting for the Wave: The Reform Party and the Conservative Movement.* 2nd ed. Montreal: McGill-Queens University Press.

Foucault, Michel. 1991. "Governmentality". In *The Foucault Effect: Studies in Governmentality,* edited by Graham Burchell, Colin Gordon and Peter Miller, 87–104. Chicago: University of Chicago Press.

Foucault, Michel. 2007. *Security, Territory, Population: Lectures at the Collège de France, 1977–1978.* Translated by Graham Burchell. Basingstoke: Palgrave Macmillan.

Foucault, Michel. 2010. *The Government of Self and Others: Lectures at the Collège de France, 1982–1983.* Translated by Graham Burchell. Basingstoke: Palgrave Macmillan.

Frankfurt, Harry. 2005. *On Bullshit.* Princeton: Princeton University Press.

Freeden, Michael. 1996. *Ideologies and Political Theory: A Conceptual Approach.* Oxford: Oxford University Press.

Freeden, Michael. 2003. *Ideology: A Very Short Introduction.* Oxford: Oxford University Press.

Freedlander, David. 2013. "Why Tea Partiers Are Boycotting Fox News". *Daily Beast,* March 23. Accessed May 28, 2013. http://www.thedailybeast.com/articles/2013/03/23/why-tea-partiers-are-boycotting-fox-news.html.

Freeland, Jonathan. 2012. "In Upcoming Elections across the Eurozone Periphery, Voters Are Likely to React to Austerity by Replacing Technocracy with Populism". *LSE EUROPP blog,* June 12. Accessed June 16, 2014. http://blogs.lse.ac.uk/europpblog/2012/06/12/austerity-elections-populism/#more-3604.

Funston, John, ed. 2009. *Thaksin's Thailand: Populism and Polarisation.* Bangkok: Institute of Security and International Studies, Thailand.

George, Alexander L., and Andrew Bennett. 2005. *Case Studies and Theory Development in the Social Science.* Cambridge: MIT Press.

Gerbaudo, Paolo. 2012. *Tweets and the Streets: Social Media and Contemporary Activism.* London: Pluto Press.

Gerring, John, and Paul A. Barresi. 2009. "Culture: Joining Minimal Definitions and Ideal Types". In *Concepts and Methods in Social Science: The Tradition of Giovanni Sartori,* edited by David Collier and John Gerring, 241–68. Abingdon: Routledge.

Gibson, Clark C., and James D. Long. 2009. "The Presidential and Parliamentary Elections in Kenya, December 2007". *Electoral Studies* 28(3): 497–502.

Gidron, Noam, and Bart Bonikowski. 2013. "Varieties of Populism: Literature Review and Research Agenda". *Weatherhead Working Paper Series* 13–0004. Cambridge: Weatherhead Center for International Affairs, Harvard University.

Ginsborg, Paul. 2004. *Silvio Berlusconi: Television, Power and Patrimony*. London: Verso.

Goffman, Erving. 1959. *The Presentation of Self in Everyday Life*. New York: Anchor Books.

Goodman, Nelson. 1975. "The Status of Style". *Critical Inquiry* 1(4): 799–811.

Gramsci, Antonio. 1971. *Selections from the Prison Notebooks*. Edited by Q. Hoare and G. Nowell Smith. New York: International.

Grandy, Gina. 2001. "Instrumental Case Study". In *Encyclopedia of Case Study Research: L—Z; Index, Volume 2*, edited by Albert J. Mills, G. Durepos and I. Wiebe, 473–75. Thousand Oaks, CA: SAGE.

Green, Jeffrey Edward. 2010. *The Eyes of the People: Democracy in an Age of Spectatorship*. New York: Oxford University Press.

Green, W. John. 2006. "The Rebirth of Populism in Latin America Poses a Powerful Challenge to the Neoliberal Order". *Council of Hemispheric Affairs*, August 22. Accessed June 12, 2012. http://www.coha.org/coha-report-the-rebirth-of-populism-in-latin-america-poses-a/.

Griggs, Steven, and David Howarth. 2008. "Populism, Localism and Environmental Politics: The Logic and Rhetoric of the Stop Stansted Expansion Campaign". *Planning Theory* 7(2): 123–44.

Grömping, Max. 2014. "'Echo Chambers': Partisan Facebook Groups during the 2014 Thai Election". *Asia Pacific Media Educator* 24(1): 39–59.

Guillermoprieto, Alma. 2005. "Don't Cry for Me, Venezuela". *New York Review of Books* 52(15): 26–34.

Gumede, William M. 2008. "South Africa: Jacob Zuma and the Difficulties of Consolidating South Africa's Democracy". *African Affairs* 107(427): 261–71.

Habermas, Jürgen. 1975. *Legitimation Crisis*. Translated by Thomas McCarthy. Boston: Beacon Press.

Hackney, Sheldon. 1971. "Introduction". In *Populism: The Critical Issues*, edited by Sheldon Hackney, vii–xxii. Boston: Little, Brown.

Hall Jamieson, Kathleen, and Joseph N. Cappella. 2010. *Echo Chamber: Rush Limbaugh and the Conservative Media Establishment*. New York: Oxford University Press.

Halvorssen, Thor. 2010. "Behind Exhumation of Simon Bolivar Is Hugo Chávez's Warped Obsession". *Washington Post*, July 25. Accessed January 17, 2012. http://www.washingtonpost.com/wp-dyn/content/article/2010/07/23/AR2010072302420.html.

Hanson, Pauline. 1996. Australia, House of Representatives, *Hansard Parliamentary Debates*. September 10. 3859–62.

Hanson, Pauline. 2004. "Enough Rope with Andrew Denton: Pauline Hanson [transcript]". Accessed April 6, 2012. http://www.abc.net.au/tv/enoughrope/transcripts/s1203646.htm.

Hanson, Pauline. 2007. *Untamed & Unashamed*. Docklands: JoJo.

Hariman, Robert. 1995. *Political Style: The Artistry of Power*. Chicago: University of Chicago Press.

Harrison, Trevor. 1995. *Of Passionate Intensity: Right-Wing Populism and the Reform Party of Canada*. Toronto: University of Toronto Press.

harrypotter86. 2008. "Meno male che Silvio c'è video ufficiale inno campagna PDL". *YouTube [online video clip]*, March 27. Accessed May 25, 2013. https://www.youtube.com/watch?v=WXf-YbsShoY.

Hart, G. 2013. "Gramsci, Geography, and the Languages of Populism". In *Gramsci: Space, Nature, Politics*, edited by M. Ekers, G. Hart, S. Kipfer and A. Loftus, 301–20. Chichester: John Wiley and Sons.

Hartleb, Florian. 2013. "Anti-Elitist Cyber Parties?" *Journal of Public Affairs* 13(4): 355–69.

Hawkins, Kirk A. 2009. "Is Chávez Populist? Measuring Populist Discourse in Comparative Perspective". *Comparative Political Studies* 42(8): 1040–67.

Hawkins, Kirk A. 2010. *Venezuela's Chavismo and Populism in Comparative Perspective*. New York: Cambridge University Press.

Hawkins, Kirk A. 2012. "Populism and Democracy in Latin America: New Data for Old Questions". XXX Congress of the Latin American Studies Association, San Francisco, May 23–26.

Hawkins, Kirk A., Scott Riding and Cas Mudde. 2012. "Measuring Populist Attitudes". *Political Concepts: Committee on Concepts and Methods Working Paper Series*, 55.

Hay, Colin. 1995. "Rethinking Crisis: Narratives of the New Right and Constructions of Crisis". *Rethinking Marxism: A Journal of Economics, Culture and Society* 8(2): 60–76.

Hay, Colin. 1999. "Crisis and the Structural Transformation of the State: Interrogating the Process of Change". *British Journal of Politics and International Relations* 1(3): 317–44.

Hay, Colin. 2007. *Why We Hate Politics*. Cambridge: Polity.

Hedman, Eva-Lotta E. 2001. "The Spectre of Populism in Philippine Politics and Society: Artista, Masa, Eraption!" *South East Asia Research* 9(1): 5–44.

Hellinger, Daniel. 2001. "Nationalism, Globalization and Chavismo". XXIII Congress of the Latin American Studies Association, Washington, DC, September 2–8.

Helms, Ludger. 2005. "The Presidentialisation of Political Leadership: British Notions and German Observations". *Political Quarterly* 76(3): 430–38.

Hernández, Juan Antonio. 2004. "Against the Comedy of Civil Society". *Journal of Latin American Cultural Studies* 13(1): 137–45.

Hess, Steve, and Richard Aidoo. 2010. "Beyond the Rhetoric: Noninterference in China's African Policy". *African and Asian Studies* 9(3): 356–83.

Hess, Steve, and Richard Aidoo. 2014. "Charting the Roots of Anti-Chinese Populism in Africa: A Comparison of Zambia and Ghana". *Journal of Asian and African Studies* 49(2): 129–47.

Hewison, Kevin. 2010. "Thaksin Shinawatra and the Reshaping of Thai Politics". *Contemporary Politics* 16(2): 119–33.

Higgins, Michael, and Philip Drake. 2006. "'I'm a Celebrity, Get Me into Politics': The Political Celebrity and the Celebrity Politician". In *Framing Celebrity: New Directions in Celebrity Culture*, edited by Su Holmes and Sean Redmond, 88–100. Abingdon: Routledge.

Hirst, Daniel. 2010. "Pauline Hanson's Muslim Ban 'Illegal'". *Sydney Morning Herald*, April 28, 2010. Accessed June 25, 2013. http://www.smh.com.au/national/pauline-hansons-muslim-ban-illegal-20100428-tqbb.html.

Hjarvard, Stig. 2008. "The Mediatization of Society: A Theory of the Media as Agents of Social and Cultural Change". *Nordicom Review* 29(2): 105–34.

Hjarvard, Stig. 2013. *The Mediatization of Culture and Society*. Abingdon: Routledge.

Hofstadter, Richard. 1965. *The Paranoid Style in American Politics and Other Essays*. New York: Knopf.

Houwen, Tim. 2011. "The Non-European Roots of the Concept of Populism". *Sussex European Institute Working Paper* 120. Brighton: Sussex European Institute, University of Sussex.

Howarth, David. 2008. "Ethos, Agonism and Populism: William Connolly and the Case for Radical Democracy". *British Journal of Politics and International Relations* 10(2): 171–93.

Howarth, David, and Steven Griggs. 2006. "Metaphor, Catachresis and Equivalence: The Rhetoric of Freedom to Fly in the Struggle over Aviation Policy in the United Kingdom". *Policy and Society* 25(2): 23–46.

Howarth, David, Aletta J. Norval and Yannis Stavrakakis, eds. 2000. *Discourse Theory and Political Analysis*. Manchester: Manchester University Press.

Howarth, David, and Yannis Stavrakakis. 2000. "Introducing Discourse Theory and Political Analysis". In *Discourse Theory and Political Analysis: Identities, Hegemony and Social Change*, edited by David Howarth, Aletta J. Norval and Yannis Stavrakakis, 1–23. Manchester: Manchester University Press.

Hutchins, Brett. 2005. "Unity, Difference and the 'National Game': Cricket and Australian National Identity". In *Cricket and National Identity in the Postcolonial Age: Following On*, edited by Stephen Wagg, 9–27. Abingdon: Routledge.

Ionescu, Ghita, and Ernest Gellner. 1969a. "Introduction". In *Populism: Its Meanings and National Characteristics*, edited by Ghita Ionescu and Ernest Gellner, 1–9. London: Weidenfeld and Nicolson.

Ionescu, Ghita, and Ernest Gellner, eds. 1969b. *Populism: Its Meanings and National Characteristics*. London: Weidenfeld and Nicolson.

Ivarsflaten, Elisabeth. 2008. "What Unites Right-Wing Populists in Western Europe?: Re-Examining Grievance Mobilization Models in Seven Successful Cases". *Comparative Political Studies* 41(1): 3–23.

Iyengar, Shanto, and Kyu S. Hahn. 2009. "Red Media, Blue Media: Evidence of Ideological Selectivity in Media Use". *Journal of Communication* 59(1): 19–39.

Izama, Angelo, and Michael Wilkerson. 2011. "Uganda: Museveni's Triumph and Weakness". *Journal of Democracy* 22(3): 64–78.

Jagers, Jan, and Stefaan Walgrave. 2007. "Populism as Political Communication Style: An Empirical Study of Political Parties' Discourse in Belgium". *European Journal of Political Research* 46(3): 319–45.

Jansen, Robert S. 2011. "Populist Mobilization: A New Theoretical Approach to Populism". *Sociological Theory* 29(2): 75–96.

Jansson, André. 2002. "The Mediatization of Consumption: Towards an Analytical Framework of Image Culture". *Journal of Consumer Culture* 2(1): 5–31.

Jenkins, Richard W. 2003. "More Bad News: News Values and the Uneasy Relationship between the Reform Party and the Media in Canada". In *The Media and Neo-Populism: A Contemporary Comparative Analysis*, edited by Gianpietro Mazzoleni, Julianne Stewart and Bruce Horsfield, 149–74. Westport, CT: Praeger.

Johnson, Carol, Steve Patten, and Hans-Georg Betz. 2005. "Identitarian Politics and Populism in Canada and the Antipodes". In *Movements of Exclusion: Radical Right-wing Populism in the Western World*, edited by Jens Rydgren, 85–100. Hauppauge, NY: Nova Science.

Jones, Erik. 2009. "Wheeler Dealers: Silvio Berlusconi in Comparative Perspective". *Journal of Modern Italian Studies* 14(1): 38–45.

Jones, Tim. 2011. "Chewing over Herman Cain's Pizza Past". *Bloomberg Businessweek*, June 16. Accessed November 21, 2012. http://www.businessweek.com/magazine/content/11_26/b4234036592835.htm.

Kagwanja, Peter. 2009. "Courting Genocide: Populism, Ethno-Nationalism and the Informalisation of Violence in Kenya's 2008 Post-Election Crisis". *Journal of Contemporary African Studies* 27(3): 365–87.

Kahl, Mary L., and Janis L. Edwards. 2009. "An Epistolary Epilogue: Learning from Sarah Palin's Vice Presidential Campaign". In *Gender and Political Communication in America*, edited by Janis L. Edwards, 267–78. Plymouth: Lexington Books.

Kalyvas, Andreas. 2005. "Popular Sovereignty, Democracy, and the Constituent Power". *Constellations* 12(2): 223–44.

Kamali, M. 2009. *Racial Discrimination: Institutional Patterns and Politics*. New York: Routledge.

Kantorowicz, Ernst H. 1957. *The King's Two Bodies: A Study in Mediaeval Political Theology*. Princeton: Princeton University Press.

Karaos, Ana Maria A. 2006. "Populist Mobilization and Manila's Urban Poor: The Case of SANAPA in the NGC East Side". In *Social Movements in the Philippines*, edited by Aya Fabros, Joel Rocamora and Djorina Velasco, 46–102. Quezon City: Institute for Popular Democracy.

Kassimir, Ronald. 1999. "Reading Museveni: Structure, Agency and Pedagogy in Ugandan Politics". *Canadian Journal of African Studies* 33(2/3): 649–73.

Kazin, Michael. 1995. *The Populist Persuasion: An American History*. New York: Basic Books.

Keane, John. 2009a. "Life after Political Death: The Fate of Leaders after Leaving High Office". In *Dispersed Democratic Leadership: Origins, Dynamics, and Implications*, edited by John Kane, Haig Patapan and Paul t' Hart, 279–98. Oxford: Oxford University Press.

Keane, John. 2009b. *The Life and Death of Democracy*. London: Simon and Schuster UK.

Keane, John. 2013. *Democracy and Media Decadence*. Cambridge: Cambridge University Press.

Kellner, Douglas. 2003. *Media Spectacle*. London: Routledge.

Kenneally, Ivan. 2009. "Technocracy and Populism". *New Atlantis* 24 (Spring): 46–60.

Khoo, Boo Teik. 2009. "The Ends of Populism: Mahathir's Departure and Thaksin's Overthrow". In *Populism in Asia*, edited by Kosuke Mizuno and Pasuk Phongpaichit, 127–43. Singapore: NUS Press.

Kim, Youngmi. 2008. "Digital Populism in South Korea? Internet Culture and the Trouble with Direct Participation". *KEI Academic Paper Series 'On Korea 2009'* 3(8): 1–7.

Kington, Tom. 2011. "Berlusconi Causes Outrage with Suggestion to Rename Party Go Pussy". *Guardian*, October 7. Accessed January 12, 2013. http://www.guardian.co.uk/world/2011/oct/07/berlusconi-go-pussy-quip-outrage.

Knight, Alan. 1998. "Populism and Neo-Populism in Latin America, especially Mexico". *Journal of Latin American Studies* 30(2): 223–48.

Knight, Alan. 2010. "Cárdenas and Echeverría: Two 'Populist' Presidents Compared". In *Populism in Twentieth Century Mexico: The Presidencies of Lázaro Cárdenas and Luis Echeverría*, edited by Amelia M. Kiddle and Maria L. O. Muñoz, 15–37. Tucson: University of Arizona Press.

Koopmans, Ruud, and Jasper Muis. 2009. "The Rise of Right-Wing Populist Pim Fortuyn in the Netherlands: A Discursive Opportunity Approach". *European Journal of Political Research* 48(5): 642–64.

Koselleck, Reinhart. 2006. "Crisis". *Journal of the History of Ideas* 67(2): 357–400.

Kovács, András. 2013. "The Post-Communist Extreme Right: The Jobbik Party in Hungary". In *Right-Wing Populism in Europe: Politics and Discourse*, edited by R. Wodak, M. Khrosravnik and B. Mral, 223–34. London: Bloomsbury Academic.

Krämer, Benjamin. 2014. "Media Populism: A Conceptual Clarification and Some Theses on Its Effects". *Communication Theory* 24(1): 42–60.

Krastev, Ivan. 2007. "The Strange Death of the Liberal Consensus". *Journal of Democracy* 18(4): 56–63.

Krauze, Enrique. 2011. *Redeemers: Ideas and Power in Latin America*. Translated by Hank Heifetz and Natasha Wimmer. New York: HarperCollins.

Kriesi, Hanspieter, Sandra Lavenex, Frank Esser, Jörg Matthes, Marc Bühlmann and Daniel Bochsler. 2013. *Democracy in the Age of Globalization and Mediatization*. Basingstoke: Palgrave Macmillan.

Krotz, Friedrich. 2007. "The Meta-Process of 'Mediatization' as a Conceptual Frame". *Global Media and Communication* 3(3): 256–60.

Krotz, Friedrich. 2009. "Mediatization: A Concept with which to Grasp Media and Societal Change". In *Mediatization: Concept, Changes, Consequences*, edited by Knut Lundby, 21–40. New York: Peter Lang.

Laclau, Ernesto. 1977. *Politics and Ideology in Marxist Theory*. London: NLB.

Laclau, Ernesto. 1980. "Populist Rupture and Discourse". *Screen Education* 34 (Spring): 87–93.

Laclau, Ernesto. 2000. "Constructing Universality". In *Contingency, Hegemony, Universality: Contemporary Dialogues on the Left*, edited by Judith Butler, Ernesto Laclau and Slavoj Žižek, 281–307. London: Verso.

Laclau, Ernesto. 2005a. "The Future of Radical Democracy". In *Radical Democracy: Political between Abundance and Lack*, edited by Lasse Thomassen and Lars Tønder, 256–62. Manchester: Manchester University Press.

Laclau, Ernesto. 2005b. *On Populist Reason*. London: Verso.

Laclau, Ernesto. 2005c. "Populism: What's in a Name?" In *Populism and the Mirror of Democracy*, edited by Francisco Panizza, 32–49. London: Verso.

Laclau, Ernesto. 2006. "Why Constructing a People Is the Main Task of Radical Politics". *Critical Inquiry* 32(4): 646–80.

Laclau, Ernesto, and Chantal Mouffe. 1985. *Hegemony and Socialist Strategy*. London: Verso.

Landman, Todd. 2008. *Issues and Methods in Comparative Politics: An Introduction*. 3rd ed. Abingdon: Routledge.

Langman, Lauren, and George Lundskow. 2012. "Down the Rabid Hole to a Tea Party". *Critical Sociology* 38(4): 589–97.

Lanzone, Maria Elisabetta. 2014. "The 'Post-Modern' Populism in Italy: The Case of the Five Star Movement". In *The Many Faces of Populism: Current Perspectives*, edited by Dwayne Woods and Barbara Wejnert, 53–78. Bingley: Emerald.

Laothamatas, Anek. 2006. *Thaksina-Prachaniyom*. Bangkok: Matichon Press.

Larmer, Miles, and Alastair Fraser. 2007. "Of Cabbages and King Cobra: Populist Politics and Zambia's 2006 Election". *African Affairs* 106(425): 611–37.

Larson, Magali Sarfatti, and Douglas Porpora. 2011. "The Resistible Rise of Sarah Palin: Continuity and Paradox in the American Right Wing". *Sociological Forum* 26(4): 754–78.

Lasswell, Harold D. 1935. *Politics: Who Gets What, When, How*. New York: McGraw-Hill.

Lasswell, Harold D. 1949. "Style in the Language of Politics". In *The Language of Politics: Studies in Quantitative Semantics*, edited by Harold D. Lasswell, Nathan Leites and Associates, 20–39. New York: George W. Stewart.

Laurence, Jonathan. 2003. "Ross Perot's Outside Challenge: New and Old Media in American Presidential Campaigns". In *The Media and Neo-Populism: A Contemporary Comparative Analysis*, edited by Gianpietro Mazzoleni, Julianne Stewart and Bruce Horsfield, 175–96. Westport, CT: Praeger.

Laycock, David. 1994. "Reforming Canadian Democracy? Institutions and Ideology in the Reform Party Project". *Canadian Journal of Political Science* 27(2): 213–47.

Laycock, David. 2005. "Populism and the New Right in English Canada". In *Populism and the Mirror of Democracy*, edited by Francisco Panizza, 172–201. London: Verso.

Laycock, David. 2012. "Populism and Democracy in Canada's Reform Party". In *Populism in Europe and the Americas: Threat or Corrective for Democracy?*, edited by Cas Mudde and Cristóbal Rovira Kaltwasser, 46–67. New York: Cambridge University Press.

Lefort, Claude. 1986. *The Political Forms of Modern Society: Bureaucracy, Democracy, Totalitarianism*. Edited by J. B. Thompson. Cambridge: Polity Press.

Leibovich, Mark. 2010. "Being Glenn Beck". *New York Times*, September 29. Accessed March 5, 2013. http://www.nytimes.com/2010/10/03/magazine/03beck-t.html?pagewanted=all&_r=0.

Leonard, Mark. 2011. *Four Scenarios for the Reinvention of Europe*. London: European Council on Foreign Relations.

Lepore, Jill. 2011. "Forget 9–9–9. Here's a Simple Plan: 1". *New York Times*, October 16, SR6.

Levitsky, Steven, and James Loxton. 2012. "Populism and Competitive Authoritarianism: The Case of Fujimori's Peru". In *Populism in Europe and the Americas:*

Threat or Corrective for Democracy?, edited by Cas Mudde and Cristóbal Rovira Kaltwasser, 160–81. New York: Cambridge University Press.

Levitsky, Steven, and James Loxton. 2013. "Populism and Competitive Authoritarianism in the Andes". *Democratization* 20(1): 107–36.

Lewis, Glen. 2006. *Virtual Thailand: The Media and Cultural Politics in Thailand, Malaysia and Singapore*. Abingdon: Routledge.

Lievrouw, Leah. 2011. *Alternative and Activist New Media*. Cambridge, MA: Polity Press.

Lijphart, Arend. 1971. "Comparative Politics and the Comparative Method". *American Political Science Review* 65(3): 682–93.

Lipset, Seymour Martin. 1960. *Political Man: The Social Bases of Politics*. Garden City, NY: Doubleday.

Lo, Clarence Y. H. 2012. "Astroturf versus Grass Roots: Scenes from Early Tea Party Mobilization". In *Steep: The Precipitous Rise of the Tea Party*, edited by Lawrence Rosenthal and Christine Trost, 98–130. Berkeley: University of California Press.

Loader, Brian D. 2008. "Social Movements and New Media". *Sociology Compass* 2(6): 1920–33.

Londra 5 Stelle. 2013. "Third European Meeting in London". Accessed February 5, 2013. http://www.londra5stelle.net/.

Lopez, Virginia, and Jonathan Watts. 2013. "Who Is Nicolás Maduro? Profile of Venezuela's New President". *Guardian*, April 15. Accessed April 26, 2013. http://www.guardian.co.uk/world/2013/apr/15/nicolas-maduro-profile-venezuela-president.

Louwerse, Tom. 2015. "Dutch Polling Indicator". *Peilingwijzer*. Accessed May 27, 2015. http://peilingwijzer.tomlouwerse.nl/p/english.html.

Lucardie, Paul. 2008. "The Netherlands: Populism versus Pillarization". In *Twenty-First Century Populism: The Spectre of Western European Democracy*, edited by Daniele Albertazzi and Duncan McDonnell, 151–65. Basingstoke: Palgrave Macmillan.

Lundby, Knut, ed. 2009. *Mediatization: Concept, Changes, Consequences*. New York: Peter Lang.

MacArthur, Julie. 2008. "How the West Was Won: Regional Politics and Prophetic Promises in the 2007 Kenya Elections". *Journal of Eastern African Studies* 2(2): 227–41.

MacRae, Donald. 1969. "Populism as an Ideology". In *Populism: Its Meanings and National Characteristics*, edited by Ghita Ionescu and Ernest Gellner, 197–211. London: Weidenfeld and Nicolson.

Maddens, Bart, and Stefaan Fiers. 2004. "The Direct PM Election and the Institutional Presidentialisation of Parliamentary Systems". *Electoral Studies* 23(4): 769–93.

Madrid, Raul. 2008. "The Rise of Ethnopopulism in Latin America". *World Politics* 60(3): 475–508.

Mair, Peter. 2002. "Populist Democracy vs Party Democracy". In *Democracies and the Populist Challenge*, edited by Yves Mény and Yves Surel, 81–98. Basingstoke: Palgrave.

Mair, Peter. 2006. "Ruling the Void? The Hollowing of Western Democracy". *New Left Review* 42 (November–December): 25–51.

Mancini, Paolo. 2008. "The Berlusconi Case: Mass Media and Politics in Italy". In *Media, Democracy, and European Culture*, edited by Ib Bondebjerg and Peter Madsen, 107–18. Bristol: Intellect Books.

Mancini, Paolo. 2011. *Between Commodification and Lifestyle Politics: Does Silvio Berlusconi Provide a New Model of Politics for the Twenty-First Century?* Oxford: Reuters Institute for the Study of Journalism.

Manin, Bernard. 1997. *The Principles of Representative Government*. Cambridge: Cambridge University Press.

March, Luke. 2007. "From Vanguard of the Proletariat to Vox Populi: Left-Populism as a 'Shadow' of Contemporary Socialism". *SAIS Review* 27(1): 63–77.

Marsh, David, Paul 't Hart, and Karen Tindall. 2010. "Celebrity Politics: The Politics of the Late Modernity?" *Political Studies Review* 8(3): 322–40.

Martin, Lawrence. 2010. "In Search of an Image: The Liberal Express Is Now Boarding". *Globe and Mail*, July 8. Accessed June 13, 2012. http://www.theglobeandmail.com/commentary/in-search-of-an-image-the-liberal-express-is-now-boarding/article1390308/.

Marx, Karl. 1981. *Capital, Volume III*. Translated by David Fernbach. London: Penguin Books.

Mason, Robert. 2010. "'Pitbulls' and Populist Politicians: Sarah Palin, Pauline Hanson and the Use of Gendered Nostalgia in Electoral Campaigns". *Comparative American Studies* 8(3): 185–99.

Mathekga, Ralph. 2008. "The ANC 'Leadership Crisis' and the Age of Populism in Post-apartheid South Africa". In *African Politics: Beyond the Third Wave of Democratisation*, edited by J. Pretorius, 131–49. Cape Town: Juta and Co.

Mayer, Nonna. 2013. "From Jean-Marie to Marine Le Pen: Electoral Change on the Far Right". *Parliamentary Affairs* 66(1): 160–78.

Mazzoleni, G. 2008. "Populism and the Media". In *Twenty-First Century Populism: The Spectre of Western European Democracy*, edited by Daniele Albertazzi and Duncan McDonnell, 49–64. Basingstoke: Palgrave Macmillan.

Mazzoleni, Gianpietro. 2014. "Mediatization and Political Populism". In *The Mediatization of Politics: Understanding the Transformation of Western Democracies*, edited by Jesper Strömbäck and Frank Esser, 42–56. Basingstoke: Palgrave Macmillan.

Mazzoleni, Gianpietro, Julianne Stewart, and Bruce Horsfield, eds. 2003. *The Media and Neo-Populism: A Contemporary Comparative Analysis*. Westport, CT: Praeger.

McCarthy, Patrick. 1996. "Forza Italia: The New Politics and Old Values of a Changing Italy". In *The New Italian Republic: From the Fall of the Berlin Wall to Berlusconi*, edited by Stephen Gundle and Simon Parker, 130–46. London: Routledge.

McClintock, Cynthia. 2013. "Populism in Peru: From APRA to Ollanta Humala". In *Latin American Populism in the Twenty-First Century*, edited by Carlos de la Torre and Cynthia Arnson, 203–38. Washington, DC: Woodrow Wilson Center Press with Johns Hopkins University Press.

McCoy, Jennifer L., and David J. Myers, eds. 2004. *The Unraveling of Representative Democracy in Venezuela*. Baltimore, MD: Johns Hopkins University Press.

McDonald, Mary G., and Samantha King. 2012. "A Different Contender? Barack Obama, the 2008 Presidential Campaign and the Racial Politics of Sport". *Ethnic and Racial Studies* 35(6): 1023–39.

McDonnell, Duncan. 2012. "Italy: The Prospects for Populism". *Policy Network*, September 3. Accessed September 4, 2012. http://www.policy-network.net/pno_detail.aspx?ID=4228&title=Italy%3a+the+prospects+for+populism.

McDonnell, Duncan. 2013. "Silvio Berlusconi's Personal Parties: From Forza Italia to the Popolo Della Libertà". *Political Studies* 61(S1): 217–33.

McDonnell, Duncan, and Benjamin Moffitt. 2013. "Berlusconi, Katter and Assange: A Very Personal Party". *Conversation*, April 16. Accessed April 16, 2013. http://the-conversation.com/berlusconi-katter-and-assange-a-very-personal-party-13164.

McManus, John H. 1994. *Market-Driven Journalism: Let the Citizen Beware?* Thousand Oaks, CA: SAGE.

Mead, Walter Russell. 2011. "The Tea Party and American Foreign Policy: What Populism Means for Globalism". *Foreign Policy* 90(2): 28–44.

Melleuish, Gregory. 2000. "The Rise of Conservative Populism". In *The Politics of Australian Society*, edited by Paul Boreham, Geoff Stokes and Richard Hall, 51–64. Melbourne: Addison, Wesley, Longman.

Mény, Yves. 2003. "From Popular Dissatisfaction to Populism: Democracy, Constitutionalism, and Corruption". In *Governing Europe*, edited by Jack Hayward and Anand Menon, 250–64. Oxford: Oxford University Press.

Mény, Yves, and Yves Surel. 2002. "The Constitutive Ambiguity of Populism". In *Democracies and the Populist Challenge*, edited by Yves Mény and Yves Surel, 1–21. Basingstoke: Palgrave Macmillan.

Meret, Susi. 2015. "Charismatic Female Leadership and Gender: Pia Kjærsgaard and the Danish People's Party". *Patterns of Prejudice* 49(1–2): 81–102.

Merton, Robert K. 1968. *Social Theory and Social Structure*. 3rd ed. New York: Free Press.

Meyer, Thomas. 2002. *Media Democracy: How the Media Colonize Politics*. Cambridge: Polity Press.

Michael, George. 2015. "A New American Populist Coalition? The Relationship between the Tea Party and the Far Right". In *The Promise and Perils of Populism: Global Perspectives*, edited by Carlos de la Torre, 265–91. Lexington: University of Kentucky Press.

Miller, Raymond. 1998. "New Zealand First". In *The New Politics of the Right: Neo-Populist Parties and Movements in Established Democracies*, edited by Hans-Georg Betz and Stefan Immersfall, 203–11. Basingstoke: Macmillan Press.

Minkenberg, Michael, and Bartek Pytlas. 2013. "The Radical Right in Central and Eastern Europe: Class Politics in Classless Societies?" In *Class Politics and the Radical Right*, edited by Jens Rydgren, 206–23. Abingdon: Routledge.

Minkoff, Debra C. 2001. "Producing Social Capital: National Social Movements and Civil Society". In *Beyond Tocqueville: Civil Society and the Social Capital Debate in Comparative Perspective*, edited by Bob Edwards, Michael W. Foley and Mario Diani, 183–93. Hanover: University Press of New England.

Mizuno, Kosuke, and Pasuk Phongpaichit. 2009. "Introduction". In *Populism in Asia*, edited by Kosuke Mizuno and Pasuk Phongpaichit, 1–17. Singapore: NUS Press.

Moffitt, Benjamin. 2015a. "Contemporary Populism & 'The People' in the Asia-Pacific: Thaksin Shinawatra & Pauline Hanson". In *The Promise and Perils of Populism: Global Perspectives*, edited by Carlos de la Torre, 293–316. Lexington: University of Kentucky Press.

Moffitt, Benjamin. 2015b. "How to Perform Crisis: A Model for Understanding the Key Role of Crisis in Contemporary Populism". *Government and Opposition* 50(2): 189–217.

Moffitt, Benjamin, and Simon Tormey. 2014. "Rethinking Populism: Politics, Mediatisation and Political Style". *Political Studies* 62(2): 381–97.

Mondon, Aurelien. 2012. "Nicolas Sarkozy's Legitimization of the Front National: Background and Perspectives". *Patterns of Prejudice* 47(1): 22–40.

Mondon, Aurelien. 2013. *The Mainstreaming of the Extreme Right in France and Australia: A Populist Hegemony?* Farnham, Surrey: Ashgate.

Monitor Online. 2014. "President Museveni's Full Speech at Signing of Anti-Homosexuality Bill". *Daily Monitor*, February 24. Accessed June 22, 2014. http://www.monitor.co.ug/News/National/Museveni-s-Anti-Homosexuality-speech/-/688334/2219956/-/vinrt7/-/index.html.

Montúfar, César. 2013. "Rafael Correa and His (Plebiscitary) Citizen Revolution". In *Latin American Populism in the Twenty-First Century*, edited by Carlos de la Torre and Cynthia Arnson, 295–322. Washington, DC: Woodrow Wilson Center Press with Johns Hopkins University Press.

Motta, Sara C. 2011. "Populism's Achilles' Heel: Popular Democracy beyond the Liberal State and the Market Economy in Venezuela". *Latin American Perspectives* 38(1): 28–46.

Mouffe, Chantal. 2000. *The Democratic Paradox*. London: Verso.

Mouffe, Chantal. 2005a. "The 'End of Politics' and the Challenge of Right-wing Populism". In *Populism and the Mirror of Democracy*, edited by Francisco Panizza, 50–71. London: Verso.

Mouffe, Chantal. 2005b. *On the Political*. Abingdon: Routledge.

Mudde, Cas. 2004. "The Populist Zeitgeist". *Government and Opposition* 39(4): 542–63.

Mudde, Cas. 2007. *Populist Radical Right Parties in Europe*. Cambridge: Cambridge University Press.

Mudde, Cas. 2010. "The Populist Radical Right: A Pathological Normalcy". *West European Politics* 33(6): 1167–86.

Mudde, Cas. 2011. "The New Radical Right: Spectre and Reality". *OpenDemocracy,* April 20. Accessed February 17, 2012. http://www.opendemocracy.net/cas-mudde/new-new-radical-right-spectre-and-reality.

Mudde, Cas, and Cristóbal Rovira Kaltwasser. 2011. "Voices of the Peoples: Populism in Europe and Latin America Compared". *Kellogg Institute Working Paper* 378. Notre Dame, IN: Kellogg Institute for International Studies, University of Notre Dame.

Mudde, Cas, and Cristóbal Rovira Kaltwasser. 2012a. "Populism and (Liberal) Democracy: A Framework for Analysis". In *Populism in Europe and the Americas: Threat or Corrective for Democracy?*, edited by Cas Mudde and Cristóbal Rovira Kaltwasser, 1–26. New York: Cambridge University Press.

Mudde, Cas, and Cristóbal Rovira Kaltwasser, eds. 2012b. *Populism in Europe and the Americas: Threat or Corrective for Democracy?* New York: Cambridge University Press.

Mudde, Cas, and Cristóbal Rovira Kaltwasser. 2012c. "Populism: Corrective *and* Threat." In *Populism in Europe and the Americas: Threat or Corrective for Democracy?*, edited by Cas Mudde and Cristóbal Rovira Kaltwasser, 205–22. New York: Cambridge University Press.

Mudde, Cas, and Cristóbal Rovira Kaltwasser. 2013a. "Exclusionary vs. Inclusionary Populism: Comparing Contemporary Europe and Latin America". *Government and Opposition* 48(2): 147–74.

Mudde, Cas, and Cristóbal Rovira Kaltwasser. 2013b. "Populism". In *Oxford Handbook of Political Ideologies*, edited by Michael Freeden, Marc Stears and Lyman Tower Sergeant, 493–512. Oxford: Oxford University Press.

Mudde, Cas, and Cristóbal Rovira Kaltwasser. 2014. "Populism and Political Leadership". In *The Oxford Handbook of Political Leadership*, edited by R. A. W. Rhodes and Paul t' Hart, 376–88. Oxford: Oxford University Press.

Mudde, Cas, and Cristóbal Rovira Kaltwasser. 2015. "Vox Populi or Vox Masculini? Populism and Gender in Northern Europe and South America". *Patterns of Prejudice* 49(1–2): 16–36.

Mughan, Anthony. 2000. *Media and the Presidentialization of Parliamentary Elections*. Basingstoke: Palgrave.

Murphy, Rex. 2010. "Rex Murphy: The New Michael Ignatieff, Fresh Off the Bus". *National Post*, September 4. Accessed June 13, 2012. http://fullcomment.nationalpost.com/2010/09/04/rex-murphy-the-new-michael-ignatieff-fresh-off-the-bus/.

Muth, Karl. 2011. "An Incomplete Treatise on Hats". *Global Policy*, December 6. Accessed July 21, 2014. http://www.globalpolicyjournal.com/blog/06/12/2011/incomplete-treatise-hats.

Mwakikagile, Godfrey. 2012. *Obote to Museveni: Political Transformation in Uganda since Independence*. Dar es Salaam: New Africa Press.

Napoli, Philip M. 2010. *Audience Evolution: New Technologies and the Transformation of Media Audiences*. New York: Columbia University Press.

Näsström, Sofia. 2007. "The Legitimacy of the People". *Political Theory* 35(5): 624–58.

Navarria, Giovanni. 2008. "Political Anomalies and Web-based Civil Antibodies in Silvio Berlusconi's *Bel Paese*". *Recerca: Revista de Pensament i Anàlisi* 8: 173–92.

Nelson, John S. 2008. "Realism as a Political Style: Noir Insights". *Poroi* 5(2): 1–46.

Neoclaus, Mark. 2003. *Imagining the State*. Maidenhead: Open University Press.

Newton-Small, Jay. 2011. "Palin's Populist Message". *Time Magazine*, February 5. Accessed March 21, 2012. http://swampland.time.com/2011/02/05/palin%E2%80%99s-populist-message/.

Noll, Michael A. 2006. *The Evolution of Media*. Lanham, MD: Rowman and Littlefield.

Norocel, Ov Cristian. 2011. "Heteronormative Constructions of Romanianness: A Genealogy of Gendered Metaphors in Romanian Radical-Right Populism 2000–2009". *Debatte: Journal of Contemporary Central and Eastern Europe* 19(1–2): 453–70.

Norocel, Ov Cristian. 2012. "'Give Us Back Sweden!' A Feminist Reading of the (Re) Interpretations of the Folkhem Conceptual Metaphor in Swedish Radical Right Populist Discourse". *NORA: Nordic Journal of Feminist and Gender Research* 21(1): 4–20.

Norris, Pippa. 2003. *A Virtuous Circle: Political Communications in Postindustrial Societies*. Cambridge: Cambridge University Press.

Nyhan, Brendan. 2010. "Why the 'Death Panel' Myth Wouldn't Die: Misinformation in the Health Care Reform Debate". *Forum* 8(1): 1–24.

Ochieng' Opalo, Kennedy. 2012. "African Elections: Two Divergent Trends". *Journal of Democracy* 23(3): 80–93.

Ochoa Espejo, Paula. 2011. *The Time of Popular Sovereignty: Process and the Democratic State*. University Park: Pennsylvania State University Press.

Ochoa Espejo, Paula. 2015. "Power to Whom? The People between Procedure and Populism". In *The Promise and Perils of Populism: Global Perspectives*, edited by Carlos de la Torre, 59–90. Lexington: University Press of Kentucky.

Ociepka, Beata, ed. 2005a. *Populism and Media Democracy*. Wroclaw: Wroclaw University Press.

Ociepka, Beata. 2005b. "Populism as 'Good Communication with People'. The Polish Case during the Referendum Campaign". In *Populism and Media Democracy*, edited by Beata Ociepka, 207–26. Wroclaw: Wroclaw University Press.

Olding, Rachel. 2013. "When Stephanie Got Her Facts Wrong: One Nation Candidate Makes Gaffe after Gaffe in TV Interview". *Sydney Morning Herald*, August 8. Accessed August 8, 2013. http://www.smh.com.au/federal-politics/federal-election-2013/when-stephanie-got-her-facts-wrong-one-nation-candidate-makes-gaffe-after-gaffe-in-tv-interview-20130808-2rive.html.

Osbourne, Roger. 2011. *Of the People, by the People: A New History of Democracy*. London: Random House.

Ostiguy, Pierre. 2009a. "Argentina's Double Political Spectrum: Party System, Political Identities, and Strategies, 1944–2007". *Kellogg Institute Working Paper* 361. Notre Dame, IN: Kellogg Institute for International Studies, University of Notre Dame.

Ostiguy, Pierre. 2009b. "The High-Low Political Divide: Rethinking Populism and Anti-Populism". *Political Concepts: Committee on Concepts and Methods Working Paper Series*, 35.

Painter, Anthony. 2013. *Democratic Stress, the Populist Signal and Extremist Threat*. London: Policy Network.

Palin, Bristol, and Nancy French. 2011. *Not Afraid of Life: My Journey So Far*. New York: HarperCollins.

Palin, Sarah. 2008. "Transcript: Gov. Sarah Palin at the RNC". *NPR*, September 3. Accessed February 17, 2012. http://www.npr.org/templates/story/story.php?storyId=94258995.

Palin, Sarah. 2009. *Going Rogue*. New York: HarperCollins.

Palin, Sarah. 2010. *America by Heart: Reflections on Family, Faith, and Flag*. New York: HarperCollins.

Palin, Sarah. 2013. *Good Tidings and Great Joy: Protecting the Heart of Christmas*. New York: HarperCollins.

Panizza, Francisco. 2000. "Neopopulism and Its Limits in Collor's Brazil". *Bulletin of Latin American Research* 19(2): 177–92.

Panizza, Francisco. 2005a. "Introduction: Populism and the Mirror of Democracy". In *Populism and the Mirror of Democracy*, edited by Francisco Panizza, 1–31. London: Verso.

Panizza, Francisco, ed. 2005b. *Populism and the Mirror of Democracy*. London: Verso.

Panizza, Francisco, and Romina Miorelli. 2009. "Populism and Democracy in Latin America". *Ethics and International Affairs* 23(1): 39–46.

Papadopoulos, Yannis. 2000. "National Populism in Western Europe: An Ambivalent Phenomenon". Accessed October 30, 2013. http://www2.unil.ch/iepi/pdfs/papadopoulos1.pdf.

Partij Voor de Vrijheid. 2012. "Hún Brussel, óns Nederland: Verkiezingsprogramma 2012 - 2017". Accessed July 30, 2012. http://www.pvv.nl/images/stories/verkiezingen2012/VerkiezingsProgramma-PVV-2012-final-web.pdf.

Pasquarelli, John. 1998. *The Pauline Hanson Story... By the Man Who Knows*. Frenchs Forest: New Holland Books.

Patten, Steve. 1996. "Preston Manning's Populism: Constructing the Common Sense of the Common People". *Studies in Political Economy* 50: 95–132.

Patton, Paul. 2008. "After the Linguistic Turn: Post-Structuralist and Liberal Pragmatist Political Theory". In *The Oxford Handbook of Political Theory*, edited by J. S. Dryzek, B. Honig and A. Phillips, 125–41. Oxford: Oxford University Press.

Pauwels, Teun. 2010. "Explaining the Success of Neo-liberal Populist Parties: The Case of Lijst Dedecker in Belgium". *Political Studies* 58(5): 1009–29.

Pauwels, Teun. 2011. "Measuring Populism: A Quantitative Text Analysis of Party Literature in Belgium". *Journal of Elections, Public Opinion and Parties* 21(1): 97–119.

Pels, Dick. 2003. "Aesthetic Representation and Political Style: Re-balancing Identity and Difference in Media Democracy". In *Media and the Restyling of Politics*, edited by John Corner and Dick Pels, 41–66. London: SAGE.

Pels, Dick, and Henk te Velde, eds. 2000. *Politieke stijl. Over presentatie en optreden in de politiek*. Amsterdam: Het Spinhuis.

Peri, Yoram. 2004. *Telepopulism: Media and Politics in Israel*. Stanford: Stanford University Press.

Pew Research Center's Project for Excellence in Journalism. 2011. "Top Newsmakers". *The Year in News 2011*. Accessed December 5, 2012. http://www.journalism.org/analysis_report/top_newsmakers.

Phillips, Tom. 2011. "Hugo Chávez Hints at US Cancer Plot". *Guardian*, December 29. Accessed January 17, 2012. http://www.guardian.co.uk/world/2011/dec/29/hugo-chavez-us-cancer-plot.

Phongpaichit, Pasuk, and Chris Baker. 2009a. *Thaksin*. 2nd ed. Chiang Mai: Silkworm Books.

Phongpaichit, Pasuk, and Chris Baker. 2009b. "Thaksin's Populism". In *Populism in Asia*, edited by Kosuke Mizuno and Pasuk Phongpaichit, 66–93. Singapore: NUS Press.

Pieper, Andrew L. 2013. "The Hermanator: Anti-Elitism and the Rise of Herman Cain". In *The 2012 Nomination and the Future of the Republican Party: The Internal Battle*, edited by William J. Miller, 103–26. Lanham, MD: Lexington Books.

Piper, Laurence. 2009. "The Zuma Watershed: From Post-Apartheid to Post-Colonial Politics in South Africa". *Representation* 45(2): 101–7.

Pirro, Andrea L. P. 2014. "Populist Radical Right Parties in Central and Eastern Europe: The Different Context and Issues of the Prophets of the Patria". *Government and Opposition* 49(4): 600–629.

Plasser, Fritz, and Peter A. Ulram. 2003. "Striking a Responsive Chord: Mass Media and Right-Wing Populism in Austria". In *The Media and Neo-Populism: A Contemporary Comparative Analysis*, edited by Gianpietro Mazzoleni, Julianne Stewart and Bruce Horsfield, 21–44. Westport, CT: Praeger.

Plate, Tom. 2011. *Conversations with Thaksin*. Singapore: Marshall Cavendish Editions.

Poguntke, Thomas, and Paul Webb. 2005. "The Presidentialization of Politics in Democratic Societies: A Framework for Analysis". In *The Presidentialization of Politics: A Comparative Study of Modern Democracies*, edited by Thomas Poguntke and Paul Webb, 1–25. Oxford: Oxford University Press.

Potter, W. James. 2009. *Arguing for a General Framework for Mass Media Scholarship*. Thousand Oaks, CA: SAGE.

Potter, W. James. 2011. "Conceptualizing Mass Media Effect". *Journal of Communication* 61(5): 896–915.

Poynting, Scott. 2002. "Bin Laden in the Suburbs: Attacks on Arab and Muslim Australians before and after 11 September". *Current Issues in Criminal Justice* 14(1): 43–64.

Precious, Brian. 2009. "A Man of Theories in the Flesh". *Morning Star Online*, December 10. Accessed January 23, 2013. http://www.morningstaronline.co.uk/index.php/news/content/view/full/84325.

Protevi, John. 2001. *Political Physics: Deleuze, Derrida and the Body Politic*. London: Athlone Press.

Quigley, Brendan. 2011. "Immunity, Italian Style: Silvio Berlusconi versus the Italian Legal System". *Hastings International and Comparative Law Review* 34(1): 435–63.

Rancière, Jacques. 2006. *Hatred of Democracy*. Translated by S. Corcoran. London: Verso.

Raquiza, Antoinette R. 2013. *State Structure, Policy Formation, and Economic Development in Southeast Asia: The Political Economy of Thailand and the Philippines*. Abingdon: Routledge.

Raventos, Jorge. 2002. "From the New Left to Postmodern Populism: An Interview with Paul Piccone". *Telos* 122: 133–52.

Reform Party of Canada. 1993. *Blue Sheet: Principles, Policies and Election Platform*. Calgary.

Reporters without Borders. 2005. "Reporters without Borders Annual Report 2005—Italy". Accessed May 2, 2014. http://www.refworld.org/publisher,RSF,,I-TA,46e690dfc,0.html.

Reporters without Borders. 2009. "Reporters without Borders in Rome as Berlusconi Gets Closer to Being Declared a 'Predator'". October 2. Accessed May 2, 2014. http://en.rsf.org/italy-reporters-without-borders-in-rome-02–10–2009,34640. html.

Resnick, Danielle. 2010. "Populist Strategies in African Democracies". In *UNU-WIDER Working Paper* 2010/114. Helsinki: United Nations University.

Resnick, Danielle. 2012. "Opposition Parties and the Urban Poor in African Democracies". *Comparative Political Studies* 45(11): 1351–78.

Reungoat, Emmanuelle. 2010. "Anti-EU Parties and the People: An Analysis of Populism in French Euromanifestos". *Perspectives on European Politics and Society* 11(3): 292–312.

Reuters. 2011. "Berlusconi Bemoans Italy Judges to Obama at G8". May 26. Accessed October 24, 2012. http://www.reuters.com/article/2011/05/26/us-berlusconi-judges-obama-idUSTRE74P7XQ20110526.

Ribbhagen, Christina. 2013. "Technocracy within Representative Democracy: Technocratic Reasoning and Justification among Bureaucrats and Politicians". Ph.D. diss., Department of Political Science, University of Gothenberg.

Ritzer, George, and Nathan Jurgenson. 2010. "Production, Consumption, Prosumption". *Journal of Consumer Culture* 10(1): 13–36.

Roberts, Kenneth M. 1995. "Neoliberalism and the Transformation of Populism in Latin America: The Peruvian Case". *World Politics* 48(1): 82–116.

Roberts, Kenneth M. 2003. "Social Correlates of Party System Demise and Populist Resurgence in Venezuela". *Latin American Politics and Society* 45(3): 35–57.

Roberts, Kenneth M. 2006. "Populism, Political Conflict, and Grass-roots Organization in Latin America". *Comparative Politics* 38(2): 127–48.

Roberts, Kenneth M. 2007. "Latin America's Populist Revival". *SAIS Review* 27(1): 3–15.

Roberts, Kenneth M. 2012. "Populism and Democracy in Venezuela under Hugo Chávez". In *Populism in Europe and the Americas: Threat or Corrective for Democracy?*, edited by Cas Mudde and Cristóbal Rovira Kaltwasser, 136–59. New York: Cambridge University Press.

Roberts, Kenneth M. 2015. "Populism, Political Mobilizations, and Crises of Political Representation". In *The Promise and Perils of Populism: Global Perspectives*, edited by Carlos de la Torre, 140–58. Lexington: University Press of Kentucky.

Robinson, Andrew. 2005. "The Political Theory of Constitutive Lack: A Critique".

Theory and Event 8(1). Accessed September 25, 2012. http://muse.jhu.edu/journals/theory_and_event/v008/8.1robinson.html.

Robinson, Andrew, and Simon Tormey. 2009. "Is 'Another World' Possible? Laclau, Mouffe and Social Movements". In *The Politics of Radical Democracy*, edited by Adrian Little and Moya Lloyd, 133–57. Edinburgh: Edinburgh University Press.

Rocamora, Joel. 2009. "Estrada and the Populist Temptation in the Philippines". In *Populism in Asia*, edited by Kosuke Mizuno and Pasuk Phongpaichit, 41–65. Singapore: NUS Press.

Rohlinger, Deana A., and Jesse Klein. 2014. "From Fervor to Fear: ICT and Emotions in the Tea Party Movement". In *Understanding the Tea Party Movement*, edited by Nella Van Dyke and David S. Meyer, 125–48. Farnham: Ashgate.

Roitman, Janet. 2011. "Crisis". *Political Concepts: A Critical Lexicon* 1 (Winter). Accessed December 20, 2012. http://www.politicalconcepts.org/2011/crisis.

Romero, Simon. 2008. "A Little Insult Is All the Rage in Venezuela: 'Pitiyanqui'". *New York Times*, September 6, A9.

Romo, Rafael. 2011. "Gadhafi's Friend to the Death, Chavez Calls Libyan Leader 'a Martyr'". *CNN International*. Accessed June 27, 2013. http://edition.cnn.com/2011/10/21/world/americas/venezuela-chavez-gadhafi.

Roncarolo, Franca. 2005. "Campaigning and Governing: An Analysis of Berlusconi's Rhetorical Leadership". *Modern Italy* 10(1): 75–93.

Rooduijn, Matthijs. 2014a. "The Mesmerising Message: The Diffusion of Populism in Public Debates in Western European Media". *Political Studies* 62(4): 726–44.

Rooduijn, Matthijs. 2014b. "The Nucleus of Populism: In Search of the Lowest Common Denominator". *Government and Opposition* 49(4): 573–99.

Rooduijn, Matthijs, Sarah L. de Lange and Wouter van der Brug. 2014. "A Populist Zeitgeist? Programmatic Contagion by Populist Parties in Western Europe". *Party Politics* 20(4): 563–75.

Rooduijn, Matthijs, and Teun Pauwels. 2010. "Measuring Populism: Comparing Two Methods of Content Analysis". *West European Politics* 34(6): 1272–83.

Rosanvallon, Pierre. 2008. *Counter-Democracy: Politics in an Age of Distrust*. New York: Cambridge University Press.

Rosanvallon, Pierre. 2011. "A Reflection on Populism". *Books and Ideas*, November 10. Accessed October 23, 2012. http://www.booksandideas.net/IMG/pdf/20111110_populism.pdf.

Rosenfeld, Sophia. 2011. "Cain's Pain". *New York Times*, November 11. Accessed June 6, 2013. http://campaignstops.blogs.nytimes.com/2011/11/11/cains-paine/.

Rousseau, Stéphanie. 2010. "Populism from Above, Populism from Below: Gender Politics under Alberto Fujimori and Evo Morales". In *Gender and Populism in Latin America: Passionate Politics*, edited by Karen Kampwirth, 140–61. University Park: Pennsylvania State University.

Rovira Kaltwasser, Cristóbal. 2012. "The Ambivalence of Populism: Threat and Corrective for Democracy". *Democratization* 19(2): 184–208.

Rovira Kaltwasser, Cristóbal. 2013. "The Responses of Populism to Dahl's Democratic Dilemmas". *Political Studies* 62(3): 470–87.

Roxborough, Ian. 1984. "Unity and Diversity in Latin American History". *Journal of Latin American Studies* 16(1): 1–26.

Ruggiero, Christian. 2012. "Forecasting in the Politics of Spectacle, from Berlusconi to Grillo: The Narrative of Impolite Politics". *Bulletin of Italian Politics* 4(2): 305–22.

Rydgren, Jens. 2006. *From Tax Populism to Ethnic Nationalism: Radical Right-Wing Populism in Sweden*. New York: Berghan Books.

Rydgren, Jens. 2008. "Sweden: The Scandinavian Exception". In *Twenty-First Century Populism: The Spectre of Western European Democracy*, edited by Daniele Albertazzi and Duncan McDonnell, 135–50. Basingstoke: Palgrave Macmillan.

Sabato, Larry J., Mark Stencel and S. Robert Linchter. 2000. *Peepshow—Media and Politics in an Age of Scandal*. Lanham, MD: Rowman and Littlefield.

Sandburg, Carl. 1970. *The Complete Poems of Carl Sandburg*. Orlando, FL: Houghton Mifflin Harcourt.

Sartori, Giovanni. 1970. "Concept Misformation in Comparative Politics". *American Political Science Review* 64(4): 1033–53.

Sarver Coombs, Danielle. 2014. *Last Man Standing: Media, Framing, and the 2012 Republican Primaries*. Plymouth: Rowman and Littlefield.

Saunders, Kay, and Katie McConnel. 2002. "The Men behind Pauline Hanson: Problematic Masculinity and Queensland Politics". In *Manning the Next Millennium: Studies in Masculinities*, edited by Sharyn Pearce and Vivienne Muller, 225–37. Bentley: Black Swan Press.

Saurette, Paul, and Shane Gunster. 2011. "Ears Wide Shut: Epistemological Populism, Argutainment and Canadian Conservative Talk Radio". *Canadian Journal of Political Science* 44(1): 195–218.

Saward, Michael. 2008. "Making Representations: Modes and Strategies of Political Parties". *European Review* 16(3): 271–86.

Saward, Michael. 2009. "Authorisation and Authenticity: Representation and the Unelected". *Journal of Political Philosophy* 17(1): 1–22.

Saward, Michael. 2010. *The Representative Claim*. Oxford: Oxford University Press.

Saward, Michael. 2011. "Slow Theory: Taking Time over Transnational Democratic Representation". *Ethics and Global Politics* 4(1): 1–18.

Saward, Michael. 2014. "Shape-Shifting Representation". *American Political Science Review* 108(4): 723–36.

Sawer, Marian, and David Laycock. 2009. "Down with Elites and Up with Inequality: Market Populism in Australia and Canada". *Commonwealth and Comparative Politics* 47(2): 133–50.

Scalmer, Sean. 1999. "The Production of a Founding Event: The Case of Pauline Hanson's Maiden Parliamentary Speech". *Theory and Event* 3(2). Accessed March 15, 2013. http://muse.jhu.edu/journals/theory_and_event/summary/v003/3.2scalmer.html.

Scalmer, Sean. 2002. *Dissent Events: Protest, the Media and the Political Gimmick in Australia*. Sydney: UNSW Press.

Schumpeter, Joseph A. 1942. *Capitalism, Socialism and Democracy*. New York: Harper and Brothers.

Seligson, Mitchell A. 2007. "The Rise of Populism and the Left in Latin America". *Journal of Democracy* 18(3): 81–95.

Severs, Eline. 2010. "Representation as Claim-Making. Quid Responsiveness?" *Representation* 46(4): 411–23.

Shields, James. 2013. "Marine Le Pen and the 'New' FN: A Change of Style or of Substance?" *Parliamentary Affairs* 66(1): 179–96.

Shils, Edward A. 1955. "Populism and the Rule of Law". In *Conference on Jurisprudence and Politics Proceedings (1954)*, edited by Scott Buchanan, 91–107. Chicago: University of Chicago Law School.

Shils, Edward A. 1956. *The Torment of Secrecy: The Background and Consequences of American Security Policies*. Glencoe, IL: Free Press.

Shils, Edward A. 1960. "The Intellectuals in the Political Development of the New States". *World Politics: A Quarterly Journal of International Relations* 12(3): 329–68.

Shirky, Clay. 2011. "The Political Power of Social Media: Technology, the Public Sphere, and Political Change". *Foreign Affairs* 90(1): 28–41.

Shogan, Colleen J. 2007. "Anti-Intellectualism in the Modern Presidency: A Republican Populism". *Perspectives on Politics* 5(2): 295–303.

Silverstone, Roger. 2002. "Complicity and Collusion in the Mediation of Everyday Life". *New Literary History* 33(5): 745–64.

Simons, Jon. 2002. "Governing the Public: Technologies of Mediation and Popular Culture". *Cultural Values* 6(1–2): 167–81.

Simons, Jon. 2011. "Mediated Construction of the People: Laclau's Political Theory and Media Politics". In *Discourse Theory and Critical Media Politics*, edited by Lincoln Dahlberg and Sean Phelan, 201–21. Basingstoke: Palgrave Macmillan.

Skocpol, Theda, and Vanessa Williamson. 2012. *The Tea Party and the Remaking of Republican Conservatism*. New York: Oxford University Press.

Smith, Ben. 2009. "Palin: 'Screw the Political Correctness'". *Politico*, June 5. Accessed April 24, 2013. http://www.politico.com/blogs/bensmith/0609/Palin_Screw_the_political_correctness.html.

Smith, Peter H. 1969. "Social Mobilization, Political Participation, and the Rise of Juan Perón". *Political Science Quarterly* 84(1): 30–49.

Smith, Rogers M. 2003. *Stories of Peoplehood: The Politics and Morals of Political Membership*. Cambridge: Cambridge University Press.

Snow, Dave, and Benjamin Moffitt. 2012. "Straddling the Divide: Mainstream Populism and Conservatism in Howard's Australia and Harper's Canada". *Commonwealth and Comparative Politics* 50(3): 271–92.

Sosa-Bucholz, Ximena. 2010. "Changing Images of Male and Female in Ecuador: José María Velasco Ibarra and Abdalá Bucaram". In *Gender and Populism in Latin America: Passionate Politics*, edited by Karen Kampwirth, 47–66. University Park: Pennsylvania State University Press.

Sosa, Ximena. 2012. "Populism in Ecuador: From Jose M. Valesco Ibarra to Rafael Correa". In *Populism in Latin America*, edited by Michael L. Conniff, 159–83. Tuscaloosa: University of Alabama Press.

Southall, Roger. 2009. "Understanding the 'Zuma Tsunami'". *Review of African Political Economy* 36(121): 317–33.

Squires, Nick. 2011. "Berlusconi Sex Party Boast: Eight Is Not Enough". *Sydney Morning Herald*, September 19. Accessed April 8, 2013. http://www.smh.com.au/world/berlusconi-sex-party-boast-eight-is-not-enough-20110918–1kg1u.html.

Stake, Robert E. 1995. *The Art of Case Study Research*. Thousand Oaks, CA: SAGE.

Stanley, Ben. 2008. "The Thin Ideology of Populism". *Journal of Political Ideologies* 13(1): 95–110.

Stanley, Tim. 2012. "Mitt Romney's Weirdness Means He Can't Connect with American Voters". *Telegraph,* March 10. Accessed June 13, 2012. http://blogs.telegraph.co.uk/news/timstanley/100142831/why-is-mitt-romney-considered-weird-but-rick-santorum-isnt/.

Stavrakakis, Yannis. 2004. "Antinomies of Formalism: Laclau's Theory of Populism and the Lessons from Religious Populism in Greece". *Journal of Political Ideologies* 9(3): 253–67.

Stavrakakis, Yannis. 2005. "Religion and Populism in Contemporary Greece". In *Populism and the Mirror of Democracy*, edited by Francisco Panizza, 224–49. London: Verso.

Stavrakakis, Yannis, and Giorgos Katsambekis. 2014. "Left-wing Populism in the European Periphery: The Case of SYRIZA". *Journal of Political Ideologies* 19(2): 119–42.

Stewart, Angus. 1969. "The Social Roots". In *Populism: Its Meanings and National Characteristics*, edited by Ghita Ionescu and Ernest Gellner, 180–96. London: Weidenfeld and Nicolson.

Stewart, Julianne, Gianpietro Mazzoleni and Bruce Horsfield. 2003. "Conclusion: Power to the Media Managers". In *The Media and Neo-Populism: A Contemporary Comparative Analysis*, edited by Gianpietro Mazzoleni, Julianne Stewart and Bruce Horsfield, 217–38. Westport, CT: Praeger.

Stewart, Michael, ed. 2013. *The Gypsy 'Menace': Populism and the New Anti-Gypsy Politics*. London: Hurst and Company.

Stokes, Geoff. 2000. "One Nation and Australian Populism". In *The Rise and Fall of One Nation*, edited by Micheal Leach, Geoff Stokes and Ian Ward, 23–41. St. Lucia: University of Queensland Press.

Streeck, Wolfgang, and Armin Schäfer, eds. 2013. *Politics in the Age of Austerity*. Cambridge: Polity Press.

Street, John. 2004. "Celebrity Politicians: Popular Culture and Political Representation". *British Journal of Politics and International Relations* 6(4): 435–52.

Strömbäck, Jesper. 2008. "Four Phases of Mediatization: An Analysis of the Mediatization of Politics". *International Journal of Press/Politics* 13(3): 228–46.

Strömbäck, Jesper, and Frank Esser. 2009. "Shaping Politics: Mediatization and Media Interventionism". In *Mediatization: Concept, Changes, Consequences*, edited by Knut Lundby, 205–24. New York: Peter Lang.

Strömbäck, Jesper, and Frank Esser, eds. 2014. *Mediatization of Politics: Understanding the Transformation of Western Democracies*. Basingstoke: Palgrave Macmillan.

Stroud, Natalie Jomini. 2008. "Media Use and Political Predispositions: Revisiting the Concept of Selective Exposure". *Political Behavior* 30(3): 341–66.

Sunstein, Cass. 2007. "On the Divergent American Reactions to Terrorism and Climate Change". *Columbia Law Review* 107: 503–58.

Sutherland, Meghan. 2012. "Populism and Spectacle". *Cultural Studies* 26(2–3): 330–45.

Szusterman, Celia. 2000. "Carlos Saúl Menem: Variations on the Theme of Populism". *Bulletin of Latin American Research* 19(2): 193–206.

t' Hart, Paul, and Karen Tindall, eds. 2009a. *Framing the Global Economic Downturn: Crisis Rhetoric and the Politics of Recessions*. Canberra: ANU EPress.

t' Hart, Paul, and Karen Tindall. 2009b. "Leadership by the Famous: Celebrity as Political Capital". In *Dispersed Democratic Leadership: Origins, Dynamics, and Implications*, edited by John Kane, Haig Patapan and Paul t' Hart, 256–78. Oxford: Oxford University Press.

Taggart, Paul. 1995. "New Populist Parties in Western Europe". *West European Politics* 18(1): 34–51.

Taggart, Paul. 1996. *The New Populism and the New Politics: New Protest Parties in Sweden in a Comparative Perspective*. London: Macmillan.

Taggart, Paul. 2000. *Populism*. Birmingham: Open University Press.

Taggart, Paul. 2002. "Populism and the Pathology of Representative Politics". In *Democracies and the Populist Challenge*, edited by Yves Mény and Yves Surel, 62–80. Basingstoke: Palgrave Macmillan.

Taggart, Paul. 2004. "Populism and Representative Politics in Contemporary Europe". *Journal of Political Ideologies* 9(3): 269–88.

Taguieff, P. 1995. "Political Science Confronts Populism: From a Conceptual Mirage to a Real Problem". *Telos* 103: 9–43.

Tamada, Yoshifumi. 2009. "Democracy and Populism in Thailand". In *Populism in Asia*, edited by Kosuke Mizuno and Pasuk Phongpaichit, 94–111. Singapore: NUS Press.

Tarchi, Marco. 2008. "Italy: A Country of Many Populisms". In *Twenty-First Century Populism: The Spectre of Western European Democracy*, edited by Daniele Albertazzi and Duncan McDonnell, 84–99. Basingstoke: Palgrave MacMillan.

Tejapira, Kasian. 2006. "Toppling Thaksin". *New Left Review* 39 (May–June): 5–37.

Telos. 1995a. "Special Issue on Populism I". *Telos* 103.

Telos. 1995b. "Special Issue on Populism II". *Telos* 104.

The 9/12 Project. 2010. "Our Mission". *The 9/12 Project*. Accessed March 5, 2014. http://the912-project.com/about/about-the-912-project/.

Thompson, Alex. 2010. *An Introduction to African Politics*. 3rd ed. Abingdon: Routledge.

Thompson, John B. 1995. *The Media and Modernity: A Social Theory of the Media*. Stanford: Stanford University Press.

Thompson, Mark R. 2010a. "Populism and the Revival of Reform: Competing Political Narratives in the Philippines". *Contemporary Southeast Asia: A Journal of International and Strategic Affairs* 32(1): 1–28.

Thompson, Mark R. 2010b. "Reformism vs. Populism in the Philippines". *Democratization* 21(4): 154–68.

Thompson, Mark R. 2013. "Class, Charisma, and Clientism in Thai and Philippine Populist Parties". In *Party Politics in Southeast Asia: Clientelism and Electoral Competition in Indonesia, Thailand and the Philippines*, edited by Dirk Tomsa and Andreas Ufen, 62–79. Abingdon: Routledge.

Tilly, Charles. 2008. *Contentious Politics*. Cambridge: Cambridge University Press.

Tormey, Simon. 2009. "Not in My Name: Representation and Its Discontents". *Arts: The Proceedings of the Sydney University Arts Association* 31: 92–107.

Tormey, Simon. 2012. "Occupy Wall Street: From Representation to Post-Representation". *Journal of Critical Globalisation Studies* 5: 132–37.

Tormey, Simon. 2015. *The End of Representative Politics*. Cambridge: Polity Press.

Townshend, Jules. 2003. "Discourse Theory and Political Analysis: A New Paradigm from the Essex School?" *British Journal of Politics and International Relations* 5(1): 129–42.

Traudt, Paul J. 2005. *Media, Audiences, Effects*. Boston: Pearson.

Traynor, Ian. 2008. "'I Don't Hate Muslims. I Hate Islam,' Says Holland's Rising Political Star". *Observer*, February 17. Accessed March 18, 2013. http://www.guardian.co.uk/world/2008/feb/17/netherlands.islam.

Turner, Eric. 2012. "The Grillini in Italy: New Horizons for Internet-based Mobilization and Participation". *Social Movement Studies* 12(2): 214–20.

Učeň, Peter. 2010. "Approaching National Populism". In *National Populism and Slovak-Hungarian Relations in Slovakia 2006–2009*, edited by Petocz Kálmán, 13–38. Šamorín-Somorja: Forum Minority Research Institute.

Urbinati, Nadia. 1998. "Democracy and Populism". *Constellations* 5(1): 110–24.

van Biezen, Ingrid, Peter Mair and Thomas Poguntke. 2012. "Going, Going,... Gone? The Decline of Party Membership in Contemporary Europe". *European Journal of Political Research* 51(1): 24–56.

van de Donk, Wim, Brian D. Loader, Paul G. Nixon and Dieter Rucht, eds. 2004. *Cyberprotest: New Media, Citizens, and Social Movements*. Abingdon: Routledge.

van der Brug, Wouter, and Anthony Mughan. 2007. "Charisma, Leader Effects and Support for Right-Wing Populist Parties". *Party Politics* 13(1): 29–51.

van der Pas, Daphne, Catherine de Vries and Wouter van der Brug. 2013. "A Leader without a Party: Exploring the Relationship between Geert Wilders' Leadership Performance in the Media and His Electoral Success". *Party Politics* 19(3): 458–76.

van Kessel, Stijn. 2015. *Populist Parties in Europe: Agents of Discontent?* Basingstoke: Palgrave Macmillan.

van Zoonen, Liesbet. 2005. *Entertaining the Citizen: When Politics and Popular Culture Converge*. Oxford: Rowman and Littlefield.

van Zoonen, Liesbet. 2012. "I-Pistemology: Changing Truth Claims in Popular and Political Culture". *European Journal of Communication* 27(1): 56–67.

Vaneigem, Raoul. 1994. *The Revolution of Everyday Life*. Translated by David Nicholson-Smith. 2nd ed. London: Rebel Press and Left Bank Books.

Verba, Sidney. 1965. "Comparative Political Culture". In *Political Culture and Political Development*, edited by Lucian Pye and Sidney Verba, 512–60. Princeton: Princeton University Press.

Verseck, Keso. 2012. "Young, Wired and Angry: A Revised Portrait of Hungary's Right-Wing Extremists". *Spiegel Online International,* February 3. Accessed March 2, 2012. http://www.spiegel.de/international/europe/0,1518,813243,00.html.

Vincent, Louise. 2009. "Moral Panic and the Politics of Populism". *Representation* 45(2): 213–21.

Vincent, Louise. 2011. "Seducing the People: Populism and the Challenge to Democracy in South Africa". *Journal of Contemporary African Studies* 29(1): 1–14.

Viroli, Maurizio. 2012. *The Liberty of Servants: Berlusconi's Italy*. Translated by Anthony Shuggar. Princeton: Princeton University Press.

Vivian, Bradford. 2011. "The Problems and Promises of Rhetorical Style". In *The Politics of Style and the Style of Politics*, edited by Barry Brummett, xi–xxv. Lanham, MD: Lexington Books.

Vona, Gábor. 2013. "Euro-Atlanticism Must Be Replaced by Eurasianism". *Jobbik: The Movement for a Better Hungary,* May 5. Accessed July 10, 2013. http://www. jobbik.com/g%C3%A1bor_vona_euro-atlanticism_must_be_replaced_eur- asianism.

Vossen, Koen. 2010. "Populism in the Netherlands after Fortuyn: Rita Verdonk and Geert Wilders Compared". *Perspectives on European Politics and Society* 11(1): 22–38.

Vossen, Koen. 2011. "Classifying Wilders: The Ideological Development of Geert Wilders and His Party for Freedom". *Politics* 31(3): 179–89.

Waisbord, Silvio. 2003. "Media Populism: Neo-Populism in Latin America". In *The Media and Neo-Populism: A Contemporary Comparative Analysis,* edited by Gianpietro Mazzoleni, Julianne Stewart and Bruce Horsfield, 197–216. Westport, CT: Praeger.

Waisbord, Silvio. 2011. "Between Support and Confrontation: Civic Society, Media Reform, and Populism in Latin America". *Communication, Culture and Critique* 4(1): 97–117.

Waisbord, Silvio. 2012. "Democracy, Journalism, and Latin American Populism". *Journalism* 14(4): 504–21.

Walgrave, Stefaan, and Knut de Swert. 2004. "The Making of the (Issues of the) Vlaams Blok". *Political Communication* 21(4): 474–500.

Wall Street Journal. 2013. "Suddenly, Banks Are Victims: In Their S&P Lawsuit, the Feds Discover a New Crisis Narrative". April 24, 2013, A14.

Ward, Ian, Micheal Leach and Geoff Stokes. 2000. "Introduction: The Rise and Fall of One Nation". In *The Rise and Fall of One Nation,* edited by Micheal Leach, Geoff Stokes and Ian Ward, 1–22. St. Lucia: University of Queensland Press.

Warren, Matthre. 2011. "Le Pen Taunts Rival with 'Paedophile' Slur". *The Local: France's News in English,* March 16. Accessed April 24, 2013. http://www.thelocal. fr/page/view/1180#.UXdcDLX-F8E.

Wasburn, Philo C., and Mara H. Wasburn. 2011. "Media Coverage of Women in Politics: The Curious Case of Sarah Palin". *Media, Culture and Society* 33(7): 1027–41.

Washington Times. 2005. "Embassy Row". February 2. Accessed January 12, 2012. http://www.washingtontimes.com/news/2005/feb/2/20050202–112810– 2421r/?page=.

Wear, Rae. 2008. "Permanent Populism: The Howard Government 1996–2007". *Australian Journal of Political Science* 43(4): 617–34.

Wear, Rae. 2014. "Astroturf and Populism in Australia: The Convoy of No Confidence". *Australian Journal of Political Science* 49(1): 54–67.

Weaver, Matthew. 2010. "Word of the Day: Sarah Palin Invents 'Refudiate'". *Guardian,* July 19. Accessed June 25, 2013. http://www.theguardian.com/news/ blog/2010/jul/19/sarah-palin-refudiate-new-word.

Weber, Max. 1978. *Economy and Society: An Outline of Interpretive Sociology*. Edited by G. Roth and C. Wittich. Berkeley: University of California Press.

Wegierski, Mark. 1998. "The Reform Party and the Crisis of Canadian Politics". *Telos* 111: 163–72.

Westlind, Dennis. 1996. *The Politics of Popular Identity: Understanding Recent Populist Movements in Sweden and the United States*. Lund: Lund University Press.

Weyland, Kurt. 1999. "Neoliberal Populism in Latin America and Eastern Europe". *Comparative Politics* 31(4): 379–401.

Weyland, Kurt. 2001. "Clarifying a Contested Concept: Populism in the Study of Latin American Politics". *Comparative Politics* 34(1): 1–22.

Weyland, Kurt. 2003. "Neopopulism and Neoliberalism in Latin America: How Much Affinity?" *Third World Quarterly* 24(6): 1095–115.

Weyland, Kurt. 2009. "Populism and Social Policy in Latin America". Populism of the Twenty-First Century conference, Woodrow Wilson International Center for Scholars, Washington, DC, October 8.

Weyland, Kurt. 2010. "Foreword". In *Gender and Populism in Latin America: Passionate Politics*, edited by Karen Kampwirth, vii–xii. University Park: Pennsylvania State University Press.

Wheeler, Mark. 2011. "Celebrity Politics and the United Kingdom's Televised 2010 Prime Ministerial General Election Debates". *Celebrity Studies* 2(1): 91–93.

Widfeldt, Anders. 2000. "Scandinavia: Mixed Success for the Populist Right". *Parliamentary Affairs* 53(3): 486–500.

Wilders, Geert. 2010a. "NYC Speech Geert Wilders". September 11. Accessed March 21, 2014. http://www.geertwilders.nl/index.php?option=com_content&task=view&id=1712.

Wilders, Geert. 2010b. "Wilders—Muhammad Was a Paedophile". *YouTube [online video clip]*, March 8. Accessed February 22, 2012. http://www.youtube.com/watch?v=eXuG4KhfCZM.

Wilders, Geert. 2012. *Marked for Death: Islam's War against the West and Me*. Washington, DC: Regnery.

Wilders, Geert. 2013a. "Speech Geert Wilders, Los Angeles, June 9, 2013". June 9. Accessed March 21, 2014. http://www.geertwilders.nl/index.php/in-de-media-mainmenu-74/nieuws-mainmenu-114/1829-speech-geert-wilders-los-angeles-june-9-2013.

Wilders, Geert. 2013b. "Speech Geert Wilders, Melbourne, Australia, Tuesday February 19, 2013". *Geert Wilders Weblog*, February 19. Accessed March 21, 2014. http://www.geertwilders.nl/index.php/in-english-mainmenu-98/in-the-press-mainmenu-101/77-in-the-press/1822-speech-geert-wilders-melbourne-australia-tuesday-february-19-2013.

Wiles, Peter. 1969. "A Syndrome, Not a Doctrine: Some Elementary Theses on Populism". In *Populism: Its Meanings and National Characteristics*, edited by Ghita Ionescu and Ernest Gellner, 166–79. London: Weidenfeld and Nicolson.

Williams, Conor. 2010. "Technocracy and Populism". *Dissent*. October 22. Accessed June 16, 2014. http://www.dissentmagazine.org/online_articles/technocracy-and-populism.

Williams, Michelle Hale. 2010. "Can Leopards Change Their Spots? Between Xenophobia and Trans-ethnic Populism among West European Far Right Parties". *Nationalism and Ethnic Politics* 16(1): 111–34.

Williamson, Vanessa, Theda Skocpol and John Coggin. 2011. "The Tea Party and the Remaking of Republican Conservatism". *Perspectives on Politics* 9(11): 25–43.

Worsley, Peter. 1964. *The Third World*. London: Weidenfeld and Nicolson.

Worsley, Peter. 1969. "The Concept of Populism". In *Populism: Its Meaning and National Characteristics*, edited by Ghita Ionescu and Ernest Gellner, 212–50. London: Weidenfeld and Nicolson.

Yin, Robert K. 2009. *Case Study Research: Design and Methods*. 4th ed. Thousand Oaks, CA: SAGE.

Zakaria, Fareed. 2013. "Can America Be Fixed? The New Crisis of Democracy". *Foreign Affairs* 92(1): 22–33.

Zaslove, Andrej. 2008. "Here to Stay? Populism as a New Party Type". *European Review* 16(3): 319–36.

Ziblatt, Daniel. 2006. "Of Course Generalize, but How? Returning to Middle-Range Theory in Comparative Politics". *American Political Science Association—Comparative Politics Newsletter* 17(2): 8–11.

Žižek, Slavoj. 1999. *The Ticklish Subject: The Absent Centre of Political Ontology*. London: Verso.

Žižek, Slavoj. 2006a. "Against the Populist Temptation". *Critical Inquiry* 32(3): 551–74.

Žižek, Slavoj. 2006b. *"Schlagend, aber nicht Treffend!" Critical Inquiry* 33(1): 185–211.

Žižek, Slavoj. 2008. *In Defense of Lost Causes*. London: Verso.

Zúquete, José Pedro. 2007. *Missionary Politics in Contemporary Europe*. Syracuse, NY: Syracuse University Press.

Zúquete, José Pedro. 2008. "The Missionary Politics of Hugo Chávez". *Latin American Politics and Society* 50(1): 91–121.

Zúquete, José Pedro. 2013. "Missionary Politics—A Contribution to the Study of Populism". *Religion Compass* 7(7): 263–71.

Zürn, Michael, and Gregor Walter-Drop. 2011. "Democracy and Representation beyond the Nation State". In *The Future of Representative Democracy*, edited by Sonia Alonso, John Keane and Wolfgang Merkel, 258–81. New York: Cambridge University Press.

Index

activism, 82; presidency, 113, 128; public spectacles, 32; technocratic populism, 154–55; television program, 84; toughness, 66

Corruption, 92, 116, 128, 138, 144

Courtly political style, 35 (table)

Crises: in democracy, 1, 113, 124, 144; elite responsibility for, 43–44, 124, 130–31; meaning, 119–20; media focus on, 77; perceived, 45, 120; performance of, 45, 114, 118, 119, 130–32, 158; as spectacularisation of failure, 114, 120, 121; temporal dimension, 119, 120, 122, 123

Crisis, populism and: audiences, 129; creating sense of crisis, 118, 158, 167n10; as external to populism, 114–18, 120; as internal feature, 114, 118, 120, 131–32; media events, 125–26; metaphors, 124; performance model, 121–30, 158; perpetuating sense of crisis, 128–30, 131; populism as response to, 113–14, 115–16; populism as trigger for, 114; scholarship on, 114–19, 120; solutions proposed, 126–28; staged events, 125–26; switching crises, 129

Crisis politics, 130–31

Critchley, Simon, 64

Cruz, Ted, 1

Debord, Guy, 96, 101–2, 104

De la Torre, Carlos, 32, 118–19, 129, 148, 154–55

Democracy: audience, 100–101, 170–71n5; body politic, 64; crisis of faith in, 1, 113, 124, 144; definition, 134; indicators, 140–41; liberal, 136, 138, 140; politics, 141–42; radical, 137; representative, 141, 144–45;

stylisation, 150–51. *See also individual countries*

Democracy, populism's relationship with: antidemocratic tendencies, 133, 142, 145–50; critique of democracy, 144–45; democratic tendencies, 133, 142–45, 149–50; equivocal approach, 138–40, 149–50, 159; future research directions, 151, 159; as negative force, 10–11, 133, 135–37, 140, 158; opportunistic, 150; as positive force, 133, 137–38; scholarship on, 134–41, 172n1

Demos, 91, 156

Developing countries, populism in, 14, 158. *See also individual countries*

Digital populism, 91. *See also* Internet

Discursive approach to populism: content analysis, 21–22, 171–72n1; elements, 166n4 (ch 2); Essex School, 166n5; future research directions, 155–56; on leadership, 53; on media roles, 71; overview, 21; political style approach and, 39–40; response to crises, 171–72n1; shortcomings, 22, 26–27

Duno-Gottberg, Luis, 103

Eco, Umberto, 95, 101

Ecuador, populist leaders, 14, 32, 65. *See also* Correa, Rafael

Elites: as crisis victims, 172n5; criticism of, 1, 44, 121, 124, 146; division from 'the people', 43–44, 130–31; liberal, 43–44; meanings, 167n7; media, 81; political advisors as, 80; responsibility for crises, 43–44, 124, 130–31

Ellinas, Antonis A., 79

Enemies, *see* Others

Lightning Source UK Ltd.
Milton Keynes UK
UKOW04f0744270817
308011UK00002B/143/P